MUHAMMAD ALI'S GREATEST FIGHT

Cassius Clay vs.
the United States of America

MUHAMMAD ALI'S GREATEST FIGHT

Cassius Clay vs. the United States of America

By Howard Bingham and Max Wallace

M. Evans and Company, Inc.

New York

M. Evans and Company, Inc.
216 East 49th Street
New York, New York 10017

Library of Congress Cataloging-in-Publication Data

Bingham, Howard L.
    Muhammad Ali's greatest fight : Cassius Clay vs. the United States of
America / by Howard Bingham and Max Wallace.
        p. cm.
    ISBN 0-87131-900-4
        1. Ali, Muhammad, 1942–   2. Boxers (Sports)—United States—
Political activity. 3. Vietnamese Conflict, 1961–1975—Conscientious
objectors. 4. Boxers (Sports)—United States—Biography. I. Wallace,
Max. II. Title.
    GV1132.A44 W24 2000   99-050269

Book design by Rik Lain Schell

Printed in the United States of America

9 8 7 6 5 4 3 2 1

Contents

To all those with the courage to take a stand

FOREWORD

INEVER THOUGHT OF MYSELF as great when I refused to go into the army. All I did was stand up for what I believed. There were people who thought the war in Vietnam was right. And those people, if they went to war, acted just as brave as I did. There were people who tried to put me in jail. Some of them were hypocrites, but others did what they thought was proper and I can't condemn them for following their consciences either. People say I made a sacrifice, risking jail and my whole career. But God told Abraham to kill his son and Abraham was willing to do it, so why shouldn't I follow what I believed? Standing up for my religion made me happy; it wasn't a sacrifice. When people got drafted and sent to Vietnam and didn't understand what the killing was about and came home with one leg and couldn't get jobs, *that* was a sacrifice. But I believed in what I was doing, so no matter what the government did to me, it wasn't a loss.

Some people thought I was a hero. Some people said that what I did was wrong. But everything I did was according to my conscience. I wasn't trying to be a leader. I just wanted to be free. And I made a stand all people, not just black people, should have thought about making, because it wasn't just black people being drafted. The government had a system where the rich man's son went to college, and the poor man's son went to war. Then, after the rich man's son got out of college, he did other things to keep him out of the army until he was too old to be drafted. So what I did was for me, but it was the kind of decision everyone has to make. Freedom means being able to follow your religion, but it also means carrying the responsibility to choose between right and wrong. So when the time came for me to make up my mind about going into the army, I knew people were dying in Vietnam for nothing and I knew I should live by what I thought was right. I wanted America to be America. And now the whole world knows that, so far as my own beliefs are concerned, I did what was right for me.

—Muhammad Ali

CHAPTER ONE:
Louisville and the Lip

THE GOLD MEDAL HADN'T LEFT his neck since he had received it at the 1960 Summer Olympics awards ceremony the day before. He ate with it, he slept with it, he showered with it, he lay on his back so it wouldn't stab him during the night. Cassius Clay strutted around the Olympic Village in Rome showing off the medal to anybody he passed. "I'm the king, I'm the king," he declared in the brash style that would soon become so familiar to so many. His fellow athletes from all over the world smiled and congratulated him—he had long since won them over with his infectious personality. "If there had been an election for mayor of the Olympic Village, Cassius would have won in a landslide," remembers one teammate.

Heading to the cafeteria, the eighteen-year-old boxer ran into a Russian reporter who decided Clay was worth a story, despite having vanquished a Soviet contender on his way to the title. But unlike those of the hundred or so reporters to whom the new champion had already granted interviews, the Russian's questions had nothing to do with boxing. He wanted to know how Clay felt as a Negro representing the United States, where he was still treated as a second-class citizen.

"The U.S.A. is the best country in the world, including yours," came the response.

Undeterred, the Russian proceeded to lecture his subject about one of the most popular topics in the Soviet media during that period. He reminded the young athlete about racial inequality and segregation in America. Clay refused to rise to the bait.

"We have our problems, sure, but tell your readers we got qualified people working on that, and I'm not worried about the outcome."

Millions of words have been written by what journalist Robert Lipsyte calls "Ali-ologists" analyzing, puzzling over, and attempting to explain how the boxer involved in that three-minute exchange of patriotism could within a decade become a national pariah, labelled a traitor and almost sent to prison—all because at some point he started to worry about the outcome.

The most logical and most facile explanation is supplied by Muhammad Ali himself in his 1975 autobiography, *The Greatest*.

Long before even going to Rome, Clay had dreamt about the homecoming he would receive returning to Louisville, Kentucky, as Olympic champion. By the time of the Games, he had already begun to compose the doggerel that would become his trademark. On the flight across the Atlantic he penned a little poem anticipating the greeting he had fantasized about for so many years.

HOW CASSIUS TOOK ROME
BY CASSIUS CLAY JR.

To make America the greatest is my goal
So I beat the Russian, and I beat the Pole
And for the USA won the Medal of Gold.
Italians said, "You're greater than the Cassius of old.
We like your name, we like your game
So make Rome your home if you will."
I said I appreciate kind hospitality
But the USA is my country still
Cause they're waiting to welcome me in Louisville.

The welcome, when it finally occurred, didn't disappoint. It included marching bands, red-white-and-blue streamers and, eventually, a reception by the mayor. "I was deeply proud of having represented America on a world stage," Ali would later write. "To me the gold medal was more than a symbol of what I had achieved for myself and my country; there was something I expected the medal to achieve for me. And during those first days of homecoming it seemed to be doing exactly that."

At the city hall reception, the mayor put his arms around the returning hometown-hero-made-good and declared, "He's our own boy, Cassius, our next world champion. Anything you want in town's yours. You hear that?" Afterwards, he told reporters, "If all young people could handle themselves as well as Clay does, we wouldn't have juvenile problems."

The mayor's promise echoing in his head, Clay and a friend decided to grab a bite to eat later that evening at a local diner. Like many establishments in Louisville at the time, the diner was for "whites only." But the gold medal would solve that, Cassius told his friend as they sat at the counter and placed their order: two hamburgers and two vanilla milkshakes.

It wasn't the first time they had eaten at the diner. Once for Halloween, they'd had a seamstress make a couple of African turbans and flowing gowns. They paraded downtown, talking "foreign English" and getting themselves admitted to "whites only" establishments. Once they were stopped at a movie house by a suspicious doorman until the white manager intervened, saying, "It's all right. They ain't Negroes."

But this was the first time they had entered a segregated establishment as "homegrown" Negroes, and the reaction was swift. The waitress bent down and whispered in Clay's ear, "We can't serve you here."

"Miss," he responded politely, believing she didn't recognize him. "I'm Cassius Clay. The Olympic champion." His friend proudly pulled the medal from under Clay's T-shirt and adjusted the red-,white-, and-blue- ribbon. He turned the medal around to show the Italian word PUGILATO embossed on the back.

Impressed, the waitress walked over to the owner and spoke in a hushed whisper.

"I don't care *who* he is. We don't serve no niggers!"

The other diners kept their heads down. The only eyes that would meet his were those of the old black woman working in the kitchen, who looked at him sadly.

His friend stared in disbelief. "They don't really know who you are," he kept saying. "They just don't know you're the champion. I ain't scared to tell them." Like an announcer in the ring, he said, "Folks, this is the champion! Louisville's Olympic champion. Just back from Italy."

"Ronnie, shut up," Clay urged. "Don't beg! Don't beg!"

He walked out the door and headed for the nearby Jefferson County Bridge. Walking to the middle of the span, Cassius removed the gold medal from around his neck and dropped it into the dark depths of the Ohio River.

This incident would neatly encapsulate Ali's sense of betrayal at the contradictions of the American dream. How could he have pride in representing a country in which he couldn't even order a hamburger where he wanted?

Unfortunately, it never happened. The diner episode was concocted by a ghostwriter named Richard Durham who was looking for just such an anecdote to explain in a thousand words the enigma of a man not easily explained. The truth was somewhat more complicated.

▶▶▶

For the black community of Louisville in the 1940s and '50s when Ali was growing up as Cassius Clay, Jim Crow was not as pervasive as it was in the deeper South—places like Georgia, Alabama, and Mississippi, where lynchings were an ever-present threat. Kentuckians served their racism with a gentler touch. But it was always on the menu.

"We were immersed in discrimination," recalls Ali's first cousin Coretta Bather. "Louisville was a very segregated town. The whites never let you forget your place. I had a friend in Georgia who used to talk about how she was afraid to look white folks in the eye. It was never *that* bad for us, but it was everywhere. There were a lot of shops we couldn't even go in downtown. We could mop their floors but we couldn't buy anything. The ones who would take our money still let us know what they thought of us. I remember Sears, Roebuck had two water fountains labeled 'whites only' and 'colored only.'"

Blacks sat in the back of the bus and in the balcony of the movie theater if they were allowed in at all. The best movies showed at the

Loews, the Brown, the Strand. They were for whites only, as were the prettiest parks and the public swimming pools.

For Cassius Marcellus Clay Sr., the segregation of Louisville was part of everyday life. Like most blacks, he didn't believe anything could be done to change it. His particular beef with the white establishment came from his conviction that they had thwarted his artistic ambitions. A prolific landscape artist, Cassius Sr. couldn't sell his artworks and had to resort to sign painting to earn his living. Turn down Market Street and you were greeted by a big sign reading KING CARL'S THREE ROOMS OF NEW FURNITURE with the immaculate lettering that announced it as one of Old Cash's creations. When you saw A. B. HARRIS M.D., DELIVERIES AND FEMALE DISORDERS, you knew you were on Dumesnil Street.

There was nothing modest about Cassius Sr., who regularly declared, "I am the Greatest" to anybody who would listen. Years later, his son would adopt this boast as his own personal motto. By all accounts, in fact, his paintings were rather mediocre, but his sign-painting abilities were unrivalled.

Each night at the dinner table, his family would listen to Cassius Sr. rail at the many injustices suffered by Negroes. For a time, he embraced the ideas of radical black nationalist Marcus Garvey and his calls for racial pride but he stopped short of endorsing Garvey's "Back to Africa" philosophy.

Years later, describing his childhood in Louisville, Ali lamented that "too many colored people wanted to be white." When Cassius Jr. was born in 1942 and his brother Rudy two years later, their father was determined that his sons wouldn't be among those people.

"Why can't I be rich?" young Cassius would ask his father as he saw the elegant Louisville whites flaunting their fancy cars and expensive clothes. "Look there," said the father, pointing to his brown hands, "that's why you can't be rich."

This reality was driven home one day when his mother Odessa, in an experience she would describe over and over again years later, took five-year-old Cassius downtown on a hot summer day. As the sun blazed down, the little boy started crying for a drink of water outside Woolworth's five-and-dime, at which blacks were allowed to shop but couldn't eat at the lunch counter. She took him in and asked the clerk for some water, only to be told, "If we serve Negroes in here, we lose our jobs."

Biographer David Remnick, in his thorough account of Ali's early years, *King of the World*, describes such incidents as the "accumulated slights of mid-century American Apartheid."

Around the same time, young Cassius asked his father, "Daddy, I go to the grocery and the grocery man is white. I go to the drugstore and the drugstore man's white. The bus driver's white. What do the colored people do?"

Odessa Clay took odd jobs as a maid in the houses of rich white Louisville families. She would get up at the crack of dawn, take a bus to the white part of town, and spend the day cooking, cleaning toilets, and looking after children. It was menial and, at four dollars a day, low-paying work. But the fact that the Clays were a two-income family has prompted most of Muhammad Ali's biographers to describe him as a product of the black middle class. Ali vigorously disputes this characterization. "The truth is that most of my life in Louisville was one of poverty—semi-poverty," he writes in his autobiography. "While there was a black middle class in Louisville, even some affluent blacks, and the neighborhoods were not as ghetto-looking as in some big cities, my part of the Clay family was not among them until my ring earnings made it possible."

Black Louisville is divided into three sections. The worst part of town, the slums, is the East End, known as "Snake Town." The black middle class lives in the "California Area," and the most populated, where the Clays lived, is the West End. Blacks quickly learned where they could and could not go.

"Growing up," Rudy (Rahaman) Clay later recalled, "the only problems Muhammad and I had with whites were if we were walking in a certain part of town. If we were in the wrong place, white boys would come up in a car and say, 'Hey, nigger, what are you doing here?'"

One of the most often-told anecdotes about the young Cassius Clay—and one of the most printed after he became known nationwide—was his habit of racing the bus to school every morning. He would tell people he was running to get into fight condition because he was going to be heavyweight champion one day. Years later, he confided the real reason. There was seldom enough money for his brother and him to both have bus fare to school. As the oldest, he let Rudy ride and he would run, too proud to reveal why.

Today Ali describes his family life as close-knit and loving but the Louisville police blotter indicates a certain discord. Odessa was forced to call the police at least three times to protect her from her husband, usually when he was drinking heavily. Cassius Sr. was arrested four times for reckless driving, twice for disorderly conduct, and twice for assault and battery. Ali, however, insists that his father never touched him.

According to a member of the family, Cassius Sr. was "a mean drunk. He took out his frustrations as a failed artist and could get very violent. His wife wouldn't put up with it and would throw him out of the house for days at a time. But he'd turn on that charm of his and she'd always take him back."

Stories still abound in Louisville about another of Cash's bad habits, his womanizing. Ali later acknowledged his father's philandering ways, calling him "a playboy with an eye for the ladies." What effect this all had on the young Cassius is a matter of speculation. Their relationship over the years ranged from coolness to estrangement to an uneasy detente, but in interviews Ali always gives his father his due for "making me what I am."

His relationship with his mother Odessa was much closer. She called him "G.G.," he called her "Bird" and the two would spend hours playing games or reading the bible. It's as if they were creating their own oasis from the harsh realities of life with Cassius Sr. and the world outside their door.

In 1954, when Cassius Clay was twelve, the United States Supreme Court handed down the historic *Brown vs. Board of Education* decision desegregating American schools. The judgment had a ripple effect throughout the South but didn't have much of an impact on the young Clay, who would attend all-black schools throughout his youth.

At around the same time *Brown* heralded a new era for American blacks, an event took place more than eight thousand miles away that would prove to have a much greater impact on the future of Muhammad Ali.

In May, French forces in Indochina were surrounded by the communist guerrilla army of Ho Chi Minh at the battle of Dien Bien Phu and forced to surrender. The resulting peace agreement led to the partition of the country into North and South Vietnam. It was the height of the Cold War. Senator Joe McCarthy was in the last stages of his witch hunt. Members of Congress were urging President Eisenhower to send U.S. troops to the region to beat back the communist threat before a domino effect could engulf Asia in a Red tide.

In America, this drumbeat towards war was raising alarm bells for the black actor, singer, and activist Paul Robeson, who expressed his views on potential American involvement.

"Shall Negro sharecroppers from Mississippi be sent to shoot brown-skinned peasants in Vietnam—to serve the interests of those who oppose Negro liberation at home and colonial freedom abroad?" asked Robeson in a remarkably prescient speech. Robeson, himself a former All-American athlete during his days at Rutgers University, would later be persecuted by the American government, labeled a traitor, and have his passport taken away for supposed un-American activities. Today Ali claims he had never heard of Robeson during this period.

Ali lore traces the beginnings of his rise as the greatest boxer in history to an incident—"*the* incident"—which took place in October of that year. Cassius Jr. had just received a brand new bike as a present from his parents—a red-and-white Schwinn. Its cost? Sixty dollars, which may explain later descriptions of Ali as a product of the black middle class. In fact, Cassius Sr. had just won a lucrative sign-painting contract and was eager to share his largesse with the family after a long period of austerity.

Eager to try out and show off his new bike, Cassius and a friend rode downtown to a black bazaar called the Louisville Home Show. The merchants were giving out free popcorn and candy and the two boys spent most of the afternoon feasting on junk food. When it was time to leave, they returned to the side of the building where they had left their bikes. The new Schwinn was gone.

Clay was fit to be tied. The usually easygoing youngster erupted in fury and started to yell for a policeman. Somebody told him there was an officer downstairs in the auditorium, which housed the Columbia Gym. In tears, he stormed down to the basement and came face-to-face with Joe Martin, an off-duty Louisville policeman who trained young boxers in his spare time. He demanded Martin arrest whoever had stolen his bike. "He said he was gonna whup whoever stole it," Martin later recalled. "And I brought up the subject, I said, 'Well, you better learn how to fight before you start challenging people that you're gonna whup.'" He invited Cassius back to the gym for some lessons.

The twelve-year-old boy was an unlikely prospect for boxing lessons. Painfully skinny at only eighty-nine pounds, he had never shown any signs of aggression before the bike was stolen.

When he walked into the gym a few days later to take Martin up on his offer, he knew he had found his calling. "When I was eight and ten years old, I'd walk out of my house at two in the morning, and look up at the sky for an angel or a revelation or God telling me what to do. I never got the answer. Then my bike got stolen and I started boxing and it was like God telling me that boxing was my responsibility," Ali told Thomas Hauser in the definitive biography/oral history *His Life and Times*.

Six weeks after joining Martin's gym, Cassius made his ring debut and won a three-round decision over another beginner named Ronnie O'Keefe. When the referee raised his arm to signal Clay had triumphed, the victorious boxer shouted to the crowd the words which would soon become a familiar refrain. "I'm gonna be the greatest of all time!" And he was going to do whatever he had to do to ensure the words were no idle boast. From then on, Cassius Marcellus Clay Jr. was a study in determination. Each morning he rose at 4:30 A.M. and ran five miles. For breakfast, he would down a quart of milk mixed with two raw eggs. He went everywhere carrying a solution of bottled water mixed with garlic, insisting it would keep his health perfect. When his mother questioned his unusual eating habits, he told her he was going to be the champion and buy her a big house one day.

While his friends experimented with drugs and alcohol, Cassius refused to do anything that might jeopardize his goals. The closest he ever came to a vice, he later admitted, was taking the cap off a gas tank and smelling the gas for a hallucinogenic sensation. "Boxing kept me out of trouble," he says.

He didn't have much use for other sports. He tried tennis a few times and wasn't bad but football definitely wasn't for him. "I tried it once, that's all," he says. "They gave me the ball and tackled me. My helmet hit the ground, pow! No sir. You got to get hit in that game, it's too tough. You don't have to get hit in boxing, people don't understand that."

Elsewhere, in the wake of *Brown vs. Board of Education,* a fuse was being ignited. A year after Clay first stepped into the ring, a black woman named Rosa Parks refused to give up her seat and move to the back of a city bus in Montgomery, Alabama, prompting the Montgomery Bus Boycott and raising a young preacher named Martin Luther King Jr. to national prominence.

Today Ali claims he wasn't paying much attention to King's activities. "I was too focused on boxing to follow all that stuff," he says. As he racked up victory after victory in the amateur ranks, the struggle for integration was beginning in earnest. For the black community of Louisville, even then, King and his new movement were being watched closely.

"We followed King and the bus boycott pretty much from the beginning," recalls Ali's cousin Coretta. "What he was doing was exciting. Remember, Louisville wasn't as bad as Montgomery, but we had to sit in the back of the bus too. We needed the voice, we needed the leadership. I guess Ali was pretty caught up in his career to follow King. Some people think that's why he never really took to the whole integration cause." The one time he marched in an integration rally, Ali remembers today, somebody dumped a bucket of water over his head.

But if Dr. King's activities failed to capture the imagination of the young Clay, it wasn't because he was unaware of the turmoil spreading throughout the South. Three months before Rosa Parks was arrested, Cassius Clay Sr. came home shaken one day with a copy of the national black magazine *Jet*, insisting his sons look at it. "This is what they do to us," he repeated over and over.

Inside, young Cassius and Rudy were shocked to see a number of gruesome photos showing the mutilated corpse of a young black boy.

In August 1955, Emmett Till was a fourteen-year-old black northerner from a middle-class neighborhood on the South Side of Chicago. His mother had relatives in the small town of Money, Mississippi, population 350. Her uncle Mose suggested she send Emmett down to visit for a couple of weeks to get some fresh air and down-home cooking before school started.

Mamie Till Bradley was nervous about sending her son to the heart of the Deep South. Chicago wasn't exactly a model of race relations—its neighborhoods were segregated, Emmett himself went to an all-Negro school, and blacks were discriminated against on a daily basis.

But Emmett had a few white friends, and the city had recently seen a number of intermarriages, which were heavily frowned upon but reluctantly tolerated by blacks and whites.

In contrast, the Mississippi Delta was the heart of Southern Jim Crow society. Four hundred sixty blacks had been lynched in the state since the Civil War, and the state's elected officials were committed racists who vowed to oppose integration at every turn. The governor, J. P. Coleman, had recently declared blacks unfit to vote. And the *Brown* desegregation decision the year before had put the state in a fighting mood. In fact, Mississippi Senator James Eastland asserted that the decision had "destroyed the Constitution" and Mississippi was not obliged to obey it. State senator Walter Givhan claimed the real purpose of the NAACP's campaign to end school desegregation was "to open the bedroom doors of our white women to Negro men."

It was into this climate that a nervous Mamie Bradley packed off her son one August day. But not before she cautioned him "not to fool with white people down there." Emmett was known to be a bit brash and fun-loving, and she warned him against his usual sass. "If you have to get on your knees and bow when a white person goes past, do it willingly," she told him.

The first few days of his visit were uneventful. He hung out with his cousin Simeon and went fishing with his great uncle Mose. He couldn't help notice the differences between his Northern friends and relatives and these new kinfolk who were openly fearful of whites and consciously subservient, answering "Ya suh" and "Naw suh" when they were spoken to. It was an oppressive atmosphere for the young teenager, but he was determined not to demean himself.

One day, hanging out with his cousin and some friends in front of Bryant's general store, Emmett—who was known as a prankster—took a picture of a white girl out of his wallet and showed it around, announcing "that's my girl."

His friends were skeptical. They told him there was a pretty white woman working in the store at that moment and dared Emmett to go inside and talk to her. Accepting the challenge, he went inside and bought some candy. On the way out, he turned to her and said loudly so his friends could hear, "Bye, baby." One witness inside the store claimed Emmett had whistled at her.

The sales clerk's husband, Roy Bryant, was out of town trucking shrimp. When he came back three days later and heard the story, he paid a visit to the hut of Emmett's great uncle Mose Wright, accompanied by his brother-in-law J. W. Milam. "We come to get the boy who done the talkin'," they announced.

Mose told them Emmett was just a visiting Northerner unaccustomed to the ways of the South. He tried to convince them to let him off with a "good whipping."

Unimpressed, they dragged Emmett out of the hut and dumped him in the back seat of the car, where they drove him to the nearby Tallahatchee River. At their destination, they made him carry a 75-pound cotton gin fan to the riverbank, ordered him to strip, beat him with a pipe, gouged out his eye, and then shot him in the head. They dumped the body into the river, where it was found so badly mangled that Mose Wright could only identify his nephew's remains from his ring.

The body was brought back to Chicago, where authorities wanted to bury it immediately. But Emmett's mother was determined to have an open casket funeral so the "world would see what they did to my boy." Hundreds of thousands of mourners came to view the body, photos were printed in the black press, white editorialists around the country condemned the savage act, and the resulting publicity captured the imagination of Americans.

When the two men went on trial for murder, the case was closely watched across America. Lynchings were commonplace throughout the South, but this was the murder of a child. The trial took place in the nearby town of Sumner, whose ironic motto was "A Good Place to Raise a Boy." Despite the testimony of Mose Wright, who bravely identified the men who kidnapped his nephew—knowing the risks of testifying against the white defendants—the men were acquitted of the crime and set free.

The verdict shocked a nation and is widely credited as a catalyst for the imminent civil rights movement.

For the young Cassius Clay, it was a traumatic event. "I felt a deep kinship to him when I learned he was born the same year and day I was," he would write. In fact, Clay was six months older, but the Till incident unquestionably had a deep impact on him and he has brought it up several times in subsequent years. In his autobiography, he describes his reaction to the verdict, although many believe this is another concoction like the diner incident, designed for effect by the ghostwriter.

"I couldn't get Emmett out of my mind, until one evening I thought of a way to get back at white people for his death. . . . It was late at night when we reached the old railroad station on Louisville's West Side. I remember a poster of a thin white man in striped pants and a top hat who pointed at us above the words UNCLE SAM WANTS YOU. We stopped and hurled stones at it. . . ." He and his friend then sabotaged the railroad track, running away as a train ripped up the railway ties.

It is possible this incident happened, and Ali insists it did. But the next words of his autobiography stretch credulity and are clearly fiction. "It took two days to get up enough nerve to go back there. A work crew was still cleaning up the debris. And the man in the poster was still pointing. I always knew that sooner or later he would confront me, and I would confront him."

While Martin Luther King Jr. and other civil rights pioneers fought for racial justice, however, Cassius Clay just kept fighting one opponent after another in the ring, racking up amateur victory after victory, including six Kentucky Golden Gloves championships, two National Golden Gloves tournaments, and two National Amateur titles before he was eighteen. Those around him were already detecting a special quality in and out of the ring. "You could see that the little smart aleck —I mean, he's always been sassy—had a lot of potential, " recalled Joe Martin, the Louisville policeman who taught the young Cassius to box and continued to cultivate the fighter. "He stood out because he had more determination than most boys. He was a kid willing to make the sacrifices necessary to achieve something worthwhile in sports. I realized it was almost impossible to discourage him. He was easily the hardest worker of any kid I ever taught."

His hard work in the ring didn't translate to the classroom, where his marks were below average. All he could think about, he says, was his boxing career. "In school, sometimes I'd pretend they were announcing my name over the loudspeaker system, saying, 'Cassius Clay, heavyweight champion of the world.'"

One often-told story has it that some of his teachers, unimpressed with their poor student's athletic ability, wanted to fail him, but the school principal, Atwood Wilson, wouldn't hear of it. It was obvious that Cassius was going places, and he wasn't going to stand in the way. At a faculty meeting one day, Wilson silenced the talk of failing the school's young star. "Cassius is not going to fail in my school," he announced. "One day the greatest claim to fame of Central High will be that we produced Cassius Clay. If every teacher in this room fails him, he's still not going to fail, not in my school. I'm going to say I taught him and I'm going to be proud."

Those who knew him at the time came to have a very different impression than the fans who were coming out in increasing numbers to watch Clay box. "Cassius was a very easy-to-get-along-with fellow," recalled Joe Martin's wife Christine who would drive him to bouts. "He was very easy to handle, very polite. Whatever you asked him to do, that's what he'd do. On trips, most of the boys were out looking around, seeing what they could get into, whistling at pretty girls. But Cassius didn't believe in that. He carried his Bible everywhere he went, and while the other boys were out looking around, he was sitting and reading his Bible."

Her description would have come as quite a surprise to those who saw him box. Already he was being dubbed the "Louisville Lip" by the media and the fans who were witnessing the evolution of his brash style. Each Saturday night, Clay's bouts were televised on a local TV show called "Tomorrow's Champions," and thousands would see Cassius taunt his opponents with cries of "You can't lay a glove on me, I'm the Greatest." Before a match, he would pay a visit to his opponents' dressing rooms and hone the psychological warfare that would infuriate his future professional nemeses. "I'm going to whup you and you're going to beg me to stop," he warned them.

When he came into the arena for a match, the crowds would root against him, yelling for his opponent to "Whip the Lip." One night he told a local reporter that his opponent wouldn't last one round, reciting a poem to make his point.

> *This guy must be done*
> *I'll stop him in one*

Sure enough, the fight lasted less than a minute and a new tradition was born, calling the round. His predictions didn't always pan out, but that didn't matter; the mystique was growing.

Amateur boxing official Chuck Bodak, who coached at the Golden Gloves tournaments, recalled the impression Clay made on him. "You had to be blind not to see how good this kid was. I told his mother once, 'Cassius must be from outer space, because I've never seen anyone like him in my life.'"

Clay himself certainly saw it. The day after out-of-town tournaments, people staying at the same hotel as the young boxer remember buying newspapers and finding the sports section missing. Cassius would be up in his room with a scissors and fifteen sports sections, cutting his own picture out of each one.

By 1960, Clay had proven himself as one of the best amateur boxers in the country but was still a relative unknown in the media. The Olympics could change that, but first he had to get by the trials, which would be held in California. And that meant taking his first airplane trip, a bumpy, turbulence-ridden flight that left the usually supremely confident Clay with white knuckles. He prevailed at the Olympic trials and qualified to represent the United States in Rome. But that meant an even longer flight, and Clay was determined never to set foot on another airplane. Nobody could change his mind. His friends and family implored him to go, arguing this was his big chance. Joe Martin finally appealed to his dream. "I finally took him out to Central Park in Louisville and we had a long talk for a couple of hours and I calmed him down and convinced him if he wanted to be heavyweight champion of the world, that he had to go to Rome and win the Olympics," Martin later recalled.

The world was about to be introduced to one of the century's most unforgettable characters.

Much has been written about Clay in Rome, strutting around the Olympic Village, making friends with athletes who didn't even speak his language, impressing the media with his unique style and personality. But beyond the brashness, the jollity, the confidence, at least one witness saw something beneath the surface of Clay's act, something almost messianic. Skeeter McClure was a fellow member of the U.S. boxing team, and Clay's roommate in Rome. The two had met several

Homecoming. Surrounded by children in his hometown of Louisville, 1963

times at tournaments, and Cassius had even visited McClure's home in Ohio for a meal after a match. "When I first saw him when he came to our home in Toledo, his pants were up at his ankles, his sports coat was too short, but it's like the clothing was irrelevant because he glowed," McClure told Thomas Hauser. "It's like there was a star when he was born that fated him to do what he was going to do and to have an impact on mankind around the globe, and there's nothing that he could have done to prevent it and nothing he could have done to make it happen."

But if there was a star guiding the boxer's destiny, it seemed to many that for the next decade it was taking him in the wrong direction.

In 1960 boxing was still a dirty business, populated by mobsters and corrupt to its core. Countless congressional and media investigations uncovered ties between organized crime and boxing's leading promoters, managers, and fighters. From the 1940s until his arrest in 1959—and from prison for years thereafter—a petty New York hood named Frankie Carbo virtually controlled boxing, including its mecca, Madison Square Garden. Fights were fixed, boxing writers supplemented their meager salaries with weekly envelopes filled with cash courtesy of Carbo, and many of the country's greatest fighters, including Joe Louis, ended up penniless while the mob reaped the benefits.

When Cassius Clay returned from Rome with his gold medal and a reputation, Cassius Clay Sr.—savvy to the sport's reputation—was determined for his son to end up in the right hands. He located a West End lawyer to safeguard his son's interests and was ready to start taking offers, which were already pouring in.

"There were a lot of people who wanted to take him over when he came back from the Olympics," recalled the elder Clay years later. "And I saw he could take care of himself in the ring, but I wanted to see he was well taken care of out of it too. He was underage, and didn't know how to handle himself in business."

The most attractive of these offers came from a group of eleven white Louisville businessmen, who called themselves the Louisville Sponsoring Group. The group represented a who's who of old-line Kentucky breeding. Ali called them the "men with the connections and the complexions." There were the oil tycoons J. D. Coleman; the steel baron Elbert Sutcliffe; the refined horse breeder Patrick Calhoun Jr., who admitted, "What I know about boxing you can put in your eye;" and plenty of tobacco and whiskey money thrown in to the mix.

None of these men needed the money, to be sure, but most of them regarded it as a bit of a lark—the chance to attach themselves to a hometown hero and have a bit of fun. Cassius Clay and his father, of course, couldn't meet to discuss the terms at the exclusive Pendennis Club, to which all of the Sponsoring Group's members belonged. The only way they could enter that Louisville institution would be by the back door as janitors or busboys.

The group represented its motivation as purely magnanimous, but one of its members, Vertner Smith, while having a drink with a reporter from *Sports Illustrated* one day, let slip his real aims.

"Let me give you the official line—we are behind Cassius Clay to improve the breed of boxing; to do something nice for a deserving, well-behaved Louisville boy; and finally to save him from the jaws of the hoodlum jackals. I think it's fifty percent true, but also fifty percent hokum. What I want to do, like a few others, is to make a bundle of money."

Each member of the syndicate contributed $2,800, a paltry sum for them, even by 1960 standards, so they didn't have a lot to lose.

Whatever their motivations, the contract they offered Clay was extremely generous and certainly met his father's objectives of safeguarding the fighter's interests. He was to receive a $10,000 signing bonus and a guaranteed draw of $4,000 a year against earnings. The group would underwrite all travel and training expenses and they would split earnings fifty-fifty. To safeguard Clay's future, 15 percent of all income would be set aside into a pension fund that he couldn't touch until age thirty-five or his retirement from boxing. It was a long way from Frankie Carbo.

Louisville is, of course, the home of the famed Kentucky Derby. Each member of the Sponsoring Group had at some time or another been involved with racehorses. But if the men thought their new acquisition could be controlled by pulling on his reins, they were in for a surprise.

CHAPTER TWO:
Those Who Came Before

ALL SPORT CAN BE SEEN AS A METAPHOR, even a proxy, for conflict and war. But none comes closer to fulfilling that metaphor—its superficial role as athletic competition to become something bigger, a more potent symbol—than boxing. From the days when gladiators fought to the death in the middle of packed Roman coliseums as part of a carefully orchestrated strategy to keep the people from revolting, organized combat between two men has transcended mere sport.

Boxing historian Budd Schulberg has observed that just as the people get the government they deserve, each era gets the heavyweight boxing champion it deserves, one who reflects the social and political currents of the day. To take his theory a step further, it can be argued that the history of black heavyweight champions has always mirrored the history of American race relations.

For Muhammad Ali, who was about to irrevocably shape his own era, there were two forebears who illustrated Schulberg's maxim perfectly, whose careers would serve as precursors for his own.

The first black boxers were plantation slaves who fought each other in vicious, anything-goes matches for the amusement of the slaveholders and the other slaves. In the most celebrated interplantation matches, the slaves gave everything they had in pursuit of the victory

prize—their freedom. Nineteenth century African-American philosopher Frederick Douglass described these matches as "among the most
effective means in the hands of the slaveholder in keeping down the
spirit of insurrection." At the peak of his career, Muhammad Ali captured Douglass's skepticism in describing how he felt when he per-
formed for the crowd: "We're just like two slaves in that ring. The mas-
ters get two of us big old black slaves and let us fight it out while they
bet: 'My slave can whup your slave.' That's what I see when I see two
black people fighting."

Following the Civil War and the liberal abolitionist spirit that accompanied it, blacks made significant gains in the sporting arena. Even in
the South, where Reconstruction forced their temporary acceptance as
full citizens, Blacks were integrated into most major sports. But the end
of Reconstruction in the 1880s saw a rapid turnaround in the way
Americans viewed Blacks. Suddenly, as historian Frederic Jaher
observed, "Court decisions, legislative and executive actions, publicly
and privately sanctioned terrorism, the 'findings' of biologists and social
scientists, and the metaphors of writers and movie makers denied
blacks economic opportunities, separated them from whites in all but
servile interactions, and stigmatized them as childlike brutes genetical-
ly incapable of participating in civilized society."

Athletics was one of the first segments of American society to feel the
changing attitudes. Blacks were formally barred from most sporting
institutions because it was believed their victories over whites would
significantly undermine the growing arguments about their inferiority.

The impact was profound: fourteen of the fifteen jockeys in the 1875
Kentucky Derby were black; by 1911, however, Blacks were completely barred from the race. Despite the widely held notion that Jackie
Robinson was the first black to break baseball's color barrier, there
were in fact several prominent Black Major League players during the
1870s. Yet the next decade saw the institution of segregation on the
nation's diamonds, a baseball apartheid that would last nearly seventy
years. As early as 1809, the former slave Tom Molineaux had fought for
the heavyweight boxing championship. By the end of the century,
however, white champions routinely insisted on only fighting men of
their own color.

There was no rule per se that Blacks could not fight for the heavy-

weight championship. But a succession of champions, the most celebrated personalities of their era, simply refused to fight a black man.
From John L. Sullivan, the first boxer to defend the title under the
Marquis of Queensbury rules, to Jim Corbett, to Bob Fitzsimmons, no
champion would risk his prestige by losing to a lowly Negro, although
blacks could still contest the crown of lower divisions. This informal
ban lasted for more than two decades, until 1905, when the so-called
"golden age of boxing" came to an end with the retirement of the
champion Jim Jeffries.

Jeffries's departure from the sport is considered by some as the end
of the greatest era of boxing. It also set the stage for the man who
would shake America to its foundations.

After the retirement of Jeffries, the championship was won by a journeyman Canadian named Tommy Burns. Boxing had lost its lustre and
the crop of white contenders was mediocre, failing to entice the fans
that had turned out in droves to see the colorful personalities of the
previous era. While there was clearly no white contender worthy of a
title bout, and more importantly none who could attract the kind of
gate that would make a promoter take notice, there was one fighter
whose feats were gaining widespread attention.

Jack Johnson was born in 1880 to former slaves in Galveston, Texas.
In the fifth grade, he dropped out of school to do odd jobs and help support his six siblings. After beating up a local bully, he began training to
box, and by 1897 he had turned professional. From 1902 to 1907,
Johnson won more than fifty matches, most of them against other black
boxers. But in 1906 he fought Bob Fitzsimmons, the ex-heavyweight
champion, and knocked him out. None of the boxers who had succeeded Fitzsimmons would agree to fight Johnson because of his color.

After Burns won the crown in 1906, there was a growing chorus of
voices arguing that Johnson deserved a chance at the title. Confident
that Johnson, nicknamed "Little Arthur," would easily be handled by his
racially superior foe—"the match will set to rest for all time the matter
of fistic supremacy between white race and colored"—the *New York Sun*
chided Burns to accept Johnson's challenge. Finally, Burns relented.

The bout was to be fought in Australia, so the expected American
outrage over a fight between a black challenger and a white champion
was somewhat tempered. Still, feelings ran strong. Jack London, author

of *Call of the Wild*, is best known as an adventure novelist and a fervent socialist. But he was also one of America's greatest boxing aficionados and would frequently cover matches for the *New York Herald*. Sent to Australia to cover the Johnson-Burns bout, scheduled for Christmas Day, 1908, London signaled the attitude of most Americans in his pre-fight dispatches. "I am with Burns all the way," he wrote. "He is a white man and so am I. Naturally I want to see the white man win."

London and millions of white Americans were shocked at the result. It was bad enough that Johnson displayed a complete mastery over the hapless Burns, knocking him out in the fourteenth round. But the way he did it made things much worse. The challenger continuously taunt-ed Burns, a smile on his face as he toyed with the champion, dancing around, jeering for his opponent to "come get me." Sixty years later, these kinds of tactics would infuriate boxing fans when employed by Muhammad Ali, who would claim to be the reincarnation of Johnson. But in 1908, reports of this kind of behavior by a Negro sent the nation into a blind rage. One letter to the editor called Johnson's victory "a calamity in this country worse than the San Francisco earthquake."

The search began in earnest for a "white hope" who could put Johnson in his place. In his report on the Burns match, London implored the former champion Jim Jeffries to come out of retirement and restore the title to white America. A series of mediocre white con-tenders came forward to challenge Johnson in 1909 and he knocked out each one in succession, delivering a taunt with every punch.

By the end of the year, cries for a Jeffries fight had reached a fevered pitch, with London leading the charge, describing the retired champi-on as the "chosen representative of the white race."

Finally, the financial lure proved too much for Jeffries to resist. Anticipating the largest gate in the history of prizefighting, a sleazy promoter named Tex Rickard offered him a huge sum of money to take on Johnson. Announcing that he was succumbing to "that portion of the white race that has been looking for me to defend its racial superi-ority," Jeffries signed on for the fight.

Rickard was anxious to exploit the growing racial fear and hostility of Americans, and he heavily promoted the fight as a battle for racial supremacy. The nation was whipped into a frenzy. Editorial cartoons portrayed Johnson as a gorilla or a watermelon-eating brute and

Jeffries as a Superman. From pulpits all over the nation, ministers took up the theme that the fight would be the salvation of white pride. One Baltimore minister warned his congregation that a Johnson victory would make it unsafe for white women and children to walk the streets. The three-time Democratic presidential nominee and fundamentalist Christian William Jennings Bryan telegraphed Jeffries before the fight: "God will forgive everything you do to that nigger in this fight. . . Jeff, God is with you."

The fight—and the hooplah leading up to it—was sending shock waves through the west coast. Originally scheduled to take place in San Francisco, it was moved to Reno, Nevada, after fifty ministers held a prayer vigil at the California State Capitol to convince the governor to reject the controversial bout.

But overwhelmingly, the country was hypnotized by the promotion of the fight as an epic duel between black and white. A song was penned by Dorothy Forrester in a typical vaudeville Italian-style dialect, popular in those days, capturing the mood of the country:

> *Commence right away to get into condish*
> *An' you punch-a da bag-a day and night*
> *An'-a-din pretty soon, when you meet-a da coon,*
> *You knock-a him clear out of sight.*
> *Chorus: Who's dat man wid-a hand like da bunch-a*
> *banan!*
> *It's da Jim-a-da-Jeff, oh! da Jim-a-da-Jeff,*
>
> *Who give-a da Jack Jonce one-a little-a tap?*
> *Who make-a him take-a one big-a long nap?*
> *Who wipe-a da Africa off-a da map?*
> *It's da Jim-a-da-Jeff!*

White Americans weren't the only ones aware of the symbolic implications of the fight. The black press used the match as a rallying cry against thirty years of backwards progress for Negro Americans. The *Chicago Defender* assured its readers that Johnson would be fighting "Race Hatred," "Prejudice" and "Negro Persecution." In a sermon the Sunday before the match, the black Chicagoan Reverend William

Ransom declared that the match had deep significance in the struggle for Negro advancement. "The darker races of mankind, and the black race in particular, will keep the white race busy for the next few hundred years in defending the interests of white supremacy. . . what Jack Johnson seeks to do to Jeffries in the roped arena will be more the ambition of Negroes in every domain of human endeavor."

The stakes were much higher than just a boxing match, and it seemed everybody in the country was anxiously awaiting the verdict. When the fight finally took place on the holiday of July 4, 1910, eighteen thousand spectators greeted Johnson as he stepped into the ring by singing another song popular that year: "All Coons Look Alike to Me." The song was inspired by Jeffries's remark several years earlier when he refused to fight Johnson.

None were more aware of the significance of the bout than Johnson himself. When the bell sounded, he answered the years of scorn, abuse, and hostility he had been forced to endure with a punishing series of blows, delivering each with a smile and a taunt. "Package being delivered, Mr. Jeff," he announced as he rained one punch after another on his humiliated opponent. As the crowds looked on in disbelief, he finally finished off Jeffries with a fifteenth-round knockout.

JEFF MASTERED BY GRINNING, JEERING NEGRO, trumpeted the headlines in the evening papers. Within hours, a race riot was raging across the nation. Eight blacks were killed as rioting broke out in most of the country's major cities, the worst urban unrest America would witness until the assassination of Martin Luther King Jr. nearly sixty years later. "The fear, frustration, and anger generated by the Reno debacle," writes historian Frederic Jaher in his analysis of the hysteria, "was not confined to criticism of the victor, blacks, and boxing; rationalizations about the meaninglessness of Jeffries's defeat; or advice to the Negroes not to depart from the servility which reassured whites about the 'race problem' in America. Violence was still the ultimate weapon against the 'uppity nigger' and many Americans were not reluctant to resort to it when they felt the need to 'keep the Negro in his place.'"

While the riots were an extreme manifestation of America's anger and largely confined to the most unruly elements of the white population, the liberal intelligentsia was not immune from racist overreaction to Johnson's victory. "For the colored population we fear that the victory of Mr. Johnson will prove a misfortune," wrote the *New York Times*. "It will be natural for Negroes to proclaim Johnson's victory as a racial triumph and in doing so they incite hostility. . . supremacy in a civilized state does not rest on physical force," the influential journal opined, adding that it hoped America had seen the "last prizefight between representatives of different races."

Such was the symbolic importance of the heavyweight championship on the nation's collective consciousness then and for many generations to come.

For some urban blacks, according to historian Lawrence Levine, "the very extent of white anger and frustration made Johnson's victory even sweeter." A popular street song sprang up, which seemed to thumb its nose at white resentment:

> *The Yankees hold the play*
> *The white man pulls the trigger*
> *But it makes no difference what the white man say*
> *The world champion's still a nigger*

A half-century later, Muhammad Ali would delight in writing similarly defiant doggerel and playfully reciting it for his critics in response to the establishment's backlash against him.

No longer content to seek out a white hope who would "send Johnson back to the jungle," the media, the clergy, and the politicians —alarmed at the waning credibility of white supremacy—decided something had to be done to curb this dangerous trend. In those pre-television days, Americans would flock to movie theaters in large numbers to see replays of championship fights. This is where the promoters made their real money from boxing. Overnight, there was a nationwide campaign to boycott or ban fight films.

The so-called forces of decency, wrote Jaher, "sought to spare American youth the spectacle of mayhem in the ring, destroy a corrupt and commercialized sport, prevent Negroes from harboring delusions of superiority and Caucasians from further humiliation, avoid racial strife, and make interracial bouts unprofitable, if not impossible."

The boycott was successful but its proponents weren't content to stop there. They persuaded Congress to debate a bill prohibiting the inter-state transportation of fight films—which would, in effect, prevent their screening—so whites couldn't witness the blow to their race. Johnson wasn't cowed by the campaign of hatred levelled against him. "I'm black and they'll never let me forget it. Sure I'm black and I'll never let them forget it," he said defiantly. On the floor of Congress, Georgia Representative Seaborn Roddenberry called the Johnson-Jeffries fight "the grossest instance of base fraud and bogus effort at a fair fight between a Caucasian brute and African piped beast. No man descended from the old Saxon race can look upon that kind of a contest without abhorrence and disgust." The bill passed in 1912.

Johnson's behavior in the ring had already infuriated white America. But it was his actions outside the ring that would prove his undoing. After the Jeffries fight, reaction calmed down somewhat and some newspapers even seemed to gain a grudging respect for the champion. In his autobiography, Johnson described the atmosphere. "The bitterness which had actuated some of those interested in boxing had subsided," he wrote. "Some of my greatest enemies were silenced and many who had been almost venomous toward me grew a little more restrained."

The truce, however, was short-lived. An uncontrollable wave of hostility was sparked in 1911 when Johnson took his substantial ring earnings and opened up an integrated night club in Chicago's red-light district. Visitors to the club were greeted by a giant painting of Johnson embracing the white woman he had married a few months earlier.

This violation of America's most sacred taboo set off a new round of vilification against the champion. Fresh from his successful crusade to ban fight films, Georgia Congressman Roddenberry proposed a bill forbidding interracial marriages. He predicted that if other blacks followed the habits of Johnson it could lead to a race conflict bloodier than the Civil War. Such unions, he raged on the floor of Congress, "make a white girl a slave of an African brute and encourage the vicious element of the Negro race, which results in the descendants of our Anglo-Saxon fathers and mothers having mixed blood descended from the far-off orangutan shores of Africa."

The news that Johnson had married a white woman caused many other blacks to reevaluate their admiration of him. The influential black writer Booker T. Washington wrote, "Jack Johnson has harmed rather than helped the race. I wish to say emphatically that his actions do not meet my approval and I'm sure they don't meet the approval of the colored race." Historian Jeffrey Sammons examined the paradox of the champion's impact on American blacks. "While Jack Johnson was clearly a source of pride to many blacks, and to some an alter ego, a man many blacks wished they could be—reckless, independent, bold and superior in the face of whites—to other blacks he was a source of embarrassment and resentment," wrote Sammons. "Many middle class, upwardly mobile blacks tended to accuse their less-refined, less-reserved, and less-cultured brethren of casting aspersions on their race . . . Johnson, in many ways, represented the 'bad nigger' whites were so willing to parade as an example of why blacks must be kept in their place. . . but while ambivalence best characterized the black community's opinion of Johnson, most whites viewed him as a menace to the established social order and to Anglo-Saxon civilization, and they were intent upon his destruction as a powerful symbol."

Like Muhammad Ali many years later, Johnson's troubles began with a lengthy investigation by the Bureau of Investigation, forerunner of the FBI. In 1913, the agency announced an eleven-count indictment against him. The charges ranged from aiding prostitution and debauchery to unlawful sexual intercourse and sodomy. He was arrested under the Mann Act, which prohibited a man from crossing a state line with a woman other than his wife for the purposes of sex. His wife had committed suicide a year earlier, and he had frequently traveled between Chicago and Pittsburgh with a woman named Belle Schreiber.

However, it was clear that the indictment and arrest were designed to persecute the man who had become a thorn in the side of white America. The trial sparked a frenzy of hatred for Johnson. A crowd of one thousand gathered outside the courthouse in Chicago, chanting, "Kill him! Lynch him!" These cries were especially troubling, considering that during Johnson's reign as heavyweight champion, 354 blacks were lynched in America, 89 for supposed offenses against white women.

The theme of miscegenation had captured the imagination of white Americans who had always harbored secret fears that black men only wanted to sleep with their women. Sordid comic books circulated with such titles as *Jack Johnson and His Girls* and *Black Ape Splitting the White Princess.* The nation's press, clergy, and politicians demanded he be sent to prison. Despite no concrete evidence against him, it took an all-white jury less than an hour to convict the despised boxer.

In sentencing Johnson to one year in prison and a $1,000 fine, Judge George Carpenter made it clear he intended to send a message to the black community. "This defendant is one of the best known men of his race. His example is far reaching and the court is bound to consider the position he occupies among his people," he declared.

Before he could serve time, Johnson escaped through Canada and made his way to Europe. America was finally rid of its embarrassing reminder of racial equality. Two years later, a broke Johnson agreed to fight the new white hope Jess Willard in Havana, Cuba. Dispirited and out of shape, Johnson was knocked out in the twenty-sixth round. White America breathed a collective sigh of relief. "The great mass of our white citizenship simply rejoiced at the outcome of the fight," editorialized the *Chicago Tribune.* "It is a point of pride with the ascendant race not to concede supremacy in anything, not even to a gorilla."

Jack Johnson would never again set foot in the ring, but his legacy would live on. Jeffrey Sammons argues that Johnson left an indelible mark on the sport and the larger society. "Those who believed that his removal from his position of influence would ease racial tensions and deter black aspirations were mistaken. Johnson was a forerunner of, and a critical ingredient in, a new social movement. Jack Johnson foreshadowed, and in some ways helped to create, the 'New Negro'—a more militant black who was disillusioned with southern segregation, northern discrimination, and the undelivered promises of the American creed."

But if Johnson's influence had an impact on American society, it would be less discernible in the ring, where it took another twenty years for a black boxer to fight again for the heavyweight title; it would be fifty years before another boxer would have the same searing impact on the collective American psyche.

▶ ▶ ▶

If Jack Johnson was the "bad nigger" in an age of strident racism, theorizes historian Frederic Jaher, then Joe Louis was "a credit to his race" in a time of patronizing tolerance.

For twenty years after Jack Johnson was put back in his place, the boxing establishment made damn sure there would be no repeat of the spectre of Little Arthur. Once again, it employed the tactic that first created the color barrier in the pre-Johnson era. Champions simply refused to fight a black challenger.

Following the First World War, a charismatic young boxer named Jack Dempsey beat Jess Willard to win the championship. At the behest of Tex Rickard—the promoter who created the atmosphere leading to the Jack Johnson race riots—the new champion immediately vowed never to step into the ring with a Negro. To this day, there is a debate whether Dempsey was a genuine racist or whether he was simply afraid of losing his title. This fear was well-founded. The leading challengers were unquestionably blacks such as Harry Wills, while the crop of white contenders was mediocre at best.

In 1923, a black Senegalese boxer known as Battling Siki defeated Georges Carpentier for the light heavyweight championship in a match fought in France. When news of Siki's victory reached the United States, one editor called it "a distinct jolt to the foundation of the world as it is today." Still haunted by the Jack Johnson era, American newspapers issued dire warnings to the French people about the danger of allowing such fights on French soil. The *Springfield Republican* warned France that its rule over African colonies depended on prestige, not force, and the victory of a black boxer might make the colonial subjects "lose their attitudes of respectful admiration for white men."

Afraid that Siki would come to America and challenge Dempsey for the heavyweight title, the media fabricated stories—a la Johnson—of Siki's playboy exploits and "savage" ways. Speculation about Siki's challenge was silenced with his murder in 1925, but another black boxer, Harry Wills, had since built up an impressive record and was considered the most formidable contender for Dempsey's title.

The prestigious boxing magazine *Ring* took up Wills's cause, arguing the black challenger deserved a title bout. Chief among its arguments was that Wills was no Jack Johnson. The articulate and humble Wills did everything he could to erase the memory of the first black champion. He publicly labelled "the talk about the menace of colored supremacy as all bunk," prompting *Ring* editor Nat Fleischer to call him "a credit to the game and to the race."

Still, Dempsey held the line and refused to fight Wills or any other Negro. But the public was getting fed up with the mediocre white opponents served up to challenge Dempsey and there was a growing chorus of calls for a Wills title bout. Sensitive to the changing mood, the New York State Athletic Commission ruled that Dempsey would have to face Wills for the heavyweight championship. The ruling raised alarm in many circles and set off a series of behind-the-scenes maneuvers—eventually successful—designed to reverse the decision, setting the scene for a match between Dempsey and Gene Tunney instead.

A committee, under the leadership of the liberal Colonel John Phelan, still had to issue each fighter a license. Phelan declared that Dempsey's license would be withheld until he agreed to fight Wills. It appeared the color barrier was about to fall. But Dempsey had vowed "never to step into the ring with a Negro," and he was determined to keep his word. He simply moved the Tunney fight to Pennsylvania where, to little consolation for Wills, Dempsey lost his title. The new champion was no more willing to entertain a black challenger, and another decade would pass before the man would emerge who was destined to change the face of boxing forever.

▶ ▶ ▶

With the onset of the Great Depression, boxing suffered a prolonged decline in attendance and prestige. This was partly due to the ascendance of other forms of popular entertainment, notably movies, which continued to attract large audiences eager to take their minds off the nation's domestic ills. But underpinning the increasing indifference to boxing was the fact that no fighter had emerged who could capture the nation's imagination and revive the sagging sport.

Tex Rickard had recently died and his protégé Mike Jacobs was determined to break the stranglehold of the Madison Square Garden establishment that had long controlled the fight game. Before he could consolidate his power, however, he needed to find the right boxer.

Around the time Jack Johnson was being hounded out of the country, Joe Louis Barrow was born to an Alabama sharecropper. His father died when he was four and his mother remarried, moving her new brood of sixteen children to Detroit, where blacks were being hired to work in the growing auto industry.

After dropping out of school in grade six, Louis was introduced to boxing by a friend and he soon discovered he had a natural talent for the sport. When he was sixteen, his mother gave him money every week for violin lessons but the teenager used the money instead to pay for a locker at the Brewster Recreation Center where Detroit's best boxers gathered and trained. His amateur career started slowly with a number of early defeats, but soon his awesome punching power was attracting attention. He made it to the Golden Gloves final in Boston in 1933 and won the amateur light heavyweight championship a year later.

His rapid rise brought Louis to the attention of a number of potential handlers—mostly mob-connected and mostly white—who were always anxious to get a piece of an up-and-coming fighter. But he was most impressed by a successful black gambling magnate named John Roxborough, who convinced him that black boxers needed somebody they could trust and that only a fellow Negro could fit that role. Roxborough brought in a Chicago numbers runner and nightclub owner named Julian Black to co-manage his new find. The two weren't exactly paragons of virtue and honesty—they were both quite prominent in the black mob—but they had a keen sense of what it would take to mold Louis so he would be acceptable to white society.

They knew their fighter must become the antithesis of Jack Johnson if he was ever to get a shot at the title. The first thing they did before turning him pro was to issue a strict set of rules he must abide by. It's as if they studied Johnson's biography before crafting the guidelines:

1. Louis was never to be photographed with a white woman.
2. He was never to enter a nightclub alone.
3. There would be no fixed fights.
4. He could never gloat over a fallen opponent.
5. He was to keep a deadpan expression in front of the cameras (in memory of the famous Johnson headline about the "grinning, jeering Negro").
6. He was to live and fight clean.

A number of physical factors helped facilitate the new image as well. Louis was very light-skinned—in photos, he appeared almost white— and thus looked much less threatening to white America than the dark-complexioned Johnson. He also had a mild speech defect and therefore rarely spoke to the media. This allowed his handlers to do most of the talking—and they took full advantage, honing a carefully crafted image of Louis as a modest, churchgoing man who hated to hurt opponents, didn't drink or smoke, and supported his large family from his earnings.

Their strategy worked. Roxborough was approached by the powerful promoter Mike Jacobs, who offered to promote Louis's fights. Jacobs sensed the potential for the "Brown Bomber"—as he was already being called—to revive the nearly bankrupt sport.

In what was to become a theme of Louis's career, world events played a pivotal role in his ascendancy. In 1934, Benito Mussolini struck the first blow for fascism by invading the African nation of Abyssinia (later Ethiopia), ruled since 1930 by Hailie Selassie, a leader who had become a hero to many American Blacks.

Mussolini had long been a boxing fan, describing punching as "an exquisitely fascist means of self-expression." In 1930, American immigration officials had threatened to deport an Italian boxer and former champion named Primo Carnera back to Italy because of his mob ties. The Italian dictator personally intervened to prevent the deportation, earning Carnera the label of "Mussolini's emissary in America." Now Jacobs decided to capitalize on the Abyssinia invasion by staging a bout between Louis and Carnera.

The media picked up on the fight as a battle between Abyssinia and Italy in the ring, but Blacks were paying the most attention. Mussolini, unlike Hitler, wasn't yet considered by most Americans to be particularly troubling. But his recent conquest of Abyssinia—which he represented as a victory of whites over the "savage race"—had turned Il Duce into a major villain in black America.

To get whites to pay attention and to garner sympathy for Louis, Jacobs donated part of the fight gate to the Milk Fund—the favorite charity of Mrs. William Randolph Hearst. This ensured the support of the powerful Hearst newspaper syndicate. Hearst reporter Quentin Reynolds, for example, told his readers that if Louis became champion, "the boxing game will have a leader of whom it will not be ashamed and the Negro race will have a representative that it can point to with pride."

On June 25, 1935, the two fighters met in Yankee Stadium and Abyssinia avenged its honor, pulverizing Italy with a sixth-round knockout. After the fight, there were reports of black youths running through the streets of Harlem, yelling "Let's get Mussolini next."

Louis made sure to react humbly to his victory, which further ingratiated him to his growing legions of supporters, Blacks and, especially, whites. The *New York Mirror* hailed Louis as "a God-fearing, Bible-reading, clean-living boy" and welcomed his "modest, quiet, and unassuming manner."

Finally, here was a black boxer who seemed to know his place. The ghost of Jack Johnson appeared to have been banished. (In fact, Johnson was still very much alive. He had returned to America to serve his time and even tried to visit Louis's training camp, where he was swiftly exorcised by Roxborough.)

The careful crafting of Louis's image was unquestionably an important factor in his growing acceptance. But times had changed considerably as well. Franklin Roosevelt was in the White House and his popular first lady Eleanor had emerged as a champion of Negro rights. Lynchings were down 80 percent since Johnson's day, and more Americans every year were expressing tolerance of integration in the annual Gallup poll. Most academics and scientists no longer believed in the genetic inferiority of Blacks, which was almost universally accepted during the Johnson years. The hostility of twenty years earlier had been replaced by a condescending tolerance, still a far cry from the acceptance of Blacks as equal.

Louis was portrayed as humble but also childlike and docile. Even in articles that praised him, the writer would often note his lack of intelligence or comment on his "animal-like" traits in the ring. In the South, he was seen by the media as a good example for Negroes because "he knew his place." But Southerners were nevertheless nervous that Louis victories might spark a surge of racial pride. Anticipating this, the *Raleigh News and Observer* counseled that "wise Negroes—as wise white men—will not put their pride in a prize fighter, but will watch the race's advance in the more important, less dramatic things by which in the long view any race or any people must be judged."

There was still considerable animosity in some circles. Editorial cartoons often portrayed Louis as a combination of savage brute and simple child. Jack Dempsey led the search for a white hope to stop him before he could get a title bout.

The most compelling evidence that America still had a long way to go toward true racial progress emerged during the fight that would represent a major setback in Louis's march towards the championship and full acceptance by white America.

By 1936, Louis seemed to have achieved all the conditions necessary to secure the right to fight for a title. *Ring* magazine had named him "boxer of the year" after he won five fights in succession. His fight with Max Baer earned boxing's first million-dollar gate, signaling a major turnaround in the fortunes of the once-moribund sport. Now Mike Jacobs only had one more obstacle for his new cash cow. Remembering the success of the Carnera fight and its symbolic implications against fascism, Jacobs plucked a former German champion named Max Schmeling out of obscurity and offered him a fight with Louis. Schmeling had long been embraced by Adolf Hitler as a model of Aryan supremacy, and Jacobs believed a fight between a "member of the master race" and his new black sensation would generate huge interest.

The media, sensing a chance to cash in on nationalistic jingoism, touted the match as a battle between America and the "tool of Hitler's oppression" rather than a fight between Black vs. White, but their support was not enough to overcome the racial divisions that still plagued parts of the country. Southern newspapers, predicting a Louis victory, reported hundreds of angry letters from readers outraged that they would champion a "darkie."

But American support for Schmeling wasn't confined to Southern crackers. This was made clear on the night of the fight. Overly optimistic, and believing the hype that he would easily vanquish Schmeling, Louis failed to train properly and was knocked out in round twelve. Frederic Jaher observed that the fight itself proved a testament to the enduring priority of racial over national affinity despite the fact that it took place in New York City, a center of American liberalism, racial tolerance, and opposition to Nazism. When Schmeling towered over his fallen opponent, he received a huge ovation from the crowd. Jack Dempsey declared his victory "the finest thing to happen to boxing in a long time." Schmeling received more congratulatory telegrams from the United States than any other country. More troubling, the media started to turn against the defeated challenger, questioning his heart, his intelligence, and his talent—as if he had betrayed them for their support.

The Nazis wasted no time in capitalizing on Schmeling's victory, hoping to convince white Americans that they and Germany were on the same side. German propagandist George Spandau declared that "through the German Schmeling the white race, Europe, and white America defeated the black race."

Meanwhile, Louis was determined to claw his way back into contention for a title shot. Putting the Schmeling fiasco behind him, he won six consecutive fights in convincing fashion. Mike Jacobs sensed the time had come for Joe Louis to take his rightful place.

On June 22, 1937, when Louis stepped into the ring with the champion James Braddock, it was the first time in twenty-two years a black boxer had fought for the heavyweight title. Media interest was subdued. Still unable to forgive him for losing to Schmeling, but recognizing the likelihood of his success, most newspaper editors counseled that a Louis victory should not be taken as a sign of black racial superiority.

Louis's handlers continued their carefully orchestrated campaign to shape their fighter's image and gain white acceptance for a black champion. His mother was quoted in the sympathetic Hearst press saying, "I know that if Joe wins the championship he is going to make Jack Johnson feel ashamed of himself again. Joe wants to win to show the white folks that a colored man can bring dignity and decency to the title just as well as a white man."

When, as expected, Louis won to reclaim the title Johnson had first claimed for blacks in 1910, the reaction was significantly muted compared to the hysteria twenty-seven years earlier. Blacks poured out onto the streets of Northern cities to celebrate, but there were few incidents of violence. In the South, the jubilant black population made sure to celebrate in their own homes for fear of provoking retaliation. Louis's characteristically modest reaction to his victory stood in stark contrast to Jack Johnson's brash gloating after he first won the title from Jim Jeffries. This, and the changing racial attitudes, helped Americans tolerate, if not fully accept, the new titleholder, even in the Deep South. The *Birmingham News* reported "less race prejudice . . . less disposition to resent a Negro heavyweight champion."

The media—and white America—continued to be lukewarm to the new champion, however, until the fight that proved to be the defining moment of his career. Since the 1936 matchup between Louis and Schmeling, Nazi Germany had annexed Austria and had made clear its intentions to take over Europe. By 1938, its brutal campaign of anti-Semitic violence had galvanized world opinion, and America's distaste for Hitler was much more intense than it had been two years earlier. In this context, Mike Jacobs arranged for a Louis–Schmeling rematch that, this time, was viewed as a contest between America and the enemy. A month before the scheduled bout, Louis was invited to the White House, where President Roosevelt told him, "Joe, we need muscles like yours to beat Germany." Both countries recognized the propaganda implications of the bout, and the hype was intense. Newspapers billed the match as Democracy vs. Fascism, Good vs. Evil. For the first time in history, the hopes of America rested on a black man.

Louis didn't let his country down. This time he was well-prepared and from the opening bell he unleashed a stunning assault on the surprised Schmeling, knocking the hope of Aryan supremacy unconscious in just 124 seconds. When the referee raised Louis's arms in victory, it elevated him from a mere boxer to a legend and, more importantly, an American hero.

Today, Reverend Jesse Jackson calls the fight the incident that freed black people "from the midst of inferiority." The media were effusive in their praise and it seemed everybody was aware of the fight's significance. *Ring* magazine declared that "Schmeling's defeat symbolized the complete deflation of any and all 'ism' or claims to natural supremacy of any particular race or group." It seemed that most Americans agreed, and for the first time ever the majority of the country told pollsters they admired a black man.

The impact of the second Louis-Schmeling fight would be felt for years to come in sports and in society at large. Jackie Robinson would credit the new acceptance of a black athlete for creating the climate that allowed him to re-break baseball's color barrier less than a decade later.

The victory was without a doubt one of the most important events in the history of American race relations, but the reaction of the celebrated sportswriter Paul Gallico underlined the reality that Louis's popularity was due in no small part to his understanding of the Negro's role in America: "Louis is what is known definitely as a 'good nigger who knows his place,'" the celebrated author wrote in the *New York Daily News*. "He has been carefully trained in the sly servility that the white man accepts as his due." If this message wasn't driven home by Gallico's assessment, it was made clear in almost every speech by every mayor who invited the champion to receive the keys to his city. The same words emerged at each reception and parade. "He's a credit to his race," they chorused—the highest praise they could imagine for the new hero. Sportswriter Jimmy Cannon underscored the liberal condescension of Louis's new admirers when he wrote, "He's a credit to his race—the human race."

If Louis was admired by white Americans, he had become a genuine icon to blacks. Years later, at the start of the civil rights movement, the generation of black Americans who grew up worshipping Joe Louis and digesting the message that they would be tolerated if they "kept in their place" were uneasy about their sons and daughters engaged in radical activities sure to incur the wrath of whites. It was this attitude of their elders that often posed the first obstacles for the young militants hungry for change.

Louis's unprecedented influence on black Americans is recalled by Martin Luther King Jr. in his manifesto *Why We Can't Wait*. He tells the story of the black convict on death row in the 1940s who was the first victim of poison gas as a method of execution. A microphone was set up to record the convict's reaction to the gas. "As the pellet dropped into the container," wrote King, "and gas curled upward, through the microphone came these words: 'Save me Joe Louis. Save me, Joe Louis. Save me, Joe Louis.'"

Louis cemented his legend after the Japanese bombed Pearl Harbor. Early on, he traveled to army bases, putting on exhibitions and entertaining the troops. He donated the entire purse from his 1942 title bout with Buddy Baer to the Navy Relief Fund, which earned him wide-

With Joe Louis, Las Vegas, 1965.

spread praise in the American media for his patriotism. In February 1942, Louis enlisted in the army, where he was assigned to Special Services, continuing his role of entertaining the troops. The U.S. government took full advantage of Louis's war effort. Almost every newsreel spotlighted his activities, and every American was aware of his patriotism, elevating his national status as a hero even higher.

But behind the government's campaign to trumpet Louis's wartime contributions was a concerted effort to mask an ugly reality. While Blacks were being urged to enlist in the army and fight for freedom, some Blacks—especially the black media—recognized the hypocrisy of the fact that the army was completely segregated. Blacks were assigned to the most menial tasks and, when they did go into battle, it was often as cannon fodder, suffering casualty rates far higher than their white counterparts.

It soon became clear that Louis's role was to convince Blacks they had a patriotic duty to go to war. Frank Capra was hired to direct a propaganda film called *The Negro Soldier,* with Sergeant Joe Louis as the centerpiece, declaring "There may be a whole lot wrong with America, but there's nothing Hitler can fix." Despite—or because of— its inaccurate implication that black soldiers had often glamorous duties and served alongside whites, the film did much to boost black morale and successfully achieved its goal of increasing enlistment.

After Louis retired in 1947, he was repaid for his patriotism and his service to the government with a massive tax bill. His white promoters had reneged on a promise to turn over their share of gate receipts to the armed forces charities to which Louis frequently contributed. As a result, his large donations were not tax exempt. Louis was no longer any use to them, and the government refused to recognize his loyal service. Louis never quite recovered from the financial hardship. He was forced to come out of retirement twice past his prime, only to suffer humiliating defeats. The rest of his life was spent in a buffoonish series of attempts to pay his back taxes, including embarrassing stints as a professional wrestler and a shill for the mob, acting as a "greeter" at various Las Vegas casinos. He died penniless in 1981.

Cassius Clay was only five years old when Joe Louis retired as heavyweight champion. Cassius Clay Sr. would later recall that "around our house, Joe was a hero. We listened to all his fights. There was no one like Joe."

No one like Joe. Within a decade and a half, much of the world would be saying the same thing about his son, Cassius Clay Jr., Muhammad Ali. And it would continue to be said for years, until Louis had faded into obscurity in the collective memory. Because as much of an impact as Joe Louis and, for that matter, Jack Johnson, had on boxing and American society in general, their legacies would pale in comparison to that of Ali, a man who—as a threat to the white establishment and a messiah to the black underclass—was a combination of Jack Johnson and Joe Louis, and then some.

CHAPTER THREE:
A Modern Crusade

WHEN HE RETURNED FROM ROME with his gold medal in 1960, Cassius Clay gave an interview to *Newsweek* sportswriter Dick Schaap. "You know I'll be a credit to my race," he declared emphatically. For the new Olympic champion, those words had a very different meaning than they did for Joe Louis.

It didn't take long for the newly minted professional to prove Rome was no fluke. In quick order and with ease, he disposed of challenger after challenger as he worked his way up the heavyweight ladder. But it wasn't his boxing skills that were attracting the most attention. It was his personality—a mixture of charm, chutzpah, and wit—that caused people to take notice. After his seventh straight knockout, he revived his old amateur trick of calling the round in which his opponent would go down.

> *They all must fall*
> *In the round I call*

When he felled the former heavyweight champion Archie Moore in round four and then proceeded to knock out pro football player Charlie Powell in round three—both as promised—the pundits stopped dismissing the brash fighter as a loudmouthed braggart.

But Clay wasn't content to let his ring exploits alone build up his

reputation. He helped his cause along whenever he could with his natural genius for self-promotion. Once, early in his pro career, a freelance
photographer named Flip Schulke shot Cassius Clay for *Sports
Illustrated*. While Schulke took photos, his subject asked him who else
he worked for. The photographer responded that he did a lot of photos
for *Life* magazine and that one of his specialties was underwater pho-
tography. "Man, how about shooting me for *Life*," the boxer pleaded.
Schulke explained he wasn't famous enough to get into *Life*—at the
time the most popular publication in America. Thinking fast, Clay concocted a story on the spot. He explained that one thing accounted for
his blinding speed. Just as runners sometimes train in weighted shoes
so they feel lighter and run faster when they put on normal sneakers,
he said he regularly trained in a swimming pool up to his neck, punching in the water. Two months later, *Life* ran a five-page photo spread of
Cassius Clay in the water up to his neck headlined HE'S ALL WET. It was
the first time he had ever set foot in a swimming pool. He couldn't
even swim.

"*Life* was convinced he trained underwater," recalled *Sports
Illustrated* writer Neil Leifer, who witnessed the deception. "Now that's
a genius you don't see in people very often. Genius and a bit of a con
man, too."

Even when Clay's fight predictions didn't come true, he found a way
to put on a positive spin. Before his fight with Doug Jones in 1963, he
prophesied:

> *This boy likes to mix*
> *So he must fall in six*

A few days later, he got cockier:

> *I'm changing the pick I made before*
> *Instead of six, Doug goes in four*

When the fight took place, Clay won—but it took a full ten rounds.
When reporters queried him about his flawed prediction, he had a
ready explanation. "First, I called it in six. Then I called it in four. Four
and six, that's ten, right?"

The Broadway Showman, Billy Rose, loved Clay's brash style, advising the young fighter "keep it up. The more obnoxious you are, the more they'll pay you to fight some white Hope. They'll pay high to see you beat. Remember the bigots got most of the money in this country."

The media and the public didn't quite know what to make of him at first. What would have passed as distasteful arrogance in most people endeared him to many sportswriters. Even the fans who came out to root for his opponents and urged them to "button the Lip" did so in a good-natured way. Clay was seen as the lovable clown, spouting doggerel as he dismissed his opponents in summary fashion. He first endeared himself to the country when he went on the *Tonight Show* in 1962 and recited a poem for host Jack Paar:

> *This is the story about a man*
> *With iron fists and a beautiful tan*
> *He talks a lot and boasts indeed*
> *Of a powerful punch and blinding speed*

But as he edged closer to a title bout, a number of observers looked beneath the clownish exterior and discovered some substance. In March 1963—a full year before he first won the heavyweight championship—*Time* magazine published a laudatory cover story entitled "Cassius Clay: The Dream."

The article credited Clay for breathing new life into a sport "which had been a bore for years." The influential publication seemed to anticipate the epic future in store for the young boxer, proclaiming, "Cassius Clay is Hercules, struggling through the twelve labors. He is Jason chasing the Golden Fleece. He is Galahad, Cyrano, D'Artagnan. When he scowls, strong men shudder, and when he smiles, women swoon. The mysteries of the universe are his tinker toys. He rattles the thunder and looses the lightning."

Cast in such heroic terms, Clay could have easily taken the message that the country was ready to accept him as another Joe Louis. The embrace of white America was his for the asking.

If *Time* magazine was the opinion-maker of the white establishment, its counterpart in the black community was *Ebony*, and the two publications saw a very different side of the same subject. The same month

Clay adorned the cover of *Time,* the popular black magazine profiled him in very different terms, declaring, "Cassius Marcellus Clay —and this fact has evaded the sportswriting fraternity—is a blast furnace of racial pride. His is a pride that would never mask itself with skin lighteners and processed hair, a pride scorched with memories of a million little burns."

It wasn't yet time to reveal the news, but *Ebony* was as good a place as any to provide a hint. Cassius Clay was trained not to let his guard down, but for years he had been harboring a secret, and he was itching to let it out.

▶ ▶ ▶

In 1897, a man named Elijah Poole was born in Georgia, the son of a Baptist minister. Poole dropped out of school in grade eight and led a fairly mundane life as a door-to-door salesman until he moved to Detroit in 1930. It was the beginning of the Depression, and blacks were suffering its devastating effects. One day, Poole encountered a mysterious man named W. D. Fard preaching his gospel on a ghetto street corner to a group of unemployed black men.

He told them he "came from the East" and recited a number of parables from the Bible. After gaining a large following, he finally revealed himself to be a Muslim from Mecca who had come to spiritually cleanse the "so-called Negroes" who were trapped in the "wilderness of North America."

Poole was soon among his most devoted followers, and Fard bestowed upon him the Muslim name Elijah Muhammad. In 1933, the mysterious Fard suddenly disappeared. But before he vanished he designated his pupil as a successor. Elijah Muhammad declared Fard to be "the person of Allah on earth" who had visited the lost-found American Negro and revealed himself to be the Messenger of Allah. He christened his movement the Nation of Islam, although his strange theology had little in common with traditional Islamic doctrine.

Each religion has its unique creation story, but few are quite as unusual as the one espoused by Elijah Muhammad, which he claimed was passed down from Fard. The Nation of Islam teaches that the black race was descended from the original tribe of Shabazz. Sixty-six hundred years ago, this tribe ruled the world, until an evil scientist named Yacub cooked up an experiment. Yacub, who was exiled to the island of Patmos with 59,999 followers because he preached dissension, inter-bred the lightest-skinned segment of the black race for hundreds of years. This resulted in a new race of blond, blue-eyed "white devils"— a people without morals or compassion. The new race set blacks against another and created so much strife that they were exiled to the caves of Europe. Two thousand years after their exile, God sent Moses to civilize the devil race. Before long, the whites took over the world, enslaving the entirety of "the darker world."

But it was prophesied that black people would give birth to someone whose power and wisdom would be infinite. W. D. Fard was that cho-sen one, and he taught that the white devil's civilization was destined to be destroyed.

The reign of the white oppressors would come to an end when a one-and-a-half-mile-wide spaceship—the Mother of Planes— appeared in the sky eight days before Allah's chosen day of retribution, which was alternately known as the Judgment, Armageddon, the fall of America, and the second Hell. The ship would drop pamphlets written in Arabic telling righteous people where to go to survive. Then 1,500 planes would emerge from the spaceship and drop deadly explosives, destroying the white race and restoring power to the original descen-dants of Shabazz.

Taking up Fard's mantle, Elijah Muhammad traveled through America's Northern ghettos preaching his doctrine, which demanded complete separation of the races. Since the white race was a race of devils, blacks should avoid them at all costs or they would be tricked by the whites' evil ways. "Integration means self-destruction," he pro-claimed. "The black people throughout the earth are seeking indepen-dence for their own, not integration into white society. . . . We want our people in America whose parents or grandparents were descendants from slaves to be allowed to establish a separate state or territory of their own—either on this continent or elsewhere. We believe that our former slave-masters are obligated to provide such land."

The fledgling movement had to compete for the allegiance of disen-chanted young blacks with a number of other nationalist organiza-tions. The most popular of these was the Harlem-based Universal

Negro Improvement Association, founded by Marcus Garvey in 1916. The UNIA was a back-to-Africa movement that stressed respect for blackness and economic help while decrying "the tragedy of white injustice." Muhammad took many of the most popular doctrines of the Garveyites and incorporated them into his own Nation of Islam.

By the beginning of World War II, the Nation could boast little success in recruiting converts and counted only a few hundred followers throughout the country. But the rhetoric being preached by Muhammad had already attracted the attention of law enforcement officials, who had infiltrated the group as early as 1941, the year Elijah Muhammad prophesied that a great conflict would erupt involving the United States. The Messenger predicted that the Japanese would cross the Pacific Ocean in the Mother Plane and "the white devils will be destroyed by dark mankind." After Pearl Harbor, he repeatedly vowed he would not fight the white man's war and repeatedly noted the segregation and discrimination rampant in the U.S. Armed Forces at the time. The army's policies gave him plenty of ammunition for his attacks. Barracks, medical centers, and training centers were all designated by race. The American Red Cross even separated blood plasma designated for the troops by skin color. His message seemed to resonate in the ghettoes where many young blacks were unimpressed by government propaganda about the fight for freedom overseas. The movement's ranks were beginning to grow.

Alarmed by Muhammad's increasingly belligerent tone and concerned about the effect his criticism might have on black enlistment, the government decided to act. On May 8, 1942, the FBI burst into Muhammad's Chicago home and arrested him for failing to register for the draft. The government agents were frank about their motives, the Messenger later recalled. "President Roosevelt doesn't want you out there in public with that kind of teaching while America is prosecuting a war. That's all we're putting you in jail for, to keep you out of the public."

Over the next four months, the government would raid each of the Nation's temples and arrest thirty-eight more of Muhammad's followers. On top of the draft evasion count, the Messenger was charged with sedition and subversion. He was convicted with dubious legal evidence to back up the charge and languished in a federal prison cell until August 1946, a full year after the war came to an end. If Muhammad was bitter toward white America before, his prison experience only served to intensify his antagonism. His biographer Claude Clegg crystallized his feelings. "The persecution and imprisonment of the Muslims seemed to confirm to Muhammad the white man's innate adverseness to truth and fairness," Clegg wrote. "In his view, he and his followers had done nothing to deserve incarceration except teach the knowledge of self and others to the so-called Negroes. No 'lost-found' had joined the German or Japanese armed forces, turned American top-secret documents over to Hitler or Hirohito or cached weapons for a fifth column offensive. They had simply practiced their religion of peace and asked for freedom, justice, and equality."

After Muhammad's release from prison, his movement struggled to regain the momentum it had begun to build up before the war. It was slow going, each convert a hard-won victory. The movement seemed destined to remain marginal—until salvation arrived in the form of a letter.

▶ ▶ ▶

Seven months before he was released from federal prison, a former hustler and petty thief named Malcolm Little was convicted in Boston of armed robbery and incarcerated for six years.

Little's parents were organizers for Marcus Garvey's Universal Negro Improvement Association and traveled the country preaching a message of racial pride. Despite these black nationalist roots, however, Little was unmoved by his parents' beliefs and his memories of childhood weren't fond ones.

"I actually believe that as anti-white as my father was, he was subconsciously so afflicted with the white man's brainwashing of Negroes that he inclined to favor the light ones, and I was his lightest child," he recalled in his autobiography, while noting that his mother treated him more harshly because his light complexion stirred memories of her own mixed-race ancestry. His parents' back-to-Africa sentiments failed to stir him as a young child. "My image of Africa, at that time, was of naked savages, cannibals, monkeys and tigers and steaming jungles."

Little's life fell apart when he was six. His father was run over by a streetcar and his mother was forced onto welfare. She managed to hold the family together for seven years, but after a nervous breakdown she was finally committed to a mental hospital. The institutionalization of his mother meant that at the age of thirteen, Malcolm was removed from his brothers and sisters and sent to reform school. Within two years, he was involved in Boston's criminal underworld. Nicknamed "Big Red," he gained a reputation as a hustler, pushing dope, playing the numbers, and peddling bootleg whiskey. Before long, he switched his operation to Harlem—the big time for a black hoodlum—where he continued his ways as "Harlem Red."

On January 12, 1946, Malcolm was arrested in a Boston jewelry store while trying to reclaim a stolen watch he had left for repair. While in prison, he received frequent visits from his three brothers and one sister, all of whom had converted to what they called "the natural religion for the black man," the Nation of Islam. They were determined to bring their brother into the fold. At first he resisted their attempts at conversion, but they persisted until one message in particular resonated—the theory that whites are devils in disguise. As he thought back over his life, he couldn't think of a single white person who hadn't been cruel to him. He especially remembered the day he informed his high school teacher that he wanted to be a lawyer, only to be told, "That's no profession for a nigger."

Profoundly moved by his new realization, Malcolm succumbed to his family's urging and devoted his life to Islam. He quit cigarettes and drugs, stopped eating pork, and finally brought himself to pray to Allah. He later described how difficult this process was for him. "Bending my knees to pray—that act—well, that took me a week. Picking a lock to rob someone's house was the only way my knees had ever been bent before. I had to force myself to bend my knees. And waves of shame and embarrassment would force me back up."

Taking advantage of the prison library, he read all he could about the "so-called Negro" people in America and the injustices they had suffered. Then, in 1949, with three years to go before he was eligible for parole, Malcolm sat down and initiated his first contact with the "Messenger of Allah" in the form of a short letter. Apologizing for his poor grammar and spelling, Malcolm introduced himself and explained he was writing at the urgence of his brothers and sisters.

A week later, Muhammad wrote back welcoming Malcolm into the "true knowledge." He enclosed a five-dollar bill as he did with all prisoners who wrote to him. The black prisoner, he wrote, symbolized white society's crime of keeping black men oppressed and deprived and ignorant, and unable to get decent jobs, turning them into criminals.

The reply had an electric effect on the young Malcolm, and he vowed to dedicate his life to the Messenger and his movement. For the next three years, Malcolm busied himself converting his fellow inmates and devouring the books in the prison library as he prepared himself to take advantage of his imminent freedom. "I still marvel at how swiftly my previous life's thinking pattern slid away from me, like snow off a roof," he would recall. Each day he wrote Elijah Muhammad, updating him on the progress of his new protégé.

When he was released in 1952, Malcolm traveled to Chicago to watch the Messenger address the faithful at a rally. "I was totally unprepared for the Messenger Elijah Muhammad's physical impact on my emotions," he wrote years later. After Muhammad addressed the cheering crowd, exhorting the black man to uplift himself and his brothers and sisters, Malcolm was shocked to hear his name mentioned from the podium. In a parable comparing his new disciple to Job, who remained faithful to God even in the face of hardship, Muhammad intoned, "We will see how Malcolm does. I believe that he is going to remain faithful." In keeping with the Nation's tradition, he urged his new devotee to shed his "slave name" Little and renamed him Malcolm X.

For a decade, Malcolm rewarded his mentor's faith in him, taking advantage of the skills he had learned in his criminal days. "As a street hustler, I was always the most articulate in the ghetto," he would write. Within a year of his release, Malcolm had been named assistant minister of the Detroit Temple, where his flare for fiery rhetoric and his ability to recruit disaffected youth was responsible for tripling membership in only a few months.

Next he was assigned to organize temples in Philadelphia and Boston, and he so impressed Muhammad with his success that within two years he was named minister of New York's Temple number 7, the largest Nation of Islam temple in the country. As he moved rapidly up the ladder of the Nation, Malcolm's relationship with Elijah Muhammad grew stronger, becoming almost like that of a father and son. Everywhere he went, he praised the Messenger in the highest of terms, comparing himself to the popular ventriloquist's dummy, Charlie McCarthy. "When you hear Charlie McCarthy speak," he would say, "you listen and marvel at what he says. What you forget is that Charlie is nothing but a dummy—a hunk of wood sitting on Edgar Bergen's lap. This is the way it is with the Messenger and me. It is my mouth working, but the voice is his."

For those ten years, Malcolm's devotion to Muhammad was absolute. His charismatic personality and flare for promotion brought thousands of new followers into the movement. Each day he would stand on a Harlem street corner and, within minutes, would be surrounded by throngs of young blacks attracted by his appealing message. In his autobiography, he explains his success. "At the bottom of the social heap is the black man in the big-city ghetto," he would tell them. "He lives night and day with the rats and cockroaches and drowns himself with alcohol and anaesthetizes himself with dope, to try and forget where and what he is. The Negro has given up all hope. He's the hardest one for us to reach, because he's the deepest in the mud. But when you get him, you've got the best kind of Muslim. Because he's the most fearless. He has nothing to lose, even his life, because he didn't have that in the first place."

The movement's rapid growth and the influence of Malcolm X took place for the most part off the media's radar screen—until 1959, when Mike Wallace produced a five-part TV series called "The Hate that Hate Produced." The highly inflammatory series vaulted the Black Muslims into the consciousness of the American public, using sensational terms to imply a threat that didn't really exist. "Black supremacy," "gospel of hate," "hate-mongers in our midst"; the series claimed the movement had at least 250,000 members "preaching hatred for the white man" and implied that the Nation was readying for a race war. Wallace chose to focus attention on Malcolm X as the chief spokesperson of the Muslims rather than the leader Elijah Muhammad. Overnight, the Nation of Islam became a national phenomenon; recruitment flourished, and the ranks of the movement swelled close to the exaggerated figure the series had portrayed.

Although this was the first time most Americans learned of the Nation's existence, it was already very familiar to one man—FBI Director J. Edgar Hoover. Long before Hoover took over the FBI, he had worked as an official in the Justice Department's General Intelligence Division. Among his assignments, he directed counterintelligence operations against the black nationalist leader Marcus Garvey. His intense racism—he alternately referred to Garvey as a "nigger" or a "jigaboo"—led to a near obsession with black militancy. During his early years at the Bureau of Investigation—the forerunner of the FBI— he refused to involve the Bureau in preventing the increasing number of lynchings rampant in the South, saying it had "no authority to protect citizens of African descent in the enjoyment of civil rights generally," according to one department memo. During the 1960s and the increasing militancy of the civil rights movement, Hoover would combine his other obsession, anti-communism, to persecute Martin Luther King Jr.—who he was convinced worked for Moscow—as "public enemy number one." But before King came to national prominence, Hoover targeted the Nation of Islam and its leaders Elijah Muhammad and Malcolm X for special scrutiny.

As early as 1952, the FBI began tapping Muhammad's phones. The same year, Hoover unsuccessfully attempted to convince the government to place the Nation of Islam on the Attorney General's list of subversive organizations. In 1959, the Justice Department refused his request to prosecute the Nation for subversive activities and concluded that the group was not a threat to national security.

Hoover insisted that all surveillance reports on the activities of Malcolm X and Elijah Muhammad be forwarded to him personally. For two decades, the FBI unsuccessfully attempted to locate W. D. Fard in an effort to prove him a hoax and discredit the movement.

After years of surveillance, the FBI could find no concrete evidence of a threat to national security. Despite their hostility towards the "white devils," members of the Nation were generally law-abiding. In 1960, agents questioned Malcolm X after he gave a particularly inflammatory speech about the spaceship that will "descend on the United States, bomb it, and destroy all the devils." An FBI account of his interrogation calls him "uncooperative" but quotes Malcolm as saying "Muslims are peaceful and they do not have guns and ammunition and they do not even carry knives."

In spite of Hoover's continuing obsession with the movement, it is clear the U.S. government didn't see a particular threat in the Nation of Islam as long as it could be successfully isolated and discredited. Malcolm X, notwithstanding his success in recruiting new members from the disenfranchised youth of the ghettoes, had no widespread national following or influence among the mainstream of black Americans and no significant forum to reach a larger audience.

That forum was about to present itself in the unlikeliest of places.

▶ ▶ ▶

In the canon of Muhammad Ali, much of the biographical information available has to be approached with caution because it has been filtered through the self-serving lens of the Nation of Islam. Even his 1975 autobiography, *The Greatest,* was ghostwritten by Richard Durham, a former editor of the Nation's newspaper, *Muhammad Speaks,* and is notoriously unreliable in places.

Among the murkiest, and most important, chapters of the early life of Cassius Clay is the question of how he first became a member of the Nation—as pivotal a moment in his life and career as the theft of his red-and-white Schwinn back in 1954.

Ali mythology traces his conversion to Miami in 1961, where he met a follower of Elijah Muhammad named "Captain Sam" while he was training for a fight. He told Thomas Hauser he had heard about Elijah Muhammad as far back as 1959 and that he once saw a copy of *Muhammad Speaks* before he went to Rome. But his first formal encounter, he insisted, was that day in Miami, "the first time I felt truly spiritual in my life."

Abdul Rahman, formerly known as Captain Sam Saxon, also recalled the alleged encounter. "I met Ali—I think it was in March of 1961—when I was selling *Muhammad Speaks* newspapers on the street. Ali saw me, said, 'Hello, brother,' and started talking. And I said, 'Hey you're into the teaching.' He told me, 'Well, I ain't been in the temple, but I know what you're talking about.' And then he introduced himself. He said, 'I'm Cassius Clay. I'm gonna be the next heavyweight champion of the world.' He was interested in himself and he was interested in Islam, and we talked about both at the same time. He was familiar in passing with some of our teachings."

There was a good reason Clay was familiar with the Nation's teachings. He had in fact been a member for at least three years prior to that day in Miami.

While Cassius Clay was making a name for himself as an amateur boxer in Louisville in the years prior to winning the Olympic gold medal, he had ample opportunity to travel and expand his horizons. Every few weeks, he would travel around the East Coast of the United States competing in boxing tournaments, usually driven by Christine Martin, the wife of his amateur coach. In October 1958, during his junior year in high school, the sixteen-year-old Clay was in Atlanta for a tournament when he stumbled upon a Nation of Islam recruiter outside a mosque, according to FBI agent Robert Nichols, who had the temple under surveillance. Ali later confirmed this encounter. "I was fished off a street corner," he recalls.

Venturing inside, he heard a message of black pride that hit home. Apart from the rantings of his father at the dinner table, he had never encountered anything like this—black people who weren't afraid to speak out against white injustice. Coming from segregated Louisville, the words were a wake-up call. Explaining the appeal years later, he said it was easy to shed the "spooks and ghosts" of his Baptist upbringing, calling traditional religion merely a white man's trick to enslave the black man on earth with a promise of "pie in the sky when you die by and by."

Returning home, he was still mesmerized by the experience. When, the following week, his high school English teacher assigned his class to write an essay about any topic about which they felt strongly, Cassius knew what he would write about—the Nation of Islam. He had no idea what kind of an uproar his choice of essay topic would cause.

When he turned in the essay a few days later, his teacher, a black woman, was livid. She marched right into principal Atwood Wilson's office and demanded disciplinary action be taken. The Principal turned the matter over to the school's guidance counselor Betty Johnston.

"You have to understand," recalls Johnston forty years later, "that most educators were usually middle of the road. When Cassius turned in a paper about the Black Muslims, his teacher was quite alarmed. She wanted to fail him. At the time, most blacks in Louisville were disturbed by the Black Muslim movement. I was quite an activist and I felt they had a place in the overall scheme of things, but most people didn't agree with me."

Nevertheless, Johnston admits she was also concerned over his choice of essay topic.

"I didn't want him to become a Black Muslim because I didn't want him to become angry. They were preaching some very negative things and he was such a gentle boy. I went to school with his parents and knew the family quite well. It was obvious from the paper that he was well-versed in the doctrine of the Muslims and that he admired them. The Principal and I talked to the teacher and defused the situation. We weren't going to let him fail. People had a feeling he was going to do something important. That's when Mr. Wilson had a meeting and made it clear Cassius was not going to fail in his school."

Previously, this meeting has been cast by Ali chroniclers as an attempt by the principal to graduate Clay despite his poor marks (see Chapter One), rather than in defense of his right to free speech.

Clay learned a lesson that week. For the time being, it was safer to keep his admiration for the Nation of Islam to himself. He didn't stop visiting the Nation's mosques; indeed, whenever he travelled to a city with a black population that was large enough and militant enough to support one, he would quietly attend the service. But, as he digested the message and as his thinking matured, they were not visits he talked about.

When he returned to the States from Rome in 1960, Clay stayed for a week in New York, where—between sightseeing—he found time to go to Harlem and watch the by-then infamous Malcolm X deliver a sermon. The new Olympic champion was captivated by the charismatic minister but was too shy to introduce himself. It would take another two years before he had the courage to approach the man who would become his mentor.

In his autobiography, Malcolm X recalled the first time the two met: "I had met Cassius Clay in Detroit in 1962. He and his brother Rudolph came into the student's luncheonette next door to the Detroit Mosque where Elijah Muhammad was about to speak at a big rally. Every Muslim was impressed by the bearing and the obvious genuineness of the handsome pair of prize-winning brothers. Cassius came up an pumped my hand, introducing himself as he later presented himself to the world, 'I'm Cassius Clay.' He acted as if I was supposed to know who he was. So I acted as though I did. Up to that moment, though, I had never even heard of him."

Malcolm X counsels his new protégé in the teachings of Islam, 1963.

From the moment of their first meeting, Malcolm and Clay formed a special bond. "I liked him," Malcolm wrote. "Some contagious quality about him made him one of the very few people I ever invited into my home. Our children were crazy about him." For the next two years, Clay would arrange his itinerary so he could come see Malcolm speak as often as possible. After the sermon, the two would spend hours discussing the Koran. Malcolm carefully nurtured his new protégé in the ways of the Nation.

Ali later described Malcolm's appeal. "He was very intelligent, with a good sense of humor, a wise man. When he talked, he held me spellbound for hours."

But Malcolm's influence over Clay extended beyond the spiritual realm. Early on, he sensed the young fighter's potential and he was quick to cultivate it. He appointed one of his officials, Archie Robinson, to act as an administrator and road manager, going over contracts and helping to run Clay's training camp.

The prominent African-American historian Jeffrey Sammons explains why Malcolm X would devote so much effort to a boxer, despite the Nation of Islam's long standing aversion to sports. "Malcolm considered prizefights exploitive affairs, in which whites gleefully permitted blacks to act like animals," he writes. "But, reasoning that mechanisms of social control worked both ways, he knew that power flowed in many directions. He sensed that the time was right to exploit the obvious link between sport and society."

As Clay inched closer to a heavyweight title fight and came increasingly under the scrutiny of the nation's sportswriters, his association with the Muslims proved harder to keep a secret. The first hint came in September 1963, when the *Philadelphia Daily News* reported that Clay attended a Nation of Islam rally in Philadelphia at which Elijah Muhammad presided. "Clay stood out in the crowd of some five thousand that heard Elijah Muhammad unleash a three-hour tirade against the white race and popularly accepted leaders," it announced. In the article, Clay denied being a Muslim but said he thought Muhammad was "great."

The timing could have been better. Only three weeks before Clay announced his admiration for the avowed black separatist who preached racial segregation, Martin Luther King Jr. had given his famous "I Have a Dream" speech in front of 250,000 followers in Washington, D.C. The positive reaction nationwide signaled a widespread acceptance in white America of the civil rights movement and its calls for integration.

Fortunately for Clay, the *Daily News* item was largely ignored or dismissed as a publicity stunt. His association continued to be a closely guarded secret until five months later when his hometown newspaper the *Louisville Courier-Journal* caught him in a candid moment. "Sure I talked to the Muslims and I'm going back again," he confided. "I like the Muslims. I'm not going to get killed trying to force myself on people who don't want me. I like my life. Integration is wrong. The white people don't want integration. I don't believe in forcing it, and the Muslims don't believe in it. So what's wrong with the Muslims?"

Ali's cousin Coretta Bather recalls the impact of that interview in Louisville. "By that time," she says, "the black community was completely caught up in the civil rights movement. Martin Luther King's brother even lived in Louisville and Dr. King was like a messiah to folks here. You can imagine that Ali's words weren't very well received. You could even say people were in shock."

None more so than his own father, Cassius Sr. In November, the world heavyweight champion Sonny Liston had agreed to a February 25 title bout against Clay in Miami Beach. On February 7, *Miami Herald* sportswriter Pat Putnam cornered Old Cash after a few drinks and asked him if the rumors were true about his son's conversion to the Nation of Islam. In a long tirade, Clay confirmed the story and complained that the Muslims had brainwashed his son to hate white people and were stealing his money. When he objected, claimed Clay Sr., the Muslims threatened to drown him.

"After my story came out," recalls Putnam, "I started getting death threats from the Muslims, really nasty stuff. I went and told Ali about it and he was pretty pissed off. The threats immediately stopped."

The resulting story in the *Herald* would send shockwaves throughout the sports world and the country.

▶ ▶ ▶

Sonny Liston (at mic) announces his intentions to take on challenger Cassius Clay at the Los Angeles press conference, 1963.

Admiring his first million dollars, Los Angeles, 1965.

The prevailing myth has always been that Ali kept his conversion a secret for fear it would jeopardize his title bout. This is a myth that was carefully cultivated after the fact by the Nation of Islam because the truth is somewhat more embarrassing.

In the highly regulated Nation of Islam, one of the strongest prohibitions set down in the strict code of behavior was attendance at sporting events. In his book *Message to the Blackman in America*, Elijah Muhammad wrote, "Poor so-called Negroes are the worst victims in this world of sport and play because they are trying to learn the white man's games of civilization. Sport and play (gambling) take away the remembrance of Allah and the doing of good, says the Holy Koran. Think over what I am teaching, my people, and judge according to justice and righteousness."

When Cassius Clay first started attending meetings of the Nation in 1958, he was still an unknown and never came to the attention of the Chicago headquarters. As he started to achieve national media attention, some members of the movement recognized the potential publicity value of his membership. One of Clay's earliest Muslim teachers was Jeremiah Shabazz, who recalled the reaction of the leadership when he first told them about Clay's involvement. "When I telephoned our national secretary to tell him, 'We got this fighter coming to our meetings,' I was roundly condemned for being involved with a boxer. The Messenger told me I'd been sent to the South to make converts, not fool around with fighters," recalled Shabazz.

On subsequent occasions, when Clay's interest in the movement was pointed out to him, the Messenger was steadfast. Sports, he maintained, "cause delinquency, murder, theft, and other forms of wicked and immoral crimes."

As Clay came under the tutelage of Malcolm X, headquarters also admonished Malcolm for his involvement in the sports domain. After the Liston title fight was announced, Malcolm traveled to Miami to spend time with Clay at his training camp, a fact noted in the *New York Herald Tribune*. The paper observed that despite Malcolm's presence, Clay had still not formally announced support for the Muslims and refused to discuss the subject publicly.

The reports of Malcolm's presence at the Miami fight camp sparked alarm in Chicago, where Elijah Muhammad and other Nation officials warned him to disassociate himself from the boxer. "They felt that Cassius hadn't a prayer of a chance to win. They felt the Nation would be embarrassed through my linking the Muslim image with him," Malcolm X wrote in his autobiography.

Indeed, nobody gave Clay much of a chance of beating the heavily favored Liston, whose powerful punch was considered unstoppable. Arthur Daley of the *New York Times* summed up the attitude of the boxing elite in his column a few days before the fight: "Cassius is a precocious master of Ballyhoo who lulls himself to sleep at night not by counting sheep but by counting money. He'll be seeing stars when Sonny Liston hits him on Tuesday."

Besides Clay himself, only one man gave the challenger any hope of winning the title. But Malcolm X had other things on his mind besides boxing. Two weeks after Clay signed to fight Liston, John F. Kennedy was assassinated in Dallas. The Nation of Islam had always been fierce in its condemnation of President Kennedy and his professed concern for Negroes. But Elijah Muhammad was acutely aware of the impact his death had on the country, and he understood it was not the right time to further alienate the white establishment at a time of national mourning. He immediately issued a directive to all his lieutenants to remain silent about Kennedy's death until further notice.

For more than a decade, the loyalty of Malcolm X to the Messenger had been absolute. He would never have dared to question or disobey an order from the man he regarded as the Divine Prophet. But a few months earlier Malcolm had learned some disturbing news. For years, it was whispered in the movement that Elijah Muhammad had fathered a number of illegitimate children by his secretaries. If true, this would have violated the Muslims' strict edict against adultery. Malcolm had always dismissed these rumors as FBI propaganda—until the spring of 1963, when he visited Muhammad at his Detroit home. When he arrived, there were three women with their children standing on the front porch. Each of the children appeared to have a common father. The women needed Muhammad's signature so the children could attend school. But the Messenger refused to sign and wouldn't allow the women in the house. The truth finally dawned on Malcolm. The man he most admired—the man he had followed faithfully for fifteen years—was an immoral hypocrite. That night he told his wife, "The foundation of my life seems to be coming apart."

From that moment, Malcolm's entire moral system was undermined to the point where he questioned the basis of his beliefs. "My faith had been shaken in a way that I can never fully describe," he later wrote. "For I had discovered Muslims had been betrayed by Elijah Muhammad himself."

He could not yet bring himself to abandon the movement that had become his life, but he began to see things differently. A number of recent positive encounters with white people had convinced him that not all whites were devils—another revelation that shattered his previous way of thinking.

By the time of Kennedy's assassination, Malcolm was no longer capable of blindly obeying Muhammad's directives. On December 1, he gave an interview about the slain president, arguing that Kennedy had merely become a victim of the violent status quo his administration had tolerated. "Being an old farm boy," he said, "chickens coming home to roost never did make me sad; they've always made me glad." These words reached Chicago quickly, infuriating Muhammad—not so much because of their potential to alienate white America but because his once loyal disciple had publicly disobeyed him.

Since May, the Messenger had known that Malcolm's loyalty had waned, and he was acutely aware of the threat posed by the movement's most popular and influential minister. It was time to signal that the real power rested in Chicago, not New York.

The next day, Muhammad summoned Malcolm to national headquarters and told him that in order to disassociate the Muslims from his remarks, he would be suspended for ninety days. Malcolm accepted his punishment stoically, knowing that the power struggle between the two charismatic men was coming to a head. "Any Muslim would have known that my 'Chickens coming home to roost' statement had been only an excuse to put into action the plan for getting me out," he would write.

While Malcolm was still under suspension, he and his wife Betty were invited by Clay to attend his Miami training camp. The sudden presence of Malcolm X at Clay's camp combined with the rumors of the boxer's conversion to Islam sent the media into an uproar, and Clay's entourage urged him to distance himself from the infamous figure until after the fight. But Clay insisted he needed Malcolm by his side. He told the media that he had given the trip to Malcolm and his wife as a sixth anniversary present. The truth was that, despite his outward bravado—"Sonny Liston is great but he'll fall in eight"—he was scared stiff of his formidable opponent. Malcolm, however, recognized the enormous potential of linking the heavyweight champion of the world to his cause, and he was determined to strengthen Clay's resolve. He reminded the challenger that Allah had already willed that he would win the fight. "This fight is the truth," he said forcefully. "It's the Cross and the Crescent fighting in the prize ring—for the first time. It's a modern Crusades. . . . Do you think Allah has brought about all this intending for you to leave the ring as anything but the champion?"

While most of the assembled media, promoters, and VIPs stayed at the exclusive Fontainbleu Hotel, Malcolm X checked in to the downscale Hampton House Motel, where Clay was staying. There may have been a political component in the choice of accommodation, but one way or another it was somewhat limited: most of the better hotels in Miami Beach, including the Fontainbleu, didn't allow Blacks. Florida was still a Jim Crow state.

Above: Miami, 1963. Outside training camp, taking his mind off upcoming Liston fight.
Below: Malcolm X photographs Ali signing autographs for Miami children, 1964.

Malcolm's wife later recalled the regular late-night pep talks her husband gave to the young fighter. "Cassius was just about hysterical with apprehension of Sonny Liston. . . . They talked continuously about how David slew Goliath, and how God would not allow someone who believed in him to fail, regardless of how powerful the opponent was. . . ."

But if Clay was afraid of his opponent, nobody would have guessed by his public behavior. At the weigh-in ceremony, he and his assistant trainer Bundini Brown stormed up to Liston screaming "Float like a butterfly, sting like a bee. We're ready to rumble, you big ugly bear! Let's get it on right now!"

Meanwhile, Chicago headquarters continued to admonish the suspended minister for associating the Nation with a losing cause. Muhammad forbade him from speaking to the huge media contingent assembled in Miami for the fight. Malcolm, who was being referred to as Clay's "spiritual advisor," told most reporters nothing beyond the fact that he believed he would be reinstated at the end of ninety days, even though he knew otherwise.

But despite the prohibition against Malcolm speaking to the media, writer George Plimpton, who was doing a profile on Clay for *Harper's* magazine, was granted an extensive interview by the renegade Black Muslim.

"The atmosphere was very bizarre," recalls Plimpton thirty-five years later. "Like most people there, I was puzzled why Clay would associate with a man like Malcolm X and was flirting with the Black Muslims, who we saw as this hate organization. I interviewed Malcolm and came away very impressed by this man. His words were still scary but his mind was fascinating. And as impressed as I was with him, he seemed equally impressed by Clay."

FBI eavesdropping reports overheard Elijah Muhammad telling his associates that week that Malcolm was trying to usurp his power and was spreading rumors of his adultery to discredit him. In his autobiography, Malcolm reports that it was at around this time that he received his first death threats from within the Nation and heard rumors of a plan to "eliminate" him.

On January 21, Clay suddenly disappeared from his fight camp. Without telling his managers, he flew to New York with Malcolm to

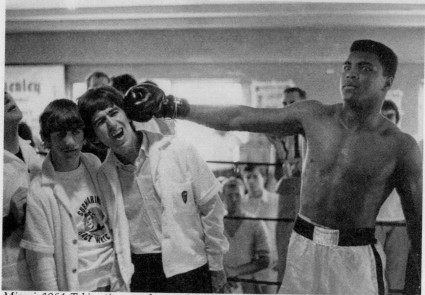

Miami, 1964. Taking time out from training to greet the Beatles, newly arrived in America. It was to be the last time Ali would be portrayed as a lovable clown.

address a Muslim rally. Because of his suspension, Malcolm himself could not speak but he stage-managed Clay's appearance—his first official function as a Muslim—for maximum effect.

Rallying support for his upcoming title bout against Liston, Clay told the crowd of 1,600, "I'm training on lamb chops and that big ugly bear is training on pork chops." He regularly praised his mentor, saying, "I'm proud to walk the streets of Miami with Malcolm X." An FBI informant, one of many who had infiltrated the movement at the behest of J. Edgar Hoover, immediately alerted the media of Clay's presence at the rally. The next day, it was all over the papers.

When Clay arrived back in Miami the following day, he was besieged by questions. Asked whether he was a card-carrying member of the Nation of Islam, he deftly avoided answering the question. "Card-carrying, what does that mean? I'm a race man and every time I go to a meeting, I get inspired." This evasive answer inspired Pat Putnam to track down Cassius Sr., whose sensational claim about his son being brainwashed finally caused the country to take notice.

Plimpton recalls the commotion. "It was chaos around the fight camp," he says. "Everybody wanted Clay to disavow the Muslims, there

With singers Chuck Jackson and Dee Dee Sharp at the Apollo Theatre, Harlem, 1964.

were rumors the fight would be called off, ticket sales ground to a halt. The only person who seemed oblivious to all the fuss was Clay himself. He just went on calmly preparing for the fight."

To deflect some of the attention from the controversy, the fight publicist Harold Conrad arranged for the Beatles, who had arrived in America that week, to show up at the Clay gym for some publicity shots. The fighter clowned around with the four young British musicians, pretending to knock them down like dominoes. "You're not as stupid as you look," Clay said to John Lennon after they were introduced. "No, but you are," Lennon replied jokingly.

The resulting media coverage of the Beatles' visit was perhaps the last time Cassius Clay was ever looked upon as the lovable clown in the eyes of America. Ironically, years later, Ali's longtime nemesis Jimmy Cannon would disparagingly label the boxer "the fifth Beatle," comparing him to the "students who get a check from dad every first of the month and the painters who copy the labels off soup cans and the surf bums who refuse to work and the whole pampered style-making cult of the bored young."

Miami, 1964. With actor Sidney Poiter (left), and brother Rudy.

▶ ▶ ▶

The day after he returned from preaching in New York, lost amidst the furor over whether he was a Muslim, Clay received a notice to report to the Armed Forces Induction Center in Coral Gables, Florida, to take a military qualifying examination.

Four years earlier, shortly after turning eighteen, Cassius Clay Jr. had routinely registered with Selective Services at his local draft board in Louisville. He was classified 1-A, available for the draft.

"I never thought much of it at the time," he remembers. "There was no war on."

As he reported to the Coral Gables induction center, Clay had more important things on his mind than the possibility of being drafted. Such as Liston. He sailed through the army physical, probably the best conditioned recruit the army doctors had ever seen. Then he was ushered into a room along with twenty other potential recruits and given a "mental aptitude test." When the fifty-minute exam ended, he exit-

Coral Gables, Florida, 1963. Ali arrives for pre-induction military exam, which he would fail.

ed the center and promptly turned his attention back to the upcoming fight, unaware that a chain of events had been set in motion that would alter the course of his career.

Miami Herald sportswriter Pat Putnam was with Clay in Coral Gables. He remembers the boxer's attitude before the exam: "He had no problem at that time with the idea of going into the army. He was in a good mood and joking around. There was certainly no talk about not going in."

Halfway across the world, fifteen thousand U.S. army "advisers" had been dispatched to Southeast Asia by President Kennedy to help contain the communist threat in a place called Vietnam. Like most Americans, Cassius Clay had never heard of it.

A few days later, fight promoter Bill McDonald confronted Clay and told him the Muslim rumors had sparked a boycott of the fight among Miami's sizable Jewish community. More than half the seats remained unsold. Unless Clay publicly denied the rumors, McDonald threatened to cancel the fight.

Since the age of twelve, Cassius Clay had dreamed of the opportunity to fight for the heavyweight title. To him at the time, the Liston fight might have seemed his only chance to realize the dream. Still, and not for the last time, he summoned up a principle rarely seen in the usually amoral world of boxing.

"My religion's more important to me than any fight," he told the stunned promoter. "Do what you have to do." With that, Clay returned to his hotel and told his entourage the fight was off. He was packing his bags.

But fight publicist Harold Conrad had invested too much time and money in the bout to let everything fall apart. He quickly moved to salvage the situation, approaching McDonald with a last-minute appeal.

"I said to him, 'Bill, you're gonna go down in history as the guy who denied a fighter a title shot because of his religion.' And McDonald told me, 'Don't start hitting me with the Constitution. This is the South. I can't operate here with these people.'"

Conrad suggested a compromise. If Malcolm X agreed to leave town, he asked, would McDonald proceed with the bout? The promoter agreed and the fight was back on. Clay returned to training camp while Malcolm quietly flew back to New York.

He'd be back.

CHAPTER FOUR:
The Making of Muhammad Ali

WHEN, ON FEBRUARY 25, 1964, a beaten and battered Sonny Liston failed to get up off his stool for the eighth round, it was clear a new era had begun in heavyweight boxing. Less obvious was the fact that a new chapter was about to be written in America's political and social history.

While Clay was pounding the supposedly invincible champion into submission, Malcolm X—who had slipped quietly back into town the night before—sat in a ringside seat, vindicated by his faith in his disciple. With a week to go until his suspension was due to end, Malcolm had already made a decision about his future. The new heavyweight champion of the world was to be an integral part of that decision.

The morning after his victory, Clay arrived at a Miami Beach press conference where hundreds of journalists awaited his verdict on the fight's shocking outcome—shocking, at least, to everyone but himself and Malcolm X. Before he would agree to answer any questions, Clay looked out on the assembled throng—none of whom had given him any chance of winning the title—and asked, "Who's the Greatest?" Silence filled the hall. Again, he asked, "Who's the Greatest of them all?" No response. Finally, he repeated the question and this time the reporters meekly answered en masse, "You are."

Satisfied, he told the media he had won the fight because he was the better boxer. But the sportswriters didn't want to talk about boxing. "Are you a card-carrying member of the Black Muslims?" came the first question.

He had still not received official word from Chicago headquarters whether it was okay to publicly proclaim his conversion. He responded with his standard nondenial answer to such a question, but this time he went a little further than he had previously. "Card-carrying; what does that mean? I believe in Allah and in peace. I don't try to move into white neighborhoods. I go to a Muslim meeting and what do I see? I see that there's no smoking and no drinking and no fornicating and their women wear dresses down to the floor. And then I come out on the street and you tell me I shouldn't be in there. Well, there must be something in there if you don't want me to go in there. I don't want to marry a white woman. I was baptized when I was twelve, but I didn't know what I was doing. I'm not a Christian anymore. I know where I'm going and I know the truth."

Then he uttered the words that would become his personal anthem, the defining philosophy for the rest of his life: "I don't have to be what you want me to be. I'm free to be what I want."

In Chicago, the Messenger and his associates were as stunned as the boxing establishment at Clay's victory. The Nation of Islam newspaper *Muhammad Speaks* was perhaps the only paper in the country that didn't cover the Liston bout. Elijah Muhammad's advisers quickly updated him on the boxer's commitment to the Nation and his close allegiance to Malcolm X. Despite the strict prohibition against following sports, a number of Nation of Islam officials had grown up following boxing and were well aware of the influential platform that came with the heavyweight title, not to mention the vast quantities of money to be made.

For some time, Elijah Muhammad was troubled by reports that Malcolm was planning to break away and form his own movement. By some accounts, this was enough of a threat to prompt the Messenger to consider having his former disciple assassinated. Now, the thought of Malcolm leaving and taking Cassius Clay with him sent alarm bells through the organization. The combination of two charismatic forces with the media platform accorded the heavyweight champion would have enormous appeal to young blacks throughout the country. Elijah

Muhammad knew it, Malcolm X knew it, and one other person knew it—J. Edgar Hoover, whose FBI wiretaps were keeping him well informed of the situation.

The only key player who didn't know that Cassius Clay was about to become a pawn in a giant power struggle was Cassius Clay, who that evening received a congratulatory phone call from the man he had revered from afar for more than five years, the Honorable Elijah Muhammad. The long-standing taboo on sports, it seems, was temporarily lifted.

The next morning, bolstered by the call officially welcoming him into the movement, Clay called a second press conference, at which he finally laid to rest any lingering doubt about his religious affiliation:

> Islam is a religion and there are 750 million people all over the world who believe in it, and I'm one of them. I ain't no Christian. I can't be when I see all the colored people fighting for forced integration get blowed up. They get hit by stones and chewed by dogs, and they blow up a Negro church and don't find the killers. I get telephone calls every day. They want me to carry signs. They want me to picket. They tell me it would be a wonderful thing if I married a white woman because this would be good for brotherhood. I don't want to be blown up. I don't want to be washed down sewers. I just want to be happy with my own kind.
>
> I'm the heavyweight champion, but right now there are some neighborhoods I can't move into. I know how to dodge booby-traps and dogs. I dodge them by staying in my own neighborhood. I'm no troublemaker. I don't believe in forced integration. I know where I belong. I'm not going to force myself into anybody's house. I'm not joining no forced integration movement, because it don't work. A man has got to know where he belongs.
>
> People brand us a hate group. They say we want to take over the country. They say we're Communists.

That is not true. Followers of Allah are the sweetest people in the world. They don't carry knives. They don't tote weapons. They pray five times a day. The women wear dresses that come all the way to the floor and they don't commit adultery. All they want to do is live in peace. They don't want to stir up any kind of trouble. All the meetings are held in secret, without any fuss or hate-mongering.

I'm a good boy. I have never done anything wrong. I have never been in jail. I have never been in court. I don't join any integration marches. I don't pay any attention to all those white women who wink at me. I don't carry signs. I don't impose myself on people who don't want me. If I go in somebody's house where I'm not welcome, I'm uncomfortable, so I stay away. I like white people. I like my own people. They can live together without infringing on each other. You can't condemn a man for wanting peace. If you do, you condemn peace itself. A rooster crows only when it sees the light. Put him in the dark and he'll never crow. I have seen the light and I am crowing.

Reaction to his declaration was swift and furious. *New York Times* reporter Robert Lipsyte, who was in Miami covering the fight, recalls the uproar. "Before the Liston fight," he says, "even the old-line columnists, the ones like Jimmy Cannon and Dick Young who were hostile to him, didn't feel threatened by Clay because they thought he was going to lose. If anything, Clay gave them a chance to fulminate about how boxing was taking yet another bad turn. First you had the criminal element, and now you had the encroachment of a show-business clown. They took boxing totally seriously, way out of proportion to its true worth. They were saying, 'This is the worst thing that ever happened to boxing.' And soon, that escalated to, 'This might be the worst thing that ever happened to the youth of America, which needs a proper role model.' Basically, what they were talking about was the heavyweight champion, usually black, always poor, being a safe role model for the underclass. When he said 'I don't have to be what you want me to be,' among the things he didn't have to be were Christian, a good soldier of American democracy in the mold of Joe Louis, or the kind of athlete-prince white America wanted."

Under normal circumstances, Clay's conversion to Islam may have been dismissed as just more foolishness from a blowhard athlete instead of sparking a national fury. But the old guard of the sports-writing fraternity were determined to elevate his Muslim ties to the level of a catastrophe for America. These were the same writers who could be seen drinking every evening with the mobsters who controlled Sonny Liston—murderers, gamblers, and pimps. But Clay's association with clean-living Muslims could not be tolerated.

The dean of boxing writers, Jimmy Cannon, fired the first salvo in the *New York Journal American.* "The fight racket, since its rotten beginnings, has been the red-light district of sports," he wrote. "But this is the first time it has been turned into an instrument of mass hate. It has maimed the bodies of numerous men and ruined their minds but now, as one of Elijah Muhammad's missionaries, Clay is using it as a weapon of wickedness in an attack on the spirit. I pity Clay and abhor what he represents. In the years of hunger during the Depression, the Communists used famous people the way the Black Muslims are exploiting Clay. This is a sect that deforms the beautiful purpose of religion."

The day after the second press conference, Elijah Muhammad publicly ushered Clay into the Muslim fold, telling five thousand followers gathered for the movement's holiday, Savior's Day, "I'm so glad that Cassius Clay admits he's a Muslim. He was able, by confessing that Allah was the God and by following Muhammad, to whip a much tougher man. Clay has confidence in Allah, and in me as his only messenger."

Malcolm X understood what was happening. He was engaged in a tug-of-war with the Messenger for the allegiance of Clay. The prize? A very important national forum, a loud media platform, and the hearts and minds of millions of young black boxing fans. He told reporters, "Clay is the finest Negro athlete I have ever known, the man who will mean more to his people than any athlete before him. He is more than Jackie Robinson was, because Robinson is the white man's hero. The white press wanted him to lose because he is a Muslim. You notice nobody cares about the religion of other athletes. But the prejudice against Clay blinded them to his ability."

Indeed, few had noted the blinding speed and dazzling footwork, nor the innate ability to think on his feet—what pundits later called "ring genius"—that had enabled the new champion to prevail against his supposedly invincible opponent.

"Before the first Liston fight, I wasn't terribly impressed by Ali's boxing skills," recalls syndicated sports columnist Jerry Izenberg. "When Liston failed to get up off that stool, I knew that I was witnessing the real deal. This kid was good."

Behind the scenes, after the fight, Malcolm confided in Clay for the first time his plan to start a new black nationalist movement and urged his young protégé to come with him. Clay was noncommittal.

Malcolm's widow Betty Shabazz recalled his efforts. "My husband was planning to break away from Elijah Muhammad and he wanted Cassius to join him. He knew that Cassius could provide the kind of publicity and influence to propel his organization into immediate success."

On March 3, an FBI surveillance report informed J. Edgar Hoover that "Malcolm X might oppose the Nation of Islam leadership of Elijah Muhammad with the assistance of Clay in the near future." Hoover immediately ordered an FBI file opened on the new heavyweight champion.

Malcolm, however, hadn't counted on one thing. For more than a decade, he had preached—and practiced—complete and total loyalty to Elijah Muhammad. When he first began to counsel Clay, he instilled this same sense of loyalty. Each spiritual lesson was preceded by, "The Honorable Elijah Muhammad teaches us. . ." As much as Clay admired Malcolm, he considered him only a conduit for the teachings of the Messenger.

NFL football star Jim Brown was a friend of Clay and remembers witnessing a crucial stage in the power struggle. "Ali took me to a little black motel with Malcolm and three or four other Muslim ministers. Malcolm said to me, 'Well, Brown, don't you think it's time for this young man to stop spouting off and get serious?' And I agreed, but that night made it clear to me that Malcolm's swan song was coming as far as Ali was concerned. Ali took me into a back room. It was just the two of us. We talked for about two hours. And he told me how Elijah Muhammad was such a little man physically but such a great man, and he was going to have to reject Malcolm and choose Elijah."

The man called Cassius Clay spent his last days with Malcolm in New York, where he announced he was changing his name to Cassius X Clay. 'X' is what the slave-masters used to be called," he said incorrectly, proving he was still slightly confused about the nomenclature of the sect. In fact, the "X" was meant to symbolize a black American's lost African identity. Malcolm and Clay toured the United Nations together, attracting a huge media throng. At the UN, Clay announced he was planning to tour Africa and Asia with Malcolm X at his side. "I'm champion of the *whole* world," he told reporters, "and I want to meet the people I'm champion of." Asked whether he thought Clay would do any formal preaching, Malcolm responded, "You don't preach our philosophy, you live it."

The same day, a small item in the *New York Times* reported a rumor that Clay had failed his army test the month before. Asked about the report, Clay said, "I tried my hardest to pass." Asked if he would consider filing for conscientious objector status, he responded, "I don't like that name. It sounds ugly—I wouldn't want to be called anything like that. "Years later he admitted he didn't know what the term meant.

At his old Harlem mosque, Malcolm told subordinates, "The Nation is finished." He believed his departure, with Clay in tow, would result in an exodus of thousands of young Muslims, causing the movement to self-destruct.

Meanwhile, back in Chicago, Elijah Muhammad was alarmed at Clay's announcement of his upcoming Africa trip. This was just the international platform Malcolm could use to launch a new movement. Incensed at the prospect, Muhammad went into action. That evening, he appeared on radio and announced that he was renaming Cassius Clay "Muhammad Ali," meaning "One who is worthy of praise." The Messenger declared, "This Clay name has no divine meaning. Muhammad Ali is the name I will give to him, as long as he believes in Allah and follows me." This move to give the champion an "original name" was very unusual, for it was one of the movement's highest honors, one not bestowed on many lifelong followers—including Malcolm X. It was Muhammad's ploy to secure the allegiance of the boxer once and for all. An FBI wiretap caught Malcolm's reaction to the move. "He did it to prevent him from coming with me," he told his associates.

Chicago 1964. With spiritual leader Elijah Muhammad, who believed sports cause "delinquency, theft and other wicked immoral crimes."

When Malcolm attempted to contact Ali that evening, his access was blocked. Elijah Muhammad had assigned his own security detail to the boxer, and their first assignment was to cut off all communications with the upstart minister. The next day, Muhammad finished the task of isolating Malcolm, informing him in a letter that his suspension was indefinite because he had not sufficiently "rehabilitated" himself.

The same day, Malcolm was secretly informed by Ali's press secretary, Leon 4X Ameer, that an order had been issued that "Malcolm had to be taken down." Ameer couldn't bear to see Malcolm harmed and felt it necessary to warn his former spiritual mentor. A member of Elijah Muhammad's powerful new inner circle, Louis X (now known as Louis Farrakhan), was assigned to take over as minister of Malcolm's former Harlem temple.

On March 8, Malcolm held a press conference formally announcing his resignation from the Nation of Islam. "Internal differences have forced me out of it. I did not leave of my own free will." He proposed to start a new black nationalist party to engage in political activities and "social action against the oppressor." In the coming months, he would launch a very public attack against the Nation of Islam, which he accused of racism. After travelling to Mecca, where he worshipped with white Muslims, he renounced many of his former views and declared that the enemy was "not white people but white racists."

Ali was shocked by what he considered the betrayal of the man who had been a father figure to him, publicly denouncing Malcolm to the media. "You just don't buck Mr. Muhammad and get away with it," he said. "I don't want to talk about him anymore."

A major battle in the power struggle was over: the Messenger had successfully pried Ali away from Malcolm X. Only now did he realize the enormous boon Ali would bring to the Black Muslim cause. Elijah Muhammad's biographer Claude Clegg summarized Ali's new appeal:

> Notwithstanding the Muslim proscription against sports, Muhammad now viewed the twenty-two-year-old boxer as a timely addition to the Nation. Having publicly announced his affiliation with the movement, Clay brought instant, but not always favorable, press coverage to the program of Muhammad and his followers. He also brought to the coffers of the Nation considerable tithes that would make the remittance of the average believer appear paltry. Most importantly, Clay was invaluable for recruitment. He revitalized the appeal of the movement among angry urban youth as well as college students, young professionals, and sports enthusiasts. His outspoken media image, though it perhaps bristled some conservative believers, was exactly the portrait of defiant black manhood that many African Americans found refreshing, especially as the civil rights movement headed toward a bloody Freedom Summer. In short, Clay was the perfect poster boy.

If the announcement of the world heavyweight champion's conversion had rankled white America and the media, then his name change gave them an excuse to exact a petty revenge. Virtually every American newspaper refused to call him by his new name. "I remember I would turn in stories referring to him as Muhammad Ali and some editor would always change it to Cassius Clay," recalls *New York Times* sports reporter Robert Lipsyte. "I apologized about this once to Ali and he just patted my head and told me not to worry, saying, "You're just the white power structure's little brother." In person, some reporters—refusing to call him Muhammad but knowing they'd be rebuffed if they used the name Cassius—compromised by calling him "Champ."

"Sports figures," notes sportswriter Thomas Hauser, "were supposed to be one-dimensional quasi-cartoon characters. Reporters were used to fighters telling them how much they weighed and what they ate for breakfast."

On March 20, 1964, Ali attended a fight between his friend Luis Rodriguez and Holly Mimms at Madison Square Garden. It was traditional for well-known boxers in attendance at a bout to be publicly introduced, but the Garden's president, Harry Markson, refused to have Ali introduced by any other name than Cassius Clay. Ali threatened to walk out if his "slave name" was used. When he heard himself introduced as Clay, he carried out his threat and left the arena to a chorus of boos from the fans.

Today Markson regrets his action, but he explains his feelings at the time: "The Black Muslims stood for some pretty awful things. There was a positive side to what they were trying to accomplish, but I felt then and still feel that a lot of what they preached was wrong. But if I had to do it over, I'd introduce him as Eleanor Roosevelt if that's what he wanted."

For Ali the name change was highly symbolic, and he was determined that his decision be respected. "Changing my name was one of the most important things that happened to me in my life," he reflects. "It freed me from the identity given to my family by slave-masters. If Hitler changed the names of people he was killing, and instead of killing them made them slaves, after the war those people would have changed their names back. That's all I was doing. People change their names all the time and no one complains. Actors and actresses change their name. The Pope changes his name."

Indeed, well-known fighters such as Joe Louis and Sugar Ray Robinson had changed their names and the press never gave it a second thought. But to white America, the name change was a slap in the face, a defiant signal that Ali would not be what they wanted him to be.

A number of papers, eager to make Ali look foolish, traced his family tree and discovered the Clay lineage was quite distinguished. His ancestors took their name from the well-known Clay family of Kentucky. His namesake, Cassius Marcellus Clay, was a three-term Kentucky legislator who freed his slaves and edited an emancipationist newspaper, crusading for the end of slavery. The misguided boxer should be proud to carry the name of a man who did so much for Negroes, the media chided.

It is true that the nineteenth century Clay campaigned for the end of slavery, but his views on race were not quite so noble. "I am of the opinion that the Caucasian or white is the superior race," he wrote in 1845. "They have a larger and better formed brain; much more developed form and exquisite structure."

Ali continued to speak his mind, despite the continuing attacks against him in the media. "People are always telling me what a good example I could set for my people if I just wasn't a Muslim. I've heard over and over, 'how come I couldn't be like Joe Louis?' Well, they're gone now and the black man's condition is just the same, ain't it? We're still catching hell."

George Plimpton remembers the furor. "People seemed to believe this man was a threat to America's values because of his affiliation with the Muslims, which was seen as a racist organization. What they didn't seem to realize is that Ali himself wasn't going around calling whites 'devils.' He seemed to have a mind of his own on that matter."

Indeed, Ali very publicly espoused a doctrine different from Elijah Muhammad's on the subject of whites. Talking about integration, he told *Boxing & Wrestling Magazine* in July 1964, "I don't believe in forcing integration. I don't want to go where I'm not wanted. If a white man comes to my house, then he's welcome. But if he doesn't want me to come to his home, then I don't want to go. I'm not mad at the white people. If they like me, I like them. Milton Berle invited me to the hotel where he was performing and I went." Publicly, Ali denounced integration but he seemed to have great respect for the efforts of Martin Luther King Jr., who was regularly denounced by the Black Muslim movement. Around this time, he secretly phoned King to express his admiration—a phone call that would later figure prominently in Ali's legal battle. To the chagrin of his Muslim handlers, many prominent members of Ali's entourage, including his trainer, Angelo Dundee, and his fight doctor Ferdie Pacheco, were white. His first teacher, Jeremiah Shabazz, recalls teaching Clay the concept of white devils and having his student respond, "What about babies? How can they be devils?"

According to sportswriter Pat Putnam, "Ali never hated another human being in his life, black, white, or yellow. He never got caught up in all that hate bullshit."

Ali even seemed to have a special fondness for Jews, despite the notorious anti-Semitism of the Nation of Islam, which preached that Moses taught white people to oppress blacks and that Jews were the first slaveholders. Malcolm X, too, was virulently anti-Semitic, even after he supposedly renounced his former racist ways. But Ali included a number of Jews in his entourage, regularly ate in kosher restaurants—Jews and Muslims share similar dietary laws—and he occasionally suggested that Jews might be spared when the prophesied white Armageddon took place.

What was the appeal for Ali, then, in a movement whose defining philosophy—its views on race—he didn't really share? Some commentators have suggested the Nation provided him with a family and fulfilled in him a desperate need to be taken seriously, a longing for respect. Today, Ali attributes the appeal of the Nation to its ability to raise the aspirations of American blacks.

"Elijah Muhammad was a good man, even if he wasn't the Messenger of God we thought he was. If you look at what our people were like then, a lot of us didn't have self-respect. We didn't have banks or stores. We didn't have anything after being in America for hundreds of years. Elijah Muhammad was trying to lift us up and get our people out of the gutter. He made people dress properly, so they weren't on the street looking like prostitutes and pimps. He taught good eating habits, and was against alcohol and drugs. I think he was wrong when he talked about white devils, but part of what he did was make people feel it was good to be black."

▶ ▶ ▶

When he announced his conversion to Islam, Ali was prepared for the wrath of the white establishment. Steeled by Malcolm X, he even welcomed it. He was somewhat taken aback, however, when a number of black leaders publicly condemned his decision.

First, the leader of Kentucky's largest Baptist church, the Reverend D. E. King, said the new champion, who had been raised a Baptist, was "not helping the soul of America." Then, Lyman Johnson, president of the Louisville chapter of the NAACP, issued a statement decrying his affiliation with the Nation. "I hope Clay will shake himself out of this delusion, lest he ruin his chance to be a great champion," Johnson said, adding that the Negro leadership was "embarrassed for Clay, who is naive."

Most leaders of the growing civil rights movement kept their views to themselves, fearful that Blacks openly criticizing Blacks would further polarize the movement.

Two weeks after Ali defeated Liston, Martin Luther King Jr. led 650 marchers through Selma, Alabama—one of the South's most notoriously racist cities. Shocked Americans watched on television as police attacked the peaceful marchers with tear gas, clubs, and bullwhips, hospitalizing more than seventy black and white participants. A nation's consciousness was profoundly moved, and polls showed a huge increase in support for integration.

While Dr. King and his followers were putting their lives on the line, however, Muhammad Ali was publicly preaching a conflicting doctrine. Julian Bond was one of the pioneers of the civil rights movement as one of the founders of the Student Non-Violent Coordinating Committee. He marched with King in Selma that day and recalls the sentiments of his fellow activists. "You have to remember that most of our activities were confined to the South, where Jim Crow still dominated," he says. "The Nation of Islam never really attracted much attention there; it was more of a Northern movement. Then when Ali announced his conversion, here was a very appealing figure to young Blacks all over the country. A lot of my colleagues resented him at first but we never really saw it as a threat."

Most American Blacks were uneasy with the militancy of the Nation of Islam and were more comfortable with the accomodationist goals of the civil rights movement. But in the North, where Blacks faced very different issues and where the style of Martin Luther King Jr., was never warmly embraced until after his assassination, many young

Blacks privately sympathized with the aims of the Nation even if they didn't formally join the movement.

The prominent African-American writer Jill Nelson, who grew up in Harlem, told David Remnick, "We weren't about to join the Nation, but we loved Ali for that supreme act of defiance. It was the defiance against having to be the good Negro, the good Christian waiting to be rewarded by the righteous white provider. We loved Ali because he was so beautiful and powerful and because he talked a lot of lip. But he also epitomized a lot of black people's emotions at the time, our anger, our sense of entitlement, the need to be better just to get to the median, the sense of standing up against the furies."

King himself, who had been labeled by the Muslims as "hungry for a place among the white race instead of his own race," was pressed for his reaction to Ali's conversion and finally offered a mild condemnation, which he would later take back. "When Cassius Clay joined the Black Muslims and started calling himself Cassius X, he became a champion of racial segregation and that is what we are fighting against."

The late African-American tennis champion is Arthur Ashe, himself a pioneering sports activist, recalled Ali's impact on some of King's colleagues. "I can tell you that Ali was definitely, sometimes unspokenly, admired by a lot of the leaders of the civil rights movement, who were sometimes even a bit jealous of the following he had and the efficacy of what he did. There were a lot of people in the movement who wished they held that sort of sway over African Americans but who did not."

Ali was bothered by some of the criticism, but his commitment to his new movement didn't founder. "I just spoke my mind; that's all," he explains. "I said things black people thought, but were afraid to say. I didn't hate. Not then; not now. What I was doing was like a doctor giving someone a needle and hurting them a little to kill an infection. In the end it helps." He traveled the country speaking at mosques, proselytizing for Elijah Muhammad.

The first indication that his conversion might have more serious repercussions than just alienating the white and black establishments came when the World Boxing Association announced it was stripping Ali of his title because of "conduct detrimental to the best interests of boxing." WBA commissioner Abe Greene issued a statement explaining the decision. "Clay should be given a chance to decide whether he

With baseball great Jackie Robinson (center left), in 1965. Robinson, a veteran of World War II, was critical of Ali's refusal to serve in the army.

wants to be a religious crusader or the heavyweight champion. As champion, he is neither a Muslim or any other religionist because sports are completely nonsectarian. Clay should be given the choice of being the fighter who won the title or the fanatic leader of an extraneous force which has no place in the sports arena. Of course Clay might be reinstated in five or six months if his conduct improves."

In Utah, news of the WBA decision reached Bill Faversham, head of the Louisville Sponsoring Group, which still held Ali's contract. Faversham and the rest of the group had hit upon a potential bonanza when their fighter won the title. But now the controversy jeopardized millions of dollars in promotional deals and other traditional financial perks that came with the heavyweight title. Putting on a brave face, Faversham told the media, "I'm amazed that the WBA is trying to take away Clay's title. He has done nothing illegal or immoral."

Indeed, the list of heavyweight champions before Ali was filled with criminals and thugs. Sonny Liston himself had served five years in prison for robbery and still consorted with an organization far more sinister than the Nation of Islam, the Cosa Nostra. Yet Ali was singled out for conduct "detrimental to boxing."

Ali seemed genuinely perplexed. "Ain't this country supposed to be where every man can have the religion he wants, even *no* religion if that's what he wants?" he asked in a *Playboy* interview. "There ain't a court in America that would take a man's job, or his title, because of his religious convictions. The Constitution forbids Congress from making any laws involving a man's religion. But they want to take away my title —for what? What have I done to hurt boxing? I've *helped* boxing. I don't smoke, I don't drink, I don't bother with nobody."

As the controversy threatened to derail what he had worked so long to achieve, Ali's defenders were few and far between. Two well-known black athletes waded into the dispute. Jackie Robinson was one of the first to rise to Ali's defense. "Many people have asked me whether I am disturbed because, ideologically, Cassius has taken on a new trainer, Malcolm X," he wrote in his syndicated column. "Why should I be disturbed? Clay has just as much right to ally himself with the Muslim religion as anyone else has to be a Protestant or Catholic. There are those who scoff at the claim by Muhammad's Muslims that they represent a religion. These people have a right to their opinion. People who are concerned over Clay's alliance with the Muslims seem mainly worried lest great flocks of young and adult Negroes will suddenly turn to the Islam ranks. I don't believe this will happen." Despite Robinson's support, he couldn't quite bring himself to use the new name.

Joe Louis wasn't quite as open-minded. "I'm against Black Muslims," he said crankily. "I've always believed every man is my brother. Clay will earn the public's hatred because of his connections to the Muslims. The heavyweight champion is the champion of all people. He has responsibilities to all people."

Then, on March 24, Ali's problems reached the floor of Congress— and he won an unlikely defender. An influential senator rose to his feet and launched an eloquent and impassioned defense of the new champion:

> Mr. President, I have pointed out before that a wave
> of intolerance accompanied by a determination to
> enforce conformity of thought and action on all men
> was sweeping through the nation. I repeat that intol-

erance and the demand for conformity poses a serious threat to the rights of every American citizen.
Cassius Clay, in common with 180 million other
American citizens, has a right to join the religious
sect of his choice without being blackmailed,
harassed, and threatened with the severe punishment of being deprived of the heavyweight championship. This is an example of the sort of intolerance
which grips this country today.

The speaker was none other than Senator Richard Russell of
Georgia, an avowed racist and segregationist who believed Martin
Luther King Jr. was a traitor to the country. Why, then, would he rise to
the defense of a black militant? The words Russell chose to read into
the *Congressional Record*, taken from Ali's recent newspaper interviews,
provide a clue to his motivation:

I don't believe in forced integration . . . we should
stay with our own . . . tigers stay with tigers, red ants
with red ants, Cubans with Cubans . . . . Why do two
Negroes have to go two miles out of the way to a
white school, upsetting the whole school . . . . We
believe that forced and token integration is but a
temporary and not an everlasting solution to the
Negro problem . . . .

Russell unwittingly revealed one of the great ironies of the Black
Muslim movement, that they shared a common goal with the racist
defenders of Jim Crow and the forced separation of the races. This reality hit home when Malcolm X revealed in his autobiography that on
behalf of the Nation of Islam, he personally had negotiated a secret
pact with the Ku Klux Klan, in which the white supremacists pledged
not to interfere with the Nation of Islam's activities in the South. FBI
files reveal that the Klan sent an annual financial contribution to the
Nation of Islam for many years.

In the end, the World Boxing Association's influence was limited,
and its decision carried little weight. Both the New York and Illinois

athletic commissions met and voted unanimously to continue recognizing Ali as the world champion, regardless of any action the WBA might take. Melvin Kurewich, chairperson of the New York State Athletic Commission, declared, "Within the limits of the Constitution, the right to freedom of speech and to religious beliefs are inviolate. No title of a world champion has ever been vacated because of religion, race, or religious beliefs." Ali told reporters, "That New York board is the smartest. It knows I'm the greatest, and that I certainly can't lose my title outside the ring."

Nevertheless, the damage was done, the outrage incurred on both sides. For the second time, a black heavyweight champion had stood up to white America and thumbed his nose at its prejudices and preconceptions. In so doing, Ali had provoked a backlash that had not been seen since the boxing establishment turned against Jack Johnson a half century earlier.

▶ ▶ ▶

Just as one major controversy was deflected, an announcement came from Washington that was about to unleash an even greater firestorm. The day after Ali announced his conversion to the Nation of Islam, J. Edgar Hoover ordered his agents to inquire about the boxer's draft status. The easiest way to keep a troublemaker in line, he figured, would be to keep him under the watchful eye of Uncle Sam for two years. The same day, the head of Ali's Louisville Draft Board told reporters the new champion would be "drafted within three weeks."

However, the results of Ali's army aptitude tests, taken six weeks earlier, had not yet been compiled. Finally, on March 20, the results were in. CASSIUS CLAY REJECTED BY ARMY! screamed the headlines.

The Pentagon had issued a communiqué which, according to the *New York Times*, was cleared through command channels "with the care normally attached to the status of missile scientists." The communiqué announced that the Department of the Army had reviewed Ali's pre-induction examination and had determined that "he is not qualified for induction into the Army under applicable standards. Tests given Clay included measurements of aptitudes and various skills needed in military service. Clay was given a second test after it was determined that the results of the initial test were inconclusive."

The official announcement explained that Ali had been tested for aptitude in "various skills needed in military service." In failing this test, Ali fell into the category of the 18.8 percent of prospective draftees who demonstrate they "lack trainability" for even limited military skills. After taking his first test in January, and failing the mathematical section, Ali had been summoned back in early March to take a second test in Louisville. This time, an army psychologist was assigned to watch him and determine whether he was deliberately attempting to fail. The expert concluded that "Clay tried his best." Among the questions asked in the mathematical question, two in particular gave him trouble:

> 1. A man works from six in the morning to three in the afternoon with one hour for lunch. How many hours did he work?
>
> a) 7   b) 8   c) 9   d) 10
>
> 2. A clerk divided a number by 3.5 when it should be multiplied by 4.5. His answer is 3. What is the correct answer?
>
> a)3.25   b) 10.50   c) 13.75   d) 47.25

Ali was embarrassed by the publicity given his poor results. "I said I was the greatest, not the smartest," he told reporters. "When I looked at a lot of them questions, I just didn't know the answers. I didn't even know how to start about finding the answers."

Reaction around the country to the news Ali had avoided the army by failing his induction test was almost as outraged and indignant as the announcement of his conversion. "Had I flunked math, I still could have peeled potatoes for the first two months of my army service—which I did," said Representative William Ayers of Ohio on the floor of Congress. "Anybody that can throw a punch like Cassius ought to be able to throw a knife around a potato."

A Georgia lawyer started up a "Draft That Nigger Clay" campaign. South Carolina Congressperson L. Mendel Rivers embarked on a speaking tour, crusading to have Ali reclassified. "Clay's deferment is an insult to every mother's son serving in the armed forces," he raged. "Here he is, smart enough to finish high school, write his kind of poetry, promote himself all over the world, make a million a year, drive around in red Cadillacs—and they say he's too dumb to tote a gun! Who's dumb enough to believe that?" A number of incensed senators and congressmen immediately called for a Senate hearing on the matter.

Behind the scenes, Ali's handlers were working furiously to deflect the latest controversy. He recalls being approached by Worth Bingham of the Louisville Sponsoring Group, who proposed a compromise. "He told me, 'Look, Cassius, let's work this thing out. They don't want you in the army as much as they want the title back in 'patriotic' hands. Let's get them off you. You pick any service you want: Army, Navy, Air Force, Marines — you name it. We'll swing a commission. You come out in the reserves, Special Services. You'll never go near a battlefield. It's done every day.'" Ali said he'd think it over.

Nobody was more suspicious of Ali's test results than J. Edgar Hoover, who had been temporarily thwarted in his plan to eliminate the new convert's national platform and, by extension, that of the Black Muslims. His agents set out to prove that Ali had been faking it. With the help of a sympathetic insider, the FBI obtained Cassius Clay's high school records. A summary of a report sent to Hoover states:

> Person X emphasized that he was furnishing information for the assistance of the U.S. government and did not want the data made public.
>
> Clay re-entered Central High School in September of 1958, and remained until he graduated June 11, 1960. He ranked 376 out of a graduating class of 391. His average grades for the 9th, 10th, 11th, and 12th years was 72.7.
>
> On January 3, 1957, Clay was given the standard California Intelligence Quotient Test and attained a rating of 83. On February 15, 1960, he took a college qualifications test and scored a percentile of 27. That is, 73 per cent of those taking the test scored better than Clay.

Person X advised that, during the time that Clay was attending high school, a passing mark was 70.

Clay earned 16 units, earning them in the following subjects:

Subject	Grades Attained
English	75, 70, 73, 74
Mechanical Drawing	70, 71
Choral Music	70, 71
Social Studies	75
General Science	70
Biology	70
General Art	70
American History	75
Algebra 1	70
Foods	83
Metal Work	93

Much to Hoover's chagrin, Ali's high school academic record seemed to vindicate the Army's test scores. From this point on, the media seemed to revel in portraying Ali as not very bright. Even some of his liberal sympathizers would regularly refer to him as "unsophisticated," "lacking book learning" and "childlike." Never lacking in confidence before, Ali was sensitive about these characterizations. "For a while, I began to believe I was stupid," he said. He was even more troubled by the fact that public reports said he failed the "mental test," making him "crazy" in many people's minds.

But according to Jerry Izenberg, who has been covering Ali since the 1960 Olympics, "You just have to spend five minutes with him to understand how bright he is. I've never encountered a quicker, or a more intuitive, mind. The truth is that he's a hell of a lot smarter than any of the reporters who covered him, and that probably includes me."

Ali later discussed his educational limitations with *Life* magazine photographer Gordon Parks. "My mother always wanted me to be something like a doctor or lawyer," he revealed. "Maybe I'd a made a good lawyer. I talk so much. I guess I got that from my father. I'm really kinda shy. Didn't get as much schooling as I wanted to. But common sense is just as good."

Malcolm X seems to have been one of the first to understand the extent of Ali's intellect. In Miami he told George Plimpton, "Not many people know the quality of the mind he's got in there. He fools them. One forgets that though a clown never imitates a wise man, the wise man can imitate the clown. He is very shrewd—with as much untapped mental energy as he has physical power."

His high school guidance counselor Betty Johnston insists that his school record and his army aptitude test do not in any way reflect his intelligence. "I now believe we failed him in high school," she says. "We only had one guidance counselor for seventeen hundred students and he kind of got passed by. It's possible he may have even had a learning disability, dyslexia perhaps, but we just didn't know about those things then. One thing is clear. This is a highly intelligent person and only a fool can't see that."

Typical Americans seemed to sense the same thing. News of Ali's draft-exempt status prompted a deluge of angry letters to President Johnson, the Commander-in-Chief. Most found it impossible to believe the quick-witted boxer wasn't smart enough for the Army. A sampling of these letters indicates the pressure the Johnson Administration faced:

"Dear Mr. Johnson: As a citizen of the most wonderful country in the world, and the mother of a young boy that has just been drafted, I would like to ask a few questions. I hope you will take the time to answer them for me," wrote one Pennsylvania housewife. "I read in the paper that Mr. Clay was not being drafted because he was not mentally acceptable. Mr. President, I can hardly believe that! Is it because he is a millionaire and pays a lot of taxes? Is it because he is heavyweight champion of the world? Is it because he is colored and colored people are being handled with 'kid gloves' these days?"

Another citizen wrote the president, "Unless Clay is drafted into the army, you will be *personally* sorry."

Johnson felt he needed a capable, high-ranking government official to deflect the furor and handle the situation, so he assigned the dossier to Secretary of the Army Stephen Ailes. In a letter to Carl Vinson, chairperson of the House Armed Services Committee, who was demanding a public hearing on the matter, Ailes explained the decision to classify Ali 1-Y. "In my judgment, we must depend on the established standards which our mental tests measure in a very accurate degree. The requirements of today's Army do not allow acceptance of those personnel not offering a reasonable value to the defense effort."

But Johnson was so sensitive to public criticism of the Ali matter that he ordered Secretary Ailes to personally write letters to some members of the public, a job usually designated to a much lower official. In one of these letters, Ailes unwittingly reveals the extraordinary attention the government paid to Ali's induction exam and certainly lends credence to the theory that the boxer was singled out.

To an Idaho man who wrote the president speculating that Ali had faked his results, Ailes wrote, "You are concerned as to whether Clay misled the army into believing he could not acquire the needed skills. So was I. For this very reason I asked that he be re-tested. Furthermore, I sent the senior Army civilian expert in the testing field to Louisville to review the test results, to observe Clay during the test, and to observe the subsequent interview between Clay and the Army psychologist. Clay's attitude was cooperative and our people were convinced that he made a sincere effort on the tests. Accordingly, we had no basis for inducting him."

In April, anxious to leave the draft controversy behind, Ali set off on his previously scheduled tour of Africa. In contrast to the chilly reception he now received in his own country, huge crowds greeted the world champion, especially in the predominantly Muslim countries where Ali was considered a hero of the faith as well as a sporting great.

When he had announced his planned African trip at the UN two months earlier, Ali had promised, "Malcolm X will be at my side." Now, however, the two were completely estranged; indeed, they had not spoken since Malcolm had announced the formation of his new movement the month before. In the meantime, the former champion of black supremacy had visited Mecca and seen white and black Muslims worshipping side by side. The sight and its significance had prompted a profound shift in his thinking. Malcolm now believed the Nation of Islam was a racist movement and that he had been misguided in his own long-held views.

By coincidence, during the course of Ali's African trip, the boxer arrived in Ghana—through which Malcolm X was passing on his way to Mecca. At one point, the two passed each other in a marketplace but didn't speak. Moments later, Ali turned to Herbert Muhammad—the Messenger's son who was travelling with him—and offered an assessment of his former teacher.

"Man, did you get a look at him? Dressed in that funny white robe and wearing a beard and walking with a cane that looked like a prophet's stick? Man, he's gone so far out he's out completely. Doesn't that just go to show that Elijah is the most powerful; nobody listens to that Malcolm anymore." This conversation was captured in an FBI surveillance report.

Ali sounds like a man trying to convince himself he had done the right thing in choosing the Messenger over Malcolm. In later years, he would feel shame about turning his back on the man who had advanced his spiritual growth, guided his thinking, and been like family to him. But the most ironic aspect of their split was that Malcolm's new philosophy—a more flexible version of black nationalism, international solidarity, and economic self-help without the racism—closely paralleled the vision of Ali, who in the years to come sounded a lot more like Malcolm X than like Elijah Muhammad.

CHAPTER FIVE:
"I Ain't Got No Quarrel
with Them Vietcong"

S HORTLY AFTER ALI RETURNED from Africa in the spring of 1964, thousands of college students—black and white—from across America began to pour into Mississippi to register black voters, who had long been denied the franchise in America's most racist state. It was the start of Freedom Summer.

On June 21, three civil rights workers—Michael Schwerner, James Chaney, and Andrew Goodman—were arrested on a trumped-up charge by Cecil Price, a deputy sheriff in Philadelphia, Mississippi, who also happened to be a member in good standing of the local Ku Klux Klan. After alerting his Klan brothers, Price released the three activists —two of them white—late at night. Twenty minutes later, they were brutally murdered on a dark road. If John F. Kennedy's assassination seven months earlier had marked the end of America's innocence, then the deaths of the three civil rights martyrs marked a transition for a generation of youth from idealism to defiance.

Eight thousand miles away, defiance was already creating Vietnam's own martyrs. Images of Buddhist monks pouring gasoline over them-selves and going up in flames to protest the brutal dictatorship of South Vietnam were helping to fuel an indigenous revolt. To quell it, President Lyndon Johnson sent five thousand American troops to South Vietnam on July 21, the first official combat troops not disingenuously designated "advisers." The United States was wedding itself to a murderous regime it considered the only alternative to communism, but whose actions were increasingly driving the people to support the communist Vietcong "liberators."

Two weeks later, on August 5, Johnson ordered retaliatory action against gunboats and "certain supporting facilities in North Vietnam" after a number of alleged attacks against American destroyers in the Gulf of Tonkin. The official story was that North Vietnamese torpedo boats launched an "unprovoked attack" against a U.S. destroyer on routine patrol in the area on August 2—and that North Vietnamese military boats followed up with a "deliberate attack" on a pair of U.S. ships two days later. But it was revealed years later that there was no second attack by North Vietnam—no "renewed attacks against American destroyers." The Johnson administration, seeking an excuse to escalate the conflict into a full-scale war, lied to Congress and the American people and set the stage for America's longest war.

The Gulf of Tonkin Resolution—the closest thing there ever was to a declaration of war against North Vietnam—sailed through Congress on August 7. The resolution authorized the president "to take all necessary measures to repel any armed attack against the forces of the United States and to prevent further aggression." Only two senators, Wayne Morse and Ernest Gruening, opposed the resolution. The overwhelming majority of Americans, believing their president, supported the new war.

Muhammad Ali had other things on his mind. "I vaguely recall hearing about the ships getting hit but I wasn't really paying much attention," he says. A month earlier, he had fallen in love with a twenty-three-year-old cocktail waitress named Sonji Roi. A week after the Gulf of Tonkin Resolution passed, the two were married in Gary, Indiana.

After a brief honeymoon, Ali signed to fight a rematch against Sonny Liston. And he persisted in proselytizing for his new faith, travelling to mosques all over the country preaching the Black Muslim message and raising the ire of the white establishment.

His new religion was already proving costly. He told *Ebony* magazine that joining the Nation of Islam had cost him "some $500,000 in possible commercial contracts. I have turned down another $500,000 from several concerns because they wanted me to do something I think is dead wrong—chase white women in films." He revealed that he had turned down an offer to play Jack Johnson in a movie because the part would have forced him to be portrayed marrying a white woman.

The media continued to register their disgust. The dean of America's boxing writers, Jimmy Cannon, called Ali's affiliation with the Nation of Islam "the dirtiest in American sports since the Nazis were shilling for Max Schmeling as representative of their vile theories of blood." For his part, Ali calmly deflected the mounting criticism as if he were fending off jabs in the ring. "Elijah isn't teaching hate when he tells us about the evil things the white man has done any more than you're teaching hate when you tell us about what Hitler did to the Jews. That's not hate, that's history."

Pat Putnam covered boxing for the *Miami Herald* during this period. He remembers the attitude of some of his colleagues. "Some of the old-line boxing writers absolutely hated him," he recalls. "He didn't fit into their mold. I think there was some racism involved. Cannon idolized Joe Louis, he believed every boxer should be like him. Here comes this brash, loud-mouthed kid and he couldn't handle it. There was this hysteria around the Muslim thing. People were afraid of the Muslims. I think some of the old block writers were saying, 'look at those scary black men, they're going to rape my sister.'"

Ali was assuming the role that Malcolm X had vacated when he left the Nation of Islam. And, like Malcolm, he was good for recruitment. Meanwhile, Malcolm continued to spread his message through his newly formed Organization of Afro-American Unity, advocating that blacks achieve their freedom "by any means necessary" and decrying the racism of his former movement. As he did so, the Nation of Islam turned against him with a fury.

As he traveled the globe, Malcolm repeatedly predicted that he would be killed by the Nation, which had accused him of high treason and labeled him the "Chief Hypocrite." And he had good reason to worry. For months he had been receiving reports from inside the Nation that an order had been issued from the highest levels for his death. In December 1964, *Muhammad Speaks* contained an article written by Louis X, the Nation's rising star who had taken over the interim ministership of Malcolm's old Mosque number seven in Harlem.

"The die is cast and Malcolm shall not escape," wrote the man later known as Louis Farrakhan. "Such a man as Malcolm is worthy of death." Two months later, on February 21, 1965, Malcolm X was assassinated by five Nation of Islam gunmen while he was speaking at the Audubon Ballroom in Harlem. Farrakhan later attempted to spread the never-substantiated theory that the FBI was actually behind the killing.

That night, while Ali was at his Massachusetts training camp, his Chicago apartment building was gutted by fire. Rumor quickly spread that, as the Nation of Islam's highest profile representative, he was being targeted for revenge by Malcolm's followers. Five FBI agents showed up at his camp and told him they were assigning a plainclothes police guard to protect him.

The Liston rematch had been postponed in November after Ali collapsed with a hernia three days before the fight. It was rescheduled for May 26 in Lewiston, Maine. Liston was a five-to-one favorite to win his title back, despite his crushing defeat a year earlier. The pundits believed the first fight was a fluke and refused to concede Ali's superiority. Some rumors even had it that the Muslims had fixed the first fight, threatening Liston if he didn't take a dive.

Syndicated columnist Jerry Izenberg, one of Ali's earliest and most ardent supporters, one of the few who insisted on calling him by his Muslim name, remembers an "ugly atmosphere" surrounding the second Liston fight. "Malcolm was dead, and there were rumors that Ali was going to be killed, maybe even in the ring, in retaliation. A lot of it was hysteria fuelled by the press but even so the fear was there . . . . Somebody asked something about Malcolm, it was a reporter who asked, 'You've heard the stories about Malcolm's people making an attempt on your life?'. . . and Ali looked up and said, 'What people? Malcolm ain't got no people.' And I remember, I got mad because in my mind Malcolm stood for certain things. And I thought, 'You son of a bitch. One minute, Malcolm is great, and then all of a sudden he's nobody because somebody tells you he's nobody.' I was really pissed about it."

It took longer to sing the national anthem than it did for Ali to knock out Sonny Liston in the first round and prove the first fight was no fluke. Despite renewed speculation by Ali's detractors that the challenger had taken a dive—the FBI investigated the rumors and found no merit to them—it was clear to the boxing world that Muhammad Ali was a force to be reckoned with.

"Even those who didn't like him—and there were plenty—had to respect him after the second Liston fight," says Robert Lipsyte. "For a little while at least, people stopped dwelling on all the controversy and began to admire his boxing skills."

A month after the Liston fight, Ali had his marriage to Sonji Roi annulled on the grounds that she had failed to follow the tenets of the Muslim religion. To many, this signaled the increasing grip of the Nation of Islam over every facet of his life. And not without some foundation: Elijah Muhammad had assigned his son Herbert to handle Ali's business affairs, and a large Muslim entourage traveled with the champion wherever he went.

"They've stolen my man's mind," Sonji charged after the annulment. "I wasn't going to take on all the Muslims. If I had, I'd probably have ended up dead."

Meanwhile, the boxing world searched in vain for somebody to send Ali back to oblivion. In Jack Johnson's day, the call had gone out for a "white hope" to silence the upstart champion. Now a similar call went out but this time with an ironic twist. The challenger this time would have to be a black "white hope"—and it looked like there was only one man to fit the bill.

Floyd Patterson had been a popular heavyweight champion before he lost the title a few years earlier to Sonny Liston in a humiliating first-round knockout. A rematch between the two fighters had ended even more quickly. In marked contrast to Ali, Patterson was soft-spoken, humble, and well-loved by the black and white establishments. He had marched for integration with Martin Luther King Jr., moved into an all-white neighborhood before being hounded out by angry neighbors, and even married a white woman. As historian Jeffrey Sammons once observed, "Ironically in Jack Johnson's era, Ali would have been the hero and Patterson the villain."

Shortly after the first Ali-Liston fight, Patterson had drawn the battle lines by announcing his intention to "bring the title back to America." This attack didn't sit well with Ali, who countered, "If you don't believe the title already is in America, just see who I pay taxes to. I'm an American. But he's a deaf dumb so-called Negro who needs a spanking . . . . We don't consider the Muslims have the title any more than the Baptists had it when Joe Louis was champ."

Ali agreed to a title match with Patterson, vowing not to let "one old

Negro make a fool of me." Patterson, a Catholic, made much of his own religious ties, and the fight was billed as a modern-day holy war between the forces of Christianity and Islam, even though the real issues had more to do with racial ideology and patriotism than religion.

At a press conference, Patterson declared, "The Black Muslim influence must be removed from boxing. I have been told Clay has every right to follow any religion he chooses, and I agree. But by the same token, I have the right to call the Black Muslims a menace to the United States and a menace to the Negro race."

While Ali surrounded himself with an entourage of Muslims, Patterson traveled with an array of civil rights workers, liberal whites, and celebrities—including Frank Sinatra, who supplied Patterson with his own personal physician. All were rooting for him to shut Ali up once and for all.

The spectacle was not lost on the outspoken champion, who was offended by Patterson's constant invocation of his civil rights credentials. "When he was champion," Ali charged, "the only time he'd be caught in Harlem was when he was in the back of a car waving in some parade. The big shot didn't have no time for his own kind, he was so busy integrating. And now he wants to fight me because I stick up for black people."

On November 22, 1965, the two fighters took their holy war into the ring. Ali had never been known as a brutal fighter. His artistry in the ring regularly reminded observers why boxing was known as "the sweet science." A few months before the Patterson fight, he had even publicly contemplated retiring from the sport, declaring, "I don't like hurting people." But the constant attacks against his religion and his character had taken their toll and he was clearly out for revenge. What seemed to irk him most was Patterson's declaration that he would never call his opponent by his Muslim name. Addressing the challenger, he vowed to "give you a whipping until you call me Muhammad Ali." Before the fight, he announced his intentions poetically:

> I'm gonna put him flat on his back
> So that he will start acting black.
> Because when he was champ he didn't do as he should.
> He tried to force himself into an all-white neighborhood.

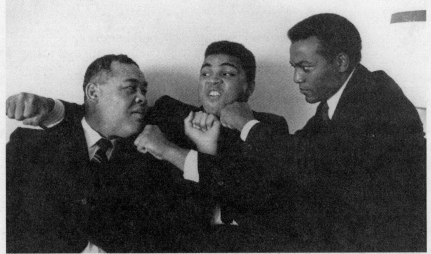

Ali mixes it up with his boyhood idol Joe Louis, left and football great Jim Brown, 1964. Louis would later turn against Ali with a vengeance.

The fight was no contest. Yet rather than putting the outmatched Patterson flat on his back quickly, Ali toyed with him, inflicting one brutal punch after another—but always holding back from ending it so as to prolong the agony. Finally, the referee showed mercy on the ex-champ and ended the fight in the twelfth round. Shocked by Ali's uncharacteristic cruelty, the media—even those few reporters previously sympathetic to him—turned against him. *Life* magazine called the fight "a sickening spectacle in the ring."

In his black cultural manifesto *Soul on Ice*—written shortly after the Patterson fight—Eldridge Cleaver explained the outpouring of negative reaction against Ali. "Muhammad Ali is the first 'free' black champion ever to confront white America," he wrote. "In the context of boxing, he is a genuine revolutionary, the black Fidel Castro of boxing. To the mind of 'white' white America and 'white' black America, the heavyweight crown has fallen into enemy hands, usurped by a pretender to the throne. Ali is conceived as 'occupying' the heavyweight kingdom in the name of a dark, alien power, in much the same way as Castro was conceived as a temporary interloper, 'occupying' Cuba."

At the time, only a handful of white reporters were willing to defend

Ali. Although he wouldn't use the same fiery rhetoric as Cleaver, Robert Lipsyte of the *New York Times* seemed to sense the parallels between Ali and Jack Johnson as far back as November 1965. Analyzing the mounting backlash against the champion, he wrote, "The public—through the press—was not ready to receive the antithesis of Louis and Patterson. Once before it had been presented with a nonconforming Negro champion, and society rejected, harassed, and eventually persecuted Jack Johnson."

Nobody was more aware of Ali's refusal to bow to the whims of the establishment than Joe Louis, who had perfected this role to become the first black man ever to be embraced by white America. Louis, who had once been Ali's hero, had showed up in Patterson's camp to give support to the challenger and took every opportunity to denounce Ali's religion and fighting skills.

"Clay has a million dollars worth of confidence and a dime's worth of courage," he said. "He can't punch; he can't hurt you . . . I would have whipped him."

Ali seemed to have Louis in mind when he later explained his rationale for speaking out. "When I first came into boxing, tied up as it was with gangster control and licensed robbers, fighters were not supposed to be human or intelligent . . . A fighter was seen but hardly heard on on any issue or idea of public importance. They could call me arrogant, cocky, conceited, immodest, a loud mouth, a braggart, but I would change the image of the fighter in the eyes of the world."

The outpouring of disgust reached the highest levels of Washington, where President Johnson continued to receive hundreds of angry letters from citizens demanding to know why Ali wasn't serving his country.

One of the most telling letters, indicating how little some racial attitudes had changed in a hundred years—not to mention the level of backwardness of the boxing establishment—was sent to General Lewis Hershey, director of the U.S. Selective Service, by the legal advisor to the World Boxing Association.

"I have watched with disgust the publicity surrounding the draft status of Cassius Clay, the boxer," wrote Robert M. Summitt. "It now appears that Clay and his *owners* are going to attempt further to evade the draft through your organization or even to the President of the United States [our italics]."

Americans still overwhelmingly supported the war in Vietnam. But, little by little, the first voices of dissent began to be heard. In June 1965, black civil rights activist Julian Bond—who had co-founded the Student Non-Violent Coordinating Committee (SNCC) five years earlier—was elected to a seat in the Georgia legislature in a special vote called to fill a vacancy. On January 6, 1966—four days before Bond was scheduled to take his seat in the legislature—SNCC issued a "white paper" on the Vietnam War denouncing the United States for its conduct in the war and calling for resistance to the draft. "We are in sympathy with and support the men in this country who are unwilling to respond to the military draft which would compel them to contribute their lives to United States aggression in the name of the 'freedom' we find so false in this country," read the controversial paper. The media descended on Bond and asked him if he endorsed the SNCC manifesto. When he answered in the affirmative, he was widely lambasted as a traitor and a renegade. By a vote of 184 to 12, the Georgia House refused to seat him. Bond had marched with Martin Luther King Jr. on the bloody battlegrounds of the fight for civil rights and considered King his mentor. But in 1965, America's most respected black leader had still not publicly come out against the war.

"At the time of the controversy, when they refused to seat me, it seemed like I was all alone," recalls Bond. "Dr. King called me to express his support. He knew the war was unjust and he wanted to take a stand but his board at the Southern Christian Leadership Conference (SCLC) wouldn't let him. President Johnson was supporting civil rights legislation and they didn't want to alienate his administration."

To challenge the legislature's unconstitutional and undemocratic action, Bond hired noted civil liberties lawyer Charles Morgan Jr., who happened to sit on the Board of King's SCLC. In doing so, he set in motion a freight train of events that would have monumental repercussions.

In July President Johnson had sent an additional 50,000 troops to Vietnam and announced that the monthly draft would increase to 17,500 men. A few years later, at the height of American escalation, the army would face severe shortages of manpower and—as in all wars — be forced to lower its eligibility standards. But in late 1965 there was still a massive draft pool to draw from, and the army could call on its most promising military recruits to fight what was still a small-scale war.

Still, inexplicably, the Pentagon issued a directive in November 1965 lowering the mental aptitude percentile on induction examinations from 30 to 15. Ali had scored 16 on his own exam two years earlier, a score that had rendered him unfit for military service. Now, by only one percentile, Ali was once again eligible for the draft.

"It was suspicious to say the least," notes Robert Lipsyte.

Immediately, the director of Selective Service in Kentucky, Colonel James Stephenson, issued a statement that Ali was likely to be drafted soon because of the new criteria. It didn't take long for the boxer's supporters to voice their opinion of the lowered standards. "The government wants to set an example of Ali and they'll even change their rules to get him," declared Elijah Muhammad. "Muhammad Ali is harassed to keep the other mentally sleeping so-called Negroes fast asleep to the fact that Islam is a refuge for the so-called Negroes in America."

But the skepticism wasn't confined to Muslims. As far away as Vietnam, U.S. soldiers were following the controversy. Marine PFC Lee Rainey told the *Chicago Tribune*, "I thought Clay's reclassification did have something to do with his involvement with the Black Muslims. He talked too much."

On February 14, 1966, Ali's lawyer, Edward Jacko, went before the Louisville draft board and requested a deferment for his client on a number of procedural grounds, including the financial hardship his family would suffer if he couldn't box. The board rendered its decision three days later.

In Congress on the morning of February 17, the Senate Foreign Relations Committee was debating an emergency appropriations bill to fund the escalating war in Vietnam. General Maxwell Taylor had been invited by the Senate to make the Johnson Administration's case for more funding. One of the earliest critics of the war, Senator Wayne Morse of Indiana, told his colleagues that America shouldn't be involved in the mounting conflict. "I want to prevent the killing of an additional thousands of boys in this senseless war," he said, adding his opinion that Americans would surely repudiate the war before long.

"That, of course, is good news to Hanoi, Senator," responded General Taylor, accusing Morse and other critics of helping to prolong the war.

"I know that is the smear tactic you militarists give to those who have honest differences of opinion," Morse fired back, "but I don't intend to get down in the gutter with you and engage in that kind of debate."

It would be the first salvo in a bitter and divisive debate in Congress and throughout the country.

While the debate raged on in the Senate, Muhammad Ali was in Miami anxiously awaiting his draft board's ruling. *New York Times* reporter Robert Lipsyte was with him when he received word of the classification decision. He recalls the atmosphere and events of that day:

> I was in Florida to do some features on Ali. I think I was doing this to justify a winter vacation. Before I headed for Ali's place, I had been watching the Senate war hearings on TV in my hotel room. Maxwell Taylor and Wayne Morse were choosing up sides for the country, and this by coincidence was the day the news arrived that he had been reclassified. He had rented a small house in a black section of Miami and when I got there it was early afternoon. He was sitting on the lawn making flirtatious comments at high school girls coming home from school. One of the Muslim women who cooked for him called him inside and when he came out, he was angry and bewildered. A wire service reporter had just informed him that he was eligible for the draft. Then the television trucks started to pull up and he was interviewed and interviewed and interviewed and he kept cranking up. He kept saying how could the government have embarrassed him for so long, saying he was a nut? They made his mother and father suffer. How could they take him out of all the thousands of eligible kids in Louisville? It was weird because, as he was sitting there, he was humming the Bob Dylan song "Blowing in the Wind."
>
> All his Muslim bodyguards and members of his entourage kept coming by and saying, "This is how the White Devils do you," "This is what the

Messenger said will happen." And a lot of these guys had been in World War Two and Korea and they had horror stories about racial discrimination in the army. They were saying, "Some fat cracker sergeant's going to drop a hand grenade down your pants." And Ali, who always had this capacity to ignite himself, kept getting hotter and hotter and saying, "Why me?"

In retrospect, as he became an icon of the anti-war movement later on, I thought how interesting it was that his first responses were so self-centered. Then things kept getting weirder. There were all kinds of rumors that an army convoy was on its way to pick him up and take him to Vietnam that night and suddenly this third wave of journalists arrived and started asking him things about the Vietcong. They were saying, "Do you know where Vietnam is?" He just sort of shrugged. He didn't know where Vietnam was, I mean I didn't even know where Vietnam was. Nobody knew where it was. It was this building, throbbing beat. You kind of get a sense of the fever that was building on that lawn. Then some reporter keeps saying, "Do you know where Vietnam is, do you know where Vietnam is?" And he said 'sure.' And the reporter says "Where?" And he just shrugged. Then somebody asks, "What do you think about the Vietcong?" By this time, he was angry, tired, pissed off and he gave his quote, which is "I ain't got nothing against them Vietcong." I had seen this build up for a few hours, it seemed an absolutely appropriate response to somebody who was being fucked over, whose intelligence, whose sanity was being questioned. And who also at that moment was afraid. His world was crumbling around him. Did this mean he wasn't going to box anymore? Did this mean he was going into the army? Did this mean he was going to be killed? The world was now really on his head. This was really the first taste of what was going to come.

There were pockets of issues and problems before but they were all boxing related, all related to his religion which he was still getting a grip on. But this was serious. Considering what happened next, it's interesting to note that Ali's remarks weren't nearly as inflammatory as Senator Morse in Congress that morning.

Lipsyte's notes reveal that Ali's initial quote was "I ain't got nothing against them Vietcong." He insists that's what he heard. But the headlines the next morning in newspapers around the world has Ali saying, "I ain't got no quarrel with them Vietcong"—the quote for which he's most famous and which was about to set off a political avalanche.

He was also quoted as asking, "How can they do this without another test to see if I'm any wiser or worser than last time? I'm fighting for the Government every day. Why are they so anxious to pay me $80 a month when the government is in trouble financially? I think it costs them $12 million a day to stay in Vietnam and I buy a lot of bullets, at least three jet bombers a year, and pay the salary of 50,000 fighting men with the money they take from me after my fights." He expressed his conviction that he was being unfairly singled out because of his affiliation with the Nation of Islam. "I'm a member of the Black Muslims and we don't go to no wars unless they're declared by Allah himself," he added.

Reaction was immediate and fierce. That night, Ali's phone rang off the hook with callers anxious to share their opinion on his remarks: "You cowardly, turncoat black rat!" yelled one caller. "If I had a bomb I would blow you to hell." Another caller, a woman, sounded hysterical as she vented her anger. "Cassius Clay? Is that you? You better'n my son? You black bastard, you. I pray to God they draft you tomorrow. Draft you and shoot you on the spot!"

The media were only marginally more restrained. In the *New York Journal American*, Murray Robinson raged, "For his stomach-turning performance, boxing should throw Clay out on his inflated head. The adult brat, who has boasted ad nauseam of his fighting skill but who squealed like a cornered rat when tapped for the Army, should be shorn of his title."

The dean of America's sportswriters, Red Smith, weighed in with his assessment. "Squealing over the possibility that the military may call him up, Cassius makes himself as sorry a spectacle as those unwashed punks who picket and demonstrate against the war," he wrote.

Syndicated sports columnist Jerry Izenberg, one of Ali's earliest and most passionate defenders, was one of the few who supported his stand. "With that one sentence about the Vietcong," he says, "Ali became the patron saint of the anti-war movement. Before that, none of the protesters could really articulate why they were against the war. He gave them the reason."

Jack Olsen of *Sports Illustrated* described the backlash, "The noise became a din, the drumbeats of a holy war. TV and radio commentators, little old ladies from Champaign-Urbana, bookies and parish priests, armchair strategists at the Pentagon and politicians all over the place joined in a crescendo of 'Get Cassius' clamor."

Ali's close friend Lloyd Wells was the first black marine drill sergeant during World War II and was wounded fighting in a segregated unit during the Korean War. He recalls his reaction to Ali's remarks. "When he said he had no quarrel with the Vietcong," says Wells, "I thought about it and realized that I had no quarrel with the North Koreans during my war either. It made a lot of sense and I immediately supported him even though I was a decorated ex-Marine."

He may not have known exactly where Vietnam was at the time, but Ali had already formed an opinion about the war. "Up to the time of my statement," he later recalled, "the extent of my involvement had been as a TV spectator. But I had seen a series of pictures in a magazine showing mangled bodies of dead Vietcong laid out on a highway like rows of logs and a white American officer walking down the aisle of the dead taking the body count. The only enemy alive was a little naked girl, searching among the bodies, her wide eyes frightened. I clipped out that picture; and the face has never quite left my mind."

Today, Ali looks back at the initial controversy with only one regret. "If I had it to do over again, I wouldn't have made the Vietcong remarks so early. I would have waited until I was about to be inducted to announce my plans."

▶ ▶ ▶

The first American soldier to be gunned down by the Redcoats in the Revolutionary War, Crispus Attucks, was a black man. Hundreds of escaped slaves were fighting for both sides. The British government had assured black men in the colonies who participated in the conflict that when the war was over their freedom would be assured, prompting George Washington—a slave-owner himself—to follow suit with his own promise of freedom. Yet once the war was over, many of the Blacks who had fought bravely for independence were actually re-enslaved. This was the first of many broken promises to come.

In 1924, the great African-American writer and philosopher W. E. B. Dubois analyzed the conflicting loyalties of the black American soldier in wartime:

> He fought because he believed that by fighting for America, he would gain the respect of the land and personal and spiritual freedom. His problem as a soldier was always peculiar; no matter for what America fought, the American Negro always fought for his own freedom and for the self-respect of his race. Whatever the cause of war, therefore, his cause was peculiarly just. He appears, therefore, in American wars always with a double motive—the desire to oppose the so-called enemy of his country along with his fellow white citizens, and before that, the motive of deserving well of those citizens, and securing justice for his folk.

When Lyndon Johnson was elected president in 1964, he vowed to wage a "War on Poverty" and to spend billions of dollars to rejuvenate the inner cities. When the Vietnam War began to escalate, however, the government diverted its financial resources to fighting the war. Poverty and unemployment continued to plague urban ghettoes in hugely disproportionate amounts. Johnson promised the black community that, when the war was won, they would reap the benefits.

But Eldridge Cleaver, reflecting a growing skepticism among black youth, refused to accept his assurances. "The black people have been tricked again and again, sold out at every turn by misleaders," he wrote. "After the Civil War, America went through a period similar to the one we are now in. The Negro problem received a full hearing. Everybody knew that the black man had been denied justice. No one doubted that it was time for changes and that the black man should be made a first class citizen. But Reconstruction ended. The lyncher and the burner received virtual license to murder Blacks at will. White Americans found a new level on which to cool the Blacks out. It has taken a hundred years of struggle up from that level of cool-out to the miserable position that black Americans find themselves in. Time is passing. The historical opportunity which world events now present to black Americans is running out with every tick of the clock . . . . The black man's interest lies in seeing a free and independent Vietnam, a strong Vietnam which is not the puppet of international white supremacy. If the nations of Asia, Latin America, and Africa are strong and free, the black man in America will be safe and secure and free to live in dignity and self-respect."

When Ali made his first controversial statements about the war, he made no explicit link between racial issues and Vietnam, despite the lately widely circulated myth that he said at the time, "No Vietcong ever called me nigger." But the whirlwind of events to follow was about to convince him that his instinctive reaction against the war had a firm basis in race politics.

As abuse was heaped on him from all quarters, Ali found himself very isolated and thoroughly confused. None of the major media had yet turned against the war, only two Senators dared to speak against it in Congress, and wide-scale student protests had not yet begun. Julian Bond, still embroiled in his own battle with the Georgia legislature, describes the mood: "When Ali said he had no quarrel against the Vietcong, I was ecstatic," he recalls. "Suddenly I didn't feel so alone. Here was a public figure with a national forum expressing something which needed to be said but which everybody was afraid to say for fear of being branded a traitor. It took tremendous courage."

It was at this point, notes sportswriter Budd Schulberg, that Ali went from reflecting his times to shaping them.

Soon after Ali's remarks, a schism erupted in the Student Non-Violent Coordinating Committee when its chairperson, Stokely Carmichael, invoked the term "Black Power" during an integration march in Mississippi. "We been saying 'Freedom' for six years," he told the marchers shortly after he was arrested and released. "What we are going to start saying now is 'Black Power'!" The term had actually been coined by black New York Congressman Adam Clayton Powell a month earlier but, out of Carmichael's mouth, it galvanized a new generation of black militants and struck fear into many whites.

Carmichael would help usher in a new era of black activism, following in the steps of Malcolm X to demand not just integration but full economic and political justice. The new slogan would eventually be taken up by the revolutionary Black Panther Party, a group that would make the Nation of Islam seem like Boy Scouts in comparison. And foremost on the agenda of the new militants was a rejection of the Vietnam War and especially the role of black Americans in the war. Carmichael crystallized the new sentiment: "Why should black folks fight a war against yellow folks so that white folks can keep a land they stole from red folks? We're not going to Vietnam. Ain't no Vietcong ever called me nigger!"

For Ali, still searching for a way to articulate a viewpoint that he had instinctively understood when he blurted out his own Vietcong remark, Carmichael's phrase resonated. From then on, he often told crowds and reporters, "No Vietcong ever called me nigger!" when pressed to explain his anti-war stand.

"At first, I was struck by how self-centered his explanations were," says Robert Lipsyte. "He would ask, 'Why are they doing this to me?' and things like that. But eventually he seemed to grow into an understanding of the issues involved and I believe he was very sincere."

Miami Herald sportswriter Pat Putnam has a slightly different view. "I don't believe he was opposing the war because of his principles. I think that when the Army rejected him for failing the intelligence tests, he was pissed off and when they reclassified him, he said to himself, 'If they don't want me, I don't want them.'"

Ali's most immediate concern was his upcoming fight with Ernie Terrell, scheduled for March 29 in Chicago. The furor over his Vietnam statement was already making waves in his recently adopted hometown, where Illinois governor Otto Kerner branded his remarks "disgusting." Echoing the editorial pages of Chicago's three daily newspapers, which unanimously called for the state athletic commission to

"Who's the prettiest of them all?"

rescind its license for the fight, Chicago Mayor Richard Daley labeled Ali a traitor and said, "I hope the fight won't be held in Chicago. The record here is that we could do well without it."

At a city council meeting, Chicago Alderman John Hoellen demanded the fight be cancelled and Ali inducted into the army immediately. "I don't see why Cassius Clay should confine his fighting to a sports arena," he said. "He deserves no better treatment than anyone else. Something is wrong with the system when the average guy gets in as fast as they can get him and guys like Clay are excluded."

Chicago's police superintendent Orlando Wilson weighed in on the dispute, urging the fight be called off because of "the unpatriotic statements attributed to Clay" and their potential to provoke public disorder.

Jim Murray of the *Los Angeles Times* called Ali a "black Benedict Arnold" and warned him "not to go near the statue of Lincoln. Those will be real tears running down his cheeks." Former heavyweight champion Jack Dempsey announced, "Muhammad Ali is finished as a fighter. Regardless of the outcome of his next fight, he is finished. He should be careful. It's not safe for him to be on the streets."

Ali clearly wasn't prepared for the turmoil he had unleashed. His declaration two years earlier that he was a Muslim was nothing compared to this. And back then, Malcolm X had helped prepare him for the backlash and given him an inner strength. The attacks this time were not only more vicious, but there was no Malcolm to counsel him.

Around the country, editorial writers heaped scorn on the boxer. He was "a self-centered spoiled brat of a child," "a sad apology for a man," "the all-time jerk of the boxing world," "the most disgusting character in memory to appear on the sports scene," "bum of the month, bum of the year, bum of all time." For once, Ali was confused about how to handle the situation.

"It was as though I had touched an electric switch that let loose the pent-up hatred and bitterness that a section of white America had long wanted to unleash on me for all my cockiness and boasting, for declaring myself 'The Greatest' without waiting for their kind approval," he later wrote. "For frustrating their desire to see me whipped 'for the good of the country.'"

To the athletic and political establishment, observes historian Randy Roberts, Ali had become the enemy.

Behind the scenes, Ali's handlers were furiously working to deflect the controversy and save the fight, which promised to be a financial bonanza. When the World Boxing Association stripped Ali of his title in 1964 after he declared his Muslim faith, Ernie Terrell had been awarded the championship in an elimination bout. Although the WBA didn't carry much weight, the upcoming match was being billed as "the undisputed heavyweight championship of the world" and, as such, it was attracting global attention. A deal was quickly struck by one of the fight promoters, Ben Bentley, without Ali's knowledge, which would have him appear before a meeting of the Illinois Athletic Commission to retreat from his anti-war remarks. Bentley had convinced the mayor, the governor, and the influential *Chicago Tribune* to back off if the recalcitrant boxer would apologize.

Ali was at first wary of the arrangement. Only that morning he had received a telegram from former heavyweight champion Gene Tunney that read, "You have disgraced your title and the American flag and the principles for which it stands. Apologize for your unpatriotic remarks or you'll be barred from the ring." Now Bentley was arguing that Tunney was right, that Ali's career was in jeopardy.

After a phone call from members of the Louisville Sponsoring Group and his lawyer Edward Jocko, Ali finally relented. He called Athletic Commission Chairperson Joe Triner and reluctantly apologized for whatever embarrassment he had caused, explaining that he had "popped off out of turn." Triner was satisfied but insisted Ali appear before the entire three-person commission to issue his apology. A meeting was scheduled for the coming Friday.

The news was immediately leaked to the media, which reported, CLAY SET TO APOLOGIZE in blaring headlines. On Friday, February 21, Ali arrived from his Miami training camp at Chicago's O'Hare airport for the Commission hearing, scheduled for noon that day. To symbolize his new "closed-mouth" policy, the promoter placed several Band-Aids over Ali's mouth to the delight of the assembled reporters.

From the airport, Ali drove to Elijah Muhammad's mansion for a meeting with his advisers. On the way, he happened to read a story in that day's *Chicago Sun-Times* claiming to be based on "secret information from inside Muslim headquarters."

The exclusive story, written by Jack Mabley, reported that "Clay's instructions, if pressed, are to give evasive answers. It is believed, however, that if it appears necessary, Clay may say at this stage that he would be willing to serve in the Armed Forces . . . if he finds it necessary to make this statement, it will be relatively simple for him to change his mind after the fight, but before he is inducted."

Ali was torn. To him, honesty was one of the cornerstones of his religion. Where did these "instructions" come from? When he arrived at the mansion, Elijah Muhammad—who, of course, had spent four years in prison for draft evasion during World War II—assured him that the decision was his. "Brother, if you felt what you said was wrong, then you should be a man and apologize for it. But if you felt what you said was right, then be a man and stand up for it," Ali reported him as saying.

At noon, Ali and his entourage arrived at the Illinois State Building, only to be greeted by a huge line of demonstrators in World War II uniforms, with signs reading, CLAY! APOLOGIZE TO AMERICA! and CLAY! LOVE AMERICA OR LEAVE IT! A small group of supporters stood across the street waving signs saying, WE AIN'T GOT NO QUARREL WITH NO VIETCONG EITHER!

As Ali was ushered down the corridor to meet the waiting commissioners, his lawyer—Edward Jacko—handed him a prepared typewritten statement outlining Ali's apology. They entered the conference room where the three commissioners presided.

"I understand you have a statement to read," Chairperson Triner said in a sympathetic tone.

At that moment, Ali came to his decision. Principle was more important than expediency. He discarded the paper and began to speak.

"I have no prepared statement. What I said in Miami, I should have said to the officials of the draft board, not to reporters. I apologize for not saying it to the proper people."

The commissioners looked shocked. One of them said, "To whom you made the remark is not important. It's the remark itself. Do you apologize for your unpatriotic remark, regardless to whom you said it?"

Beside him, Edward Jacko was apoplectic. He whispered into his client's ear, "Tell them you apologize. Go on. Tell them."

Triner again intervened. "Cassius Clay," he said from his podium, "do you apologize to the American people, to the governor of this state, to the mayor of this city? Do you apologize for your unpatriotic remark?"

Ali was resolute. "No, I do not apologize for what I said. I do not apologize."

Turning red, Triner began, "Cassius Clay . . . ."

"The name is Muhammad Ali," he said, getting up and heading for the door. The hearing was over. So was the boxing career of Muhammad Ali, declared the national press the next morning.

"The glove was thrown and I had picked it up," Ali reflected. "I had no apologies inside me."

For Ali's part, his sudden turnaround seemed to give him a new strength, a clearer vision of his anti-war sentiments. For the first time since he was reclassified 1-A, he seemed almost anxious to confront the white media and explain his stand, linking his actions to the plight of American blacks.

"The Negro's been lynched, killed, raped, burned, dragged around all through the city hanging on the chains of cars, alcohol and turpentine poured into his wounds," he told *Sports Illustrated*. "That's why the Negroes are so full of fear today. Been put into him from the time he's a baby. Imagine! Twenty-two million Negroes in America, suffering, fought in wars, got more worse treatment than any human being can even imagine, walking the streets of America in 1966, hungry with no food to eat, walk the streets with no shoes on, existing on relief, living in charity and poorhouses, twenty-two million people who faithfully served America and who have worked and who still loves his enemy are still dogged and kicked around." The influential magazine—the bible of the American sports world—seemed unsympathetic, labeling his attitude on race "a tortured confusion of truth, half-truth and untruth based on hatred and distrust of the oppressing whites."

Shortly after the hearing, Illinois Attorney General William Clark ruled that the Ali-Terrell bout violated state law on a number of dubious grounds, including the fact that Ali had not signed his legal name when applying for his license. The fight was off.

As state after state refused to sanction the bout—Ali "should be held in utter contempt by every patriotic American," said the governor of Maine—the boxing pariah became increasingly defiant, refining his controversial anti-war remarks into his trademark doggerel whenever reporters came to call:

> *Keep asking me, no matter how long*
> *On the war in Vietnam, I sing this song*
> *I ain't got no quarrel with the Vietcong*

His hometown of Louisville expressed strong interest in hosting the Terrell fight until local veterans groups threatened to launch mass demonstrations if the fight went ahead. The Kentucky Senate quickly passed a resolution expressing its opinion on the bout and Ali's character: "His attitude brings discredit to all loyal Kentuckians and to the names of the thousands who gave their lives for this country during his lifetime."

A half century earlier, Jack Johnson had been forced to fight outside of the United States because America wanted nothing to do with a black champion who spoke his mind. Now Ali was receiving the same treatment. Still, there was a larger world beyond the borders of the United States. Toronto, Canada, came forward and offered to host the fight, but Terrell announced he would have no part of it. He was to have been paid a percentage of the receipts, but veterans groups had succeeded in convincing most theaters to back out of closed-circuit telecasts. Therefore, there was no financial incentive for Terrell to fight. Instead, Canadian champion George Chuvalo was chosen to challenge Ali.

Even relocating the fight to another country didn't satisfy Ali's detractors. Arthur Daley of the *New York Times* urged a boycott."Clay could have been the most popular of all champions. But he attached himself to a hate organization, and antagonized everyone with his boasting and his disdain for the decency of even a low-grade patriotism," he wrote. "This fight should not be patronized either in person or on theater TV. Not a nickel should be contributed to the coffers of Clay, the Black Muslims, or the promoters who jammed this down so many unwilling throats."

On the floor of Congress, Representative Frank Clark joined the attack: "The heavyweight champion of the world turns my stomach. To welch or back off from the commitment of serving his country is as unthinkable as surrendering to Adolf Hitler or Mussolini would have been in my days of military service."

With the media, the government, and the entire boxing establishment bearing down on their client, Ali's legal team decided to change course. Drawing on the central teachings of the Koran and the tenets of the Nation of Islam, they filed a request for conscientious objector status.

▶ ▶ ▶

In 1658, a Maryland Quaker named Richard Keene became the first conscientious objector in American history when he refused to participate in the colonial militia because his religious beliefs opposed military activities. Like Keene, most of the other early conscientious objectors were Quakers and Mennonites, who believed the Bible forbade them from participating in wars of any kind.

The first nationwide draft by the U.S. federal government came in 1863, during the American Civil War. President Lincoln was sympathetic to conscientious objectors and introduced legislation that acknowledged the validity of their objections and permitted them to perform public service in hospitals as an alternative.

During World War I, many objectors refused to cooperate with the war in any way, including alternative service, and the War Department ordered all conscientious objectors court-martialed. Of the 450 who were found guilty, 142 were sentenced to life in prison.

In 1917, the Draft Act officially exempted men who objected to war for religious reasons, but the exemption applied only to those who belonged to a "well recognized religious sect or organization . . . whose existing creed or principles forbade its members to participate in war in any form."

During World War II, 72,000 Americans requested objector status and more than 6,000 were sent to prison for refusing alternative service, including Elijah Muhammad and many of his followers.

During the Korean War, Malcolm X had registered as a conscientious objector. He later recounted his response when officials asked him if he knew what the term meant: "I told them that when the white man asked me to go off somewhere and fight and maybe die to preserve the way the white man treated the black man in America, then my conscience made me object."

The Vietnam War created a new type of conscientious objector, one who did not condemn all military activities, just a specific war. This provided a new challenge for the courts to interpret the validity of an individual's objection.

When Ali's legal team filed its first request for draft exempt status in February 1966, it stuck to strictly procedural grounds. But on March 17, Ali appeared before the Louisville Draft Board with a new argument. Once again he testified that his parents would suffer undue financial hardship if he entered the army and earned only eighty dollars a month. But for the first time, he invoked his religion, saying that the Holy Koran forbids Muslims from fighting wars on the side of unbelievers. The presiding officer was skeptical and questioned his famous applicant's sincerity.

"I am sincere in every bit of what the Holy Koran and the teachings of Elijah Muhammad tell us and it is that we are not allowed to participate in wars on the side of non-believers," Ali responded. "This is a Christian country, not a Muslim country, and history and the facts show that every move towards the Honorable Elijah Muhammad is made to distort and to ridicule him . . . . We do not take part in any part of war unless declared by Allah himself or unless it's an Islamic World War, or a Holy War, and we are not to even so much as aid the infidels or the non-believers in Islam . . . . This is not me talking to get the draft board or to dodge nothing."

Back in Washington the Johnson White House, the FBI, and the military establishment watched Ali's actions nervously. Anxious to deflect the fallout, newspapers in cities with large black populations were issued press releases reflecting the government line. The *Atlanta Journal* carried a story that unwittingly helped make the case for black critics of the war: "Pentagon officials are praising the Negro as a gallant, hard-fighting soldier. New figures show that proportionately more Negro soldiers have died in Vietnam than military personnel of other races."

In fact, more than 29 percent of all soldiers who died in Vietnam that year were black, even though Blacks made up only 11 percent of the country's population. At the same time, large numbers of middle-class whites were being exempted from military service because of student deferments, prompting Stokely Carmichael to charge, "Blacks are being used as cannon fodder for a white man's war."

In late March, Ali's draft exemption request was again denied, prompting an appeal six weeks later before the Kentucky Appeal Board. By law, before the appeal board could make a decision, it was required to refer Ali's file to the U.S. Justice Department for an advisory recommendation. This would require a special hearing at which the appellant would be allowed to testify and call witnesses.

Hearing the case would be a retired Kentucky judge named Lawrence Grauman. In order to prevail, Ali would have to convince Grauman of his "character and good faith." He would also have to satisfy three basic tests of conscientious objector status as set out by the Selective Service Act. First, he must show that he is conscientiously opposed to war in any form. Second, he must show that this opposition is based on religious training and belief, as interpreted in two key Supreme Court rulings. Third, he must show that his objection is sincere.

Since his announcement two years earlier that he had joined the Nation of Islam, the FBI had compiled an extensive dossier on Ali, documenting his public statements, his friends, and his travels. These were based mostly on newspaper clippings and information supplied by informants. But in May 1966, J. Edgar Hoover ordered Ali to be placed under official FBI surveillance—the first boxer so honored since Jack Johnson, fifty years earlier.

Agents interviewed more than thirty-five friends, acquaintances, and family members. According to the FBI report, "These people all spoke highly of Clay and none of them provided any information that would have supported a denial of his [conscientious objector] claims." While Hoover himself was consorting with mobsters, gambling heavily, and engaging in a homosexual relationship while purging gay agents from the FBI, the thorough investigation turned up nothing more damaging against Ali than seven traffic violations over a five-year period. This information was turned over to the appeal board, along with a report that Ali had purchased a gun at a Miami pawn shop in 1964—which a member of his entourage promptly threw into the ocean—and a summary of Ali's recent appearance on the *Tonight Show*, hosted by Johnny Carson.

On August 23, 1966, the special hearing was convened. After Grauman heard from Ali's parents and a minister from the Nation of Islam, the reluctant recruit testified under oath:

> Sir, I said earlier and I'd like to again make that plain, it would be no trouble for me to go into the Armed Services, boxing exhibitions in Vietnam or traveling the country at the expense of the government or living the easy life and not having to get out in the mud and fight and shoot. If it wasn't against my conscience to do it, I would easily do it. I wouldn't raise all this court stuff and I wouldn't go through all of this and lose the millions that I gave up and my image with the American public that I would say is completely dead and ruined because of us in here now. I wouldn't jeopardize my life walking the streets of the South and all of America with no bodyguard if I wasn't sincere in every bit of what the Holy Koran and the teachings of Elijah Muhammad tell us and it is that we are not to participate in wars on the side of nonbelievers. We are not, according to the Holy Koran, to even as much as aid in passing a cup of water to the wounded. This is there before I was born and it will be there when I'm dead and we believe in not only part of it, but all of it.

In denying his 1966 claim for conscientious Objector status, the government claimed Ali was never a Minister of the Nation of Islam. Here he is seen preaching at a Chicago Mosque.

Since his first draft exemption request, the Nation of Islam had secured the services of a lawyer named Hayden Covington Jr., who had made his reputation successfully representing Jehovah's Witnesses seeking religious deferments during World War II. When he took on Ali as a client, Covington decided his previous lawyers had made a fundamental error in strategy. Initially, they had applied for conscientious objector status, which—under the nation's current laws—would have still required Ali to perform two years of alternative service in a noncombat role. Covington amended the request to seek exemption for Ali as a Muslim minister. Members of the clergy were exempted from military service of any form.

A convincing case could be made that Ali was a genuine minister. For more than two years, he had traveled the country preaching sermons at Nation of Islam mosques throughout the country. Thousands of Muslims heard him expound on his favorite topic, in what became known as the "pork-eating lecture," about one of the faith's greatest taboos. His repertoire included snuffling pig sounds and blackboard cartoons of "the nastiest animal in the world, the swine, a mouthful of maggots and pus. They bred the cat and the rat and the dog and came up with the hog." After witnessing his sermons, it was hard to doubt that he was a legitimate minister. In front of Judge Grauman, he proceeded to make this case.

"You see this?" he said, holding up a copy of the Koran. "These are the writings which we Muslims believe are revelations made to Muhammad by Allah."

He contended that 90 percent of his time was devoted to "preaching and converting people" and only 10 percent was taken up by boxing. "At least six hours of the day I'm somewhere walking and talking at Muslim temples and there are fifty odd mosques all over the United States that I am invited to minister at right now, and constantly."

When Ali finished, Judge Grauman took a short break before delivering the judgment which would shock the hearing room, the United States government, and Ali himself.

> I believe that the registrant is of good character, morals, and integrity, and sincere in his objection on religious grounds to participation in war in any form. I recommend that the registrant's claim for conscientious objector status be sustained.

James Nabrit III, who would later join Ali's legal defense team, described the general reaction. "Nobody expected the hearing to go for Ali. These things are usually pretty routine and they normally uphold the original decision. In this case, Ali was at his lowest point of popularity and he was arguing this religious doctrine which needless to say wasn't very popular in a Christian state like Kentucky."

Ali had been warned by his legal team that he was unlikely to prevail. When Grauman delivered his surprise judgment, he thought his grueling battle had finally come to an end. "For a very short time, I actually thought the system had worked," Ali recalls. "When that judge said I was sincere, I thought he was supporting the principles of our faith, he was telling America that we were legitimate, that we had as much right as the Christians to our beliefs."

But Grauman's ruling was only a recommendation. In Washington, the Justice Department wasted little time ensuring that the Appeal

Board ignored the judge's opinion. It wrote a letter to the Selective Service Board arguing that Ali had failed to satisfy the most important tenet of conscientious objection—that he was opposed to war in any form.

"It seems clear that the teachings of the Nation of Islam preclude fighting for the United States not because of objections to participation in war in any form but rather because of political and racial objections to policies of the United States as interpreted by Elijah Muhammad .... These constitute only objections to certain types of war in certain circumstances rather than a general scruple against participation in war in any form," wrote T. Oscar Smith, chief of the conscientious objector section of the Justice Department.

Pointing out that Ali had made no mention of his religious status at his first draft exemption hearing in February, the department argued that his beliefs were a matter of convenience and not "sincerely held," manifesting themselves only when military service became imminent.

Two days after the hearing, the chairperson of the House Armed Service Committee, L. Mendel Rivers, addressed a convention of the Veterans of Foreign Wars in New York. He threatened a complete over-haul of religious deferments if Ali's conscientious objector claim was upheld.

"Listen to this," he bellowed. "If that great theologian of Black Muslim power, Cassius Clay, is deferred, you watch what happens in Washington. We're going to do something if that board takes your boy and leaves Clay home to double-talk. What has happened to the leadership of our nation when a man, any man regardless of color, can with impunity advise his listeners to tell the President when he is called to serve in the armed forces, 'Hell no, I'm not going.'"

After a lengthy delay, the appeal board issued its decision. Ignoring Grauman's recommendation completely, Ali's request for conscientious objector status was denied. He would have to report for induction when his name came up.

United States Attorney Carl Walker, who would later prosecute Ali, is convinced the board's decision to deny the objector claim was political. "This is the only case I ever encountered where the hearing examiner recommended conscientious objector status and it was turned down," he says. "At that time, I'm convinced the government truly believed they would have to make an example of Ali or it would start a chain reaction of black men refusing to join the army. They were ignoring the Constitution—freedom of religion is very clear—and I thought it was wrong. But you have to understand those times."

The day the board's decision was announced, Ali knew he was left with only two choices—go into the army or go to jail.

CHAPTER SIX:
The Step

IN 1966 THE REPERCUSSIONS of his anti-war stand continued to haunt Ali, overshadowing his dominance in the ring. Like Jack Johnson a half century earlier, pariah status forced the unpopular champion into a self-imposed exile as it became increasingly obvious he was unwelcome in his own country. After beating George Chuvalo in Toronto, he successfully defended his title overseas three times within the space of six months, twice in England and once in Germany.

Syndicated sports columnist and longtime Ali defender Jerry Izenberg covered the Chuvalo fight in Toronto. "I went to Toronto to ask Ali one question," he recalls. "All these guys had been running to Canada to avoid the draft and here was Ali forced to leave his own country because of his attitude toward the war. I thought maybe he was going to stay in Canada. So when I got to Toronto for the Chuvalo fight, I asked him that question and I still remember his answer. He said, 'America is my birth country. They make the rules, and if they want to put me in jail, I'll go to jail. But I'm an American and I'm not running away.'"

But leaving behind the hostility of America for adoring crowds in Europe, Ali seemed to regain his old spirit, temporarily forgetting his legal troubles back home, although he lamented to the British press that he had "been driven out of my country because of my religious beliefs." In London to fight Henry Cooper, he began to write poetry again. For one journalist, he recited:

> *Since I won't let critics seal my fate*
> *They keep hollering I'm full of hate*
> *But they don't really hurt me none*
> *'Cause I'm doing good and having fun*
> *And fun to me is something bigger*
> *Than what those critics fail to figure*
> *Fun to me is lots of things*
> *And along with it some good I bring*
> *Yet while I'm busy helping my people*
> *These critics keep writing I'm deceitful*
> *But I can take it on the chin*
> *And that's the honest truth my friend*
> *Now from Muhammad you just heard*
> *The latest and the truest word*
> *So when they ask you "What's the latest?"*
> *Just say, "Ask Ali. He's still the greatest."*

But the fun was short-lived. Back home, his lawyers were studying tactics to delay the inevitable draft call, which now seemed imminent. The anti-war movement was picking up steam as thousands of college students demonstrated against the escalating war, shouting Stokely Carmichael's slogan—originally referring to black draftees— "Hell no, we won't go!" Ali watched these developments on television, and his resolve to stay out of the army intensified. On a side trip to Cairo, he told reporters, "My main concern now is to go back to the States and try to beat the draft."

After accompanying him for several days, during which he seemed to ignore his legal problems, *Life* magazine photographer Gordon Parks finally asked Ali, "What about your draft situation?"

"What about it?" came the reply. "How can I kill somebody when I pray five times a day for peace? Answer me. For two years the Army told everybody I was a nut. I was ashamed! My mother and father was ashamed! Now, suddenly, they decide I'm very wise—without even testing me again. I ain't scared. Just show me a soldier who'd like to be in that ring in my place. I see signs saying, 'L.B.J., how many kids did you kill today?' Well, I ain't said nothing that bad. Elijah Muhammad teaches us to fight only when we are attacked. My life is in his hands. That's the way it is. That's the way it's got to be."

Back in America, college students weren't the only ones questioning the legitimacy of the war. Martin Luther King Jr. was in the process of debating his conscience and his SCLC Board, which was still reluctant to incur the wrath of the Johnson Administration and its support of the civil rights agenda.

King had begun to shift his priorities from the battle against segregation in the South to the fight for economic justice in the rest of the country, acknowledging that his movement's legislative and judicial victories "did very little to improve the lot of millions of Negroes in the teeming North." The civil rights leader was at first uncomfortable with the increasing militancy of the new generation of young black leaders, labeling Black Power a "slogan without a program" and fearing it would lead to violence. Indeed, black ghetto unrest had already resulted in a number of urban race riots as increasing numbers of blacks began to see Dr. King's call for nonviolence as irrelevant to their situation. In October 1966, the Black Panther Party for Self Defense was formed in Oakland, California—the most militant of the Black Power groups to date. Their members carried rifles—to defend themselves against police brutality, they claimed.

Martin Luther King Jr. rejected the tactics of the Black Panthers and other militant Black Power groups. But on one issue he was becoming increasingly sympathetic. In 1964, King had been awarded the Nobel Peace Prize for his work in civil rights. Privately, he would often note the irony that he was given the world's most prestigious symbol of peace but could not speak out against the brutal war in Vietnam. In fact, he had made his personal views known in a number of interviews, but he had not yet linked the civil rights movement with the burgeoning peace movement.

"Martin really agonized over the decision of whether he should come out sooner than he did," recalls his widow Coretta Scott King. "He said, 'People who were with me on civil rights will not be with me on this issue, and we have to count those costs.' It was very difficult for him because he really felt very strongly from the very beginning on this whole issue of the Vietnam War and he could see the injustice of it all and how the people who were the poorest people in the country were more directly affected by it."

King was somewhat reticent about militant black leaders such as Stokely Carmichael. But he always seemed to have a soft spot for Muhammad Ali, despite the boxer's early advocacy of black separatism and his rejection of integration—the cause to which King had devoted his life. "King was the only black leader who sent me a telegram congratulating me after I won the title from Liston," Ali recalls.

Attorney Charles Morgan Jr. served on the board of King's Southern Christian Leadership Conference and was one of the few board members who advocated a public anti-war stand. Morgan, the only white on the board, also represented Julian Bond, who was still fighting to be seated in the Georgia legislature because of the outcry over his comments about Vietnam. He remembers that King greatly admired Ali's courage in speaking out against the war.

"Martin had opposed the war for a long time but his hands were tied by our Board," recalls Morgan. "Then Ali spoke out publicly, he took the consequences, and I believe it had an influence on Martin. Here was somebody who had a lot to lose and was willing to risk it all to say what he believed."

Sitting with Morgan on the board of the SCLC was fellow lawyer Chauncey Eskridge, who had been retained by the Nation of Islam to represent Ali in his fight to stay out of the army. Eskridge, who also represented King, regularly reported developments in the Ali case to the civil rights leader, who was seriously considering a public declaration against Vietnam. Eskridge eventually recruited Morgan onto the boxer's legal team, and together the two continued to persuade the board to come out against the war.

The popular black entertainer Harry Belafonte was a close friend and political supporter of Dr. King and the most important financial contributor to the civil rights movement, repeatedly bailing King and other freedom marchers out of jail after they had been arrested for civil disobedience. He believes Ali's public stand had an important impact on King's own evolution. "Muhammad Ali was the genuine product of what the movement inspired," Belafonte says. "He took on all of the characteristics and was the embodiment of the thrust of the movement. He was courageous. He put the class issues on the line. He didn't care about money. He brought America to its most wonderful and naked moment. He said, 'I will not play in your game of war. I will not kill on your behalf. What you ask is immoral and unjust, and I stand here to attest to that fact. Do with me what you will.' He was very inspirational. He was in many ways as inspiring as Dr. King, as inspiring as Malcolm. Out of the womb of oppression, he was our phoenix. He stood courageously and said, 'I put everything on the line for what I believe in.' They could not break his spirit nor deny his moral imperative."

As King grappled with one of his greatest dilemmas, Ali's case worked its way slowly through the system. His lawyers attempted a series of last-minute legal maneuvers to keep him out of the army. The media continued to portray him as a hate-monger for his affiliation with the Nation. But those who spent time with him saw a different side.

Gordon Parks recalls a scene he witnessed while Ali was training in Miami. "I never witnessed the hate he is assumed to have for whites. But I did see him stand in the burning sun for an hour, signing autographs for Southern white children."

Miami Herald sportswriter Pat Putnam echoes Ali's affinity for children. "It's amazing," he says. "Ali has always been drawn to kids and they have always been drawn to him. He has infinite patience for children and will never refuse a request for an autograph or a request to visit a kid in the hospital. Kids can always spot a phony but they are always drawn to him."

In February, Ali fought Ernie Terrell in the bout that had been cancelled a year earlier because of his Vietcong remarks. During the prefight hype, Terrell refused to call Ali by his Muslim name, prompting the champion to label his opponent an Uncle Tom and vowing, "I want to torture him. A clean knockout is too good for him."

The fight itself was brutal. Ali repeatedly pounded his opponent, screaming, "What's my name?" with each punch. "What's my name? Uncle Tom! You white man's nigger!"

The media's reaction was somewhat ironic. The very same reporters who were mercilessly attacking Ali for not going to war were now lambasting him for being too violent in the ring.

Gene Ward of the *New York Daily News* called the fight "a disgusting exhibition of calculating cruelty, an open defiance of decency, sportsmanship, and all the tenets of right vs. wrong." Jimmy Cannon, Ali's long-time nemesis, wrote, "It was a bad fight, nasty with the evil of religious fanaticism. This wasn't an athletic contest. It was a kind of lynching." Responding to reports that Ali had applied for military exemption as a minister, Cannon wrote, "What kind of clergyman is he? The Black Muslims demand that Negroes keep their place. They go along with the Klan on segregation. It seemed right that Cassius Clay had a good time beating up another Negro. The heavyweight champion is a vicious propagandist for a spiteful mob that works the religious underworld."

Ali was puzzled about the commotion, explaining he was merely plying his trade. "It's just a job," he said. "Grass grows, birds fly, waves pound the sand. I beat people up."

Even before the fight, the Nation of Islam and Ali's legal team had known that, for his conscientious objector claim to be taken seriously, it was essential to convince the world he was a legitimate minister. Ali's apparent cruelty in the ring didn't make this task any easier. But the Black Muslim public relations machine did its bit.

On March 3, the Nation's newspaper, *Muhammad Speaks,* carried a story headlined WORLD CHAMPION MOVES STEP CLOSER TO FULL-TIME TASK AS MUHAMMAD'S MINISTER. The article announced that Ali "took complete charge" of the Muslim mosque in Houston, replacing the regular minister while he went on a leave of absence.

"Reaction to the young athlete's assumption of his spiritual duties," the article declared, "was not only highly favorable among the believers, but exclamations of admiration were many among leaders of the black community here."

Until that point, only two heavyweight champions had failed to receive an invitation to meet the president at the White House, Jack Johnson and Muhammad Ali. On March 14, however, Ali received a different kind of invitation from President Johnson. It read:

Cassius Clay vs. the United States of America 139

ORDER FOR TRANSFERRED MAN TO REPORT
FOR INDUCTION

FROM: The President of the United States
TO: Mr. Cassius Marcellus Clay Jr.
AKA Muhammad Ali
5962 Ardmore Street
Houston, Texas 77022

Greetings:

Having heretofore been ordered to report for induction by Local Board No. 47, State of Kentucky, Louisville, Kentucky, which is your local board of origin, and
having been transferred upon your own request to
Local Board No. 61, State of Texas, Houston, Texas,
which is your Local Board of Transfer for delivery to an
induction station, you will therefore report to the last
named Local Board at 3rd Floor, 701 San Jacinto St.
Houston, Texas 77022 on April 28, 1967, at 8:00 A.M.

The induction had been originally scheduled for April 11 in
Louisville, but Ali's attorneys had requested a transfer to Houston,
Texas, because he had taken up residence there to assume his minis-
tership duties at the mosque.

Still, the day after Ali received his induction notice he was in
Chicago, where, walking through the streets, he was accosted by a
group of American Legionnaires as they emptied out of a tavern.

"Hey, is that Cassius Clay? That looks like Cassius Clay!" one shouted. A drunken member of the group waved a small American flag in his
face, exclaiming, "They gotcha! They gotcha! Sonofabitch! Thank God
they gotcha." Another waved that day's edition of the *Sun Times* with
its headline: ARMY TELLS CLAY—PUT UP OR SHUT UP!

A week later he was to take on Zora Folley at Madison Square
Garden. The marquee there also referred to the induction controversy
swirling around the champ. "Last chance to see Ali before he gets one
to three," it read, referring to the traditional sentence for draft evasion.

In Congress, Representative Robert Michel took to the floor and
complained to his colleagues:

I find it interesting, albeit depressing, to note that the illustrious Cassius Clay has scheduled another alleged bout to milk a few more thousand dollars out of dodging the draft. Apparently Cassius will fight anybody but the Vietcong.

The week of the fight (in which Ali would easily dispose of Folley), *Ring* magazine—the sport's bible—refused to designate a "Fighter of the Year" for the first time in its history. Instead it announced who *wasn't* getting the honor. "Most emphatically is Cassius Clay of Louisville, Kentucky, not to be held up as an example to the youngsters of the United States," it declared.

Even Ernie Terrell, who had been humiliated by Ali two months earlier, recognized the hypocrisy of the magazine's decision. "It's illegitimate reasoning, and it's out of the realm of the *Ring*. This will all be used as a stepping stone for the Muslims to say they achieved something. If Clay did something illegal, put him in jail. But he didn't. I dislike what Clay stands for, using boxing to further an extremist cause. But it's not against the law to be a clown."

Following the Folley fight, Ali returned to his hometown of Louisville for a rest. The scheduled induction was a month away and he wanted to weigh his options.

Ali's visit coincided with a scheduled board meeting of Martin Luther King's Southern Christian Leadership Conference taking place in Louisville, where Dr. King's brother resided and where tensions had been running high over a divisive open-housing campaign staged by the city's black community.

Ali had never met the civil rights leader face to face, although they had talked on the phone three years earlier. Elijah Muhammad had repeatedly condemned King's tactics, as well as the aims of the civil rights movement. He counseled his followers to steer clear of "the white man's dupe." Now, King requested a private meeting with the boxer at his hotel. After thirty minutes, in which he thanked the defiant draftee for the "courage of your actions," the two emerged and were questioned by the local media. King issued a clear signal that he sympathized with Ali's stand against the draft, telling the *Louisville Defender*, "As Muhammad Ali has said, we are all victims of the same system of oppression." The two embraced and Ali called King "my brother."

Later that day, Ali appeared at a local open-housing protest and told the marchers, "I came to Louisville because I could not remain silent in Chicago while my own people—many of whom I grew up with, went to school with, and some of whom are my blood relatives—were being beaten, stomped and kicked in the streets simply because they want freedom, justice, and equality in housing. I know the difference between a fair fight and a foul one—and this fight with cowardly white hoodlums, partly supported by the police, against peaceful black people, who seek only what should be granted to every human being, is a foul one."

His appearance at the housing rally was all the more remarkable given his speech about integrated housing only three years earlier. On that occasion, he announced, "I don't believe in forced integration. I know where I belong. I'm not going to force myself into anybody's house. I'm not joining no forced integration movement, because it don't work. A man has got to know where he belongs."

It was clear that his thinking had evolved significantly since then and that he had a clearer understanding of the social forces that powered American society. That afternoon, he made a clear link between his anti-war stand and the plight of his people. "Why should they ask me, another so-called Negro, to put on a uniform and go ten thousand miles from home and drop bombs and bullets on brown people in Vietnam while so-called Negro people in Louisville are treated like dogs and denied simple human rights?" he told reporters who questioned him about his impending decision. "I will not disgrace my religion, my people, or myself by becoming a tool to enslave those who are fighting for justice, equality, and freedom. I have been warned that to take such a stand would put my prestige in jeopardy and cause me to lose millions of dollars which should accrue to me as the champion. But I have said it once and I will say it again. The real enemy of my people is right here. If I thought the war was going to bring freedom and equality to twenty-two million of my people, they wouldn't have to draft me, I'd join tomorrow. But I have to either obey the laws of the land or the laws of Allah. I have nothing to lose by standing up for my beliefs. So I'll go to jail. We've been in jail for four hundred years."

While Ali was lending his unprecedented support to a civil rights protest, King was preparing to undergo his own remarkable political metamorphosis as the SCLC Board convened. That morning, the Pentagon had reported 274 American deaths in Vietnam the week before—the highest casualty figures of the war to date. Now, King and his board were finally ready to respond. After a somewhat divisive debate the SCLC endorsed a document calling the war "morally and politically unjust" and charged that it had "drowned the Negro's cry for equal rights." The document emphasized the unfairness of the draft, which "discriminates against the poor and places Negroes in the front lines in disproportionate numbers and from there to racially segregated cemetery plots in the deep south." The author of the landmark document was Muhammad Ali's lawyer, Charles Morgan Jr.

Three days later, free at last to speak publicly about the issue that had plagued him since 1965, Dr. King appeared at New York's Riverside Church and gave one of his most eloquent speeches. "Over the past two years, as I have moved to break the betrayal of my own silences and to speak from the burnings of my own heart, as I have called for radical departures from the destruction of Vietnam, many persons have questioned me about the wisdom of my path," he began. "Since I am a preacher I suppose it is not surprising that I have seven major reasons for bringing Vietnam into the field of my moral vision."

For almost an hour, he proceeded to outline these reasons, directly linking the goals of the civil rights movement to ending the war. "There is at the outset a very obvious and facile connection between the war in Vietnam and the struggle I, and others, have been waging in America. A few years ago it seemed there was a real promise of hope for the poor—both black and white—through the Poverty Program. Then came the build-up in Vietnam and I watched the program broken and eviscerated as if it were some idle political plaything of a society gone mad on war . . . . Somehow this madness must cease. I speak as a child of God and brother to the suffering poor of Vietnam and the poor of America who are paying the double price of smashed hopes at home and death and corruption in Vietnam . . . . The choice is ours and though we might prefer it otherwise we must choose in this crucial moment of human history."

In one of the most controversial passages of his landmark speech, King used language far stronger than anything Muhammad Ali or even Stokely Carmichael had uttered to date, calling the United States "the greatest purveyor of violence in the world today."

Reaction was swift and fierce, unleashing what King's lieutenant Andrew Young called "a torrent of hate and venom." Like Ali when he first spoke out against the war, King was attacked from all sides. The establishment reacted predictably. The *New York Times* called King's speech "reckless" and accused him of whitewashing Hanoi. But to his surprise, some of the harshest criticism came from the leadership of the black community.

The sixty-member board of the NAACP unanimously passed a resolution declaring, "To attempt to merge the civil rights movement with the peace movement, or to assume that one is dependent on the other, is in our judgment a serious tactical mistake. It will serve the cause neither of civil rights nor of peace."

Ironically, Julian Bond—who had recently won his fight to be seated in the Georgia legislature after his own anti-war stand—is today the national chairperson of the NAACP. He recalls the attitude of the black establishment: "When Dr. King was marching against segregation, everybody could embrace him. It was almost a motherhood issue for liberals. But when he came out against the war, all of a sudden he was a pariah. This was considered very radical at the time and there were accusations that he was a communist. The black establishment didn't want to be associated with this controversy. Some of them thought it was unpatriotic, some of them thought it would hurt the civil rights cause. One thing was for sure. It felt pretty good that I wasn't alone anymore and I'm sure Muhammad Ali felt the same way. It was actually a terribly important milestone in the movement."

J. Edgar Hoover was incensed by King's speech, writing President Johnson, "He's an instrument in the hands of subversive forces seeking to undermine our nation."

Harry Belafonte believes the attacks on King for his anti-war stand helped create "a climate of hate and distortion" that led to his assassination a year later.

Meanwhile, King's sentiments were being echoed by a growing minority of vocal black militants and white students, who were turning against the war in increasing numbers. On April 15, two weeks before Ali's scheduled induction date, the largest anti-Vietnam demonstrations up to that point took place throughout the United States and Europe. In New York's Central Park, more than one hundred thousand protesters gathered to announce they had no intention of going to war. The protest saw the largest ever mass-burning of draft cards by more than two hundred young men. Martin Luther King Jr. attended the rally and vowed, "This is just the beginning of a massive outpouring of concern and protest activity against this illegal and unjust war." An increasingly paranoid President Johnson warned that the FBI was "keeping an eye on anti-war activity."

The same day, outside the U.S. Embassy in London's Grosvenor Square, a twenty-one-year-old Oxford University student named Bill Clinton joined thousands of British demonstrators protesting American involvement in Vietnam in his first-ever political demonstration. Among the leaflets handed out that day was one reading, "LBJ Don't Send Muhammad Ali to War." Thirty years later, Clinton—whose own draft evasion had come back to haunt him—would invite Ali to the White House and praise his "courage and inspiration."

Two days after the anti-war rallies, the Supreme Court refused to grant Ali's request for an injunction to block his induction. His lawyers had argued that he had been the victim of discrimination as a Negro by the Kentucky Selective Service system.

Now that his last, best chance to stay out of the Army was thwarted, Ali was asked by reporters if he would refuse induction by not taking the oath. "I'm not saying that," he replied, "but I've made my decision and I will give it at that time. You can make your own conclusions when I say I will stand on my religious beliefs and will be ready to face any punishment in following them."

As King came under attack for his comments about Vietnam, Ali's induction date loomed ever closer, and he too was feeling the heat from all sides. If it wasn't the patriots expressing their disgust, it was the students yelling, "Hell no, don't go! Hell no, don't go!" or "Stand up to them! Stand up!" every time he showed his face in public. But neither side was going to make his decision for him. Nor were his lawyers and their reminder of the grave consequences if he didn't report—five years in prison and the loss of his heavyweight title.

If public sentiment and dire warnings didn't influence Ali, however, there is no doubt that he was listening to his mentor, Elijah Muhammad, with whom he continued to meet regularly at the Nation of Islam's Chicago headquarters. It was almost exactly twenty-five years since the Messenger had been arrested by the FBI for advising his followers not to register for World War II. Now he reminded Ali to follow his conscience, mindful of the consequences should he counsel Ali to break the law. Ali's spiritual teacher Jeremiah Shabazz insists that Elijah didn't tell his most famous follower what to do.

"Nobody put pressure on Ali not to go into the Army," he said. "The Messenger might have counseled him regarding what to say and not to say, but the final decision was all his own. Now you know and I know that once Ali starts going in a direction, sometimes it's like a bulldozer with no driver. He just keeps going and going."

Asked by reporters what he had told Ali about the draft, the Messenger replied, "Every one of my followers is free to make his own choice. I gave him no more advice than I gave the faithful ones who followed me to the penitentiary in 1942."

As powerful an influence as Elijah Muhammad was, however, there was one person Ali respected even more, his mother Odessa. He knew she was against his decision, and it troubled him. It was against this backdrop of conflicting emotions that he made plans to fly to Houston on April 27 for his fateful encounter.

As he and his lawyer Chauncey Eskridge arrived at O'Hare Airport for the flight to Texas, the boxer was swarmed by journalists wanting to know what he planned to do.

"Will you give up the title?"

"Don't you think it's your duty to defend your country?"

"Are you going to take that step?"

The step they referred to was the traditional step forward draftees are required to take when their names are called at the army induction center. For the time being, he was keeping the answer to himself, although it was clear to those around him that he hadn't changed his mind.

As the plane took off, the captain announced over the intercom, "Ladies and gentlemen, the Heavyweight Champion of the World is your travelling companion. Have a delightful trip." But even thirty thousand feet in the air, Ali couldn't escape the explosive impact of his impending decision.

The first hour of the trip proved uneventful as Ali signed autographs for his fellow passengers and chatted with his lawyer about what would happen the next day. Suddenly the plane ran into heavy turbulence, sending trays flying through the cabin. Many passengers panicked.

Across the aisle, a woman had a Bible and was praying out loud. As her eyes met Ali's, she pointed a finger and started screaming at him, "God is punishing us because he's on the plane! He's punishing us because we're helping His enemy! Cassius Clay, you turned against the true Christian God! God wants you off this plane. O forgive us, O Lord!"

Her ominous hysteria notwithstanding, the plane finally landed safely. Ali and Eskridge were met by Ali's other lawyer, Hayden Covington Jr. and the three took a taxi to the Rice Hotel to have lunch. A hearing had been scheduled that afternoon in Federal District Court where his legal team were seeking a restraining order to prevent the Selective Service board from reporting Ali delinquent if he refused to take the step forward the next day. Otherwise, he would be automatically liable to criminal charges and could face indictment and arrest within thirty days. The motion asked for the court to wait until his request for an exemption could be ruled on in civil court.

As they ate, Covington told stories about his big day in 1943 when he won thirteen separate Supreme Court decisions involving the Jehovah's Witnesses and their right to religious exemption from the military. Ali mocked his lawyer and pretended to snore in boredom. "Big Boss, this ain't 1943 anymore. It's '67, no longer are you in heaven," he joked.

Waiting outside the courtroom for the 2 P.M. hearing to begin, Ali held forth with a number of journalists and fans, talking about his future plans and a possible movie career.

"I turned down $500,000 to play the life of Jack Johnson because he wasn't the right type of person. I'd want to control my own scripts. I don't like movies. I like real-life drama. Like what's going on here today. This is history you're witnessing. Why, people are betting money on this just like a fight." Some Texas Southern University students approached him and vowed to engage in civil disobedience if Ali was jailed, to which he responded, "I don't want you suffering just because I suffer. Don't get hurt. They're talking about filling the jails."

When the hearing began, both sides made their opening arguments. A Justice Department lawyer underscored the government's concern about the high-profile case, arguing that if Ali were to prevail, "all the Muslims will refuse to take the oath and where will we get the soldiers?"

Then Ali was called to the stand. Judge Allan Hannay seemed a bit star-struck having the heavyweight champion in his courtroom and treated him with extra courtesy as he patiently allowed Ali to explain his conversion to the Muslim cause, even though religion wasn't at issue that afternoon.

Wearing a blue suit and an Islamic tie clasp, Ali told the Court how he had been approached by the Muslims in 1961 and had finally been sold on the faith shortly before the first Liston fight in 1964. He said "Old McDonald" (promoter Bill McDonald) had tried to make him renounce his religion, but he had refused, instead climbing aboard his bus to leave Miami Beach before McDonald relented.

After that demonstration of his sincerity, Ali testified, he was given the name Muhammad Ali—meaning "one who is worthy of praise." He then became a minister of his religion, one that is known as the "Lost Found Nation of Islam in North America." He told the judge that there were seventy-five Muslim mosques in the U.S. and he had spoken at eighteen of them. He said his job was as a Muslim minister, at which he spent 160 hours per month. "My sideline is being the heavyweight champion of the world," he explained to the amusement of the courtroom.

Ali finished his plea with an explanation of why he couldn't serve in the armed forces: "It's against the teachings of the Holy Koran. I'm not trying to dodge the draft. We are not supposed to take part in no wars unless declared by Allah or by the Messenger. Muhammad was a warrior fourteen hundred years ago but he was a holy warrior fighting in the name of Allah. We don't take part in Christian wars or wars of any unbelievers. We aren't Christian or Communist."

The judge seemed intrigued by his explanation. He bent forward and asked, "In a conflict between Communism and Christianity, which side would you take?"

"Neither side, judge," came the reply.

The prosecutors argued that Ali had not yet exhausted his administrative remedies—the legal criterion for being granted a restraining order. The judge agreed and denied the motion, as expected.

As Ali left the courthouse with his entourage in tow, he contemplated the consequences of the next day's induction ceremony out loud. "I want to know what is right, what'll look good in history. I'm being tested by Allah. I'm giving up my title, I'm giving up my wealth, maybe my future. Many great men have been tested for their religious belief. If I pass this test, I'll come out stronger than ever. I've got no jails, no power, no government, but six hundred million Muslims are giving me strength. Will they make me the leader of a country? Will they give me gold? Will the Supreme Being knock down the jails with an earthquake, like He could if He wanted? Am I a fool to give up all this and go to prison? Am I a fool to give up good steaks? Do you think I'm serious? If I am, then why can't I worship as I want to in America? All I want is justice. Will I have to get that from history?"

Parting from the group, Ali's assistant trainer Bundini Brown went across the street with a white friend to the Brown Derby Lounge for a drink. When his friend placed their order for two drinks, the barmaid informed him, "Sorry, señor, we don't serve no colored people."

There was a car waiting for Ali and his two lawyers, and they sped off to discuss their next step. Ali asked to be driven to Texas Southern University, where Stokely Carmichael had led a student riot a few days earlier. Ali usually got his best receptions on college campuses, and he was anxious for a sympathetic audience the day before his big decision. As they arrived on campus, Ali jumped out of the car, yelling, "I'm ready to rumble."

About a hundred students were milling about and they instantly recognized their famous visitor.

"Hi, soul," somebody yelled.

"Hi, brother," shouted Ali.

"Stokely, he tell the world to burn Whitey," said one student.

"I'm telling you religion," Ali countered.

"Naw, not religion. We want to burn Whitey."

"Don't do nothing violent. We're not violent," Ali counseled.

"This is rebellion, man. They take you in the Army, they see a rebellion."

"Stokely say burn their babies."

"We don't want violence, " Ali repeated.

"You don't put down a black brother," said a student defiantly.

Finally, Ali returned to the car. "They're a bunch of young fools," he told his lawyers. "I don't want any of this violence. I hear there'll be demonstrations tomorrow morning in New York, Chicago, London, Egypt. There are sixteen thousand Muslims in Cleveland who'll demonstrate. Nearly every Negro is a Muslim at heart. The trouble is, first thing you got to do to be a Muslim is live a righteous life. Most people, white or black, don't want to do that."

When they arrived back at the hotel, there was a message for Ali to call his mother.

"G.G., do the right thing," she implored, using the pet name she had given to him as a child. "If I were you, I would go ahead and take the step. If I were you, I would join the Army. Do you understand me, son?"

Ali reassured her that he understood how she felt. "Mama, I love you. Whatever I do, Mama, remember I love you." As she began to cry, he hung up, visibly shaken by the exchange.

He went to the hotel coffee shop for dinner, followed by a bevy of reporters. As he ate his soup, they peppered him with questions about his intentions. Ali handled his inquisitors the way he received his opponents' blows in the ring, sometimes deftly deflecting their queries, often meeting them head-on, his quick mind as agile as his famous footwork.

Somebody pointed out that he would be in danger whether he went into the army or jail. "Every day they die in Vietnam for nothing. I might as well die right here for something," he replied.

One reporter asked, "What about just playing the game like other big-time athletes? You wouldn't be sent to the front lines. You could give exhibitions and teach physical fitness." Ali was constantly being reminded of this option, the same one given to his boyhood idol, Joe Louis, when he was drafted into the army during World War II. Louis avoided combat by boxing exhibitions and entertaining the troops. Lately Louis had been publicly badmouthing Ali for his lack of patriotism, implying Ali was afraid to go to Vietnam, to which Ali responded, "Louis is the one without courage. Louis, he doesn't know what the words mean. He's a sucker."

Now, Ali dismissed the reporter's question, making it clear that putting on an army uniform was tantamount to going to battle against an enemy with whom he "had no quarrel."

He leaned forward to make his point. "What can you give me, America, for turning down my religion? You want me to do what the white man says and go fight a war against some people I know nothing about, get some freedom for some other people when my own people can't get theirs here?

"You want me to be so scared of the white man I'll go and get two arms shot off and ten medals so you can give me a small salary and pat my head and say, 'Good boy, he fought for his country'?"

A report earlier that week had disclosed that the Pentagon was expecting fifty thousand civilian casualties in Vietnam that year. Statistics like these, which he would often cite to underscore his opposition, seemed to fuel Ali's decision as much as his Muslim beliefs. He was also fond of pointing out that black Americans accounted for a disproportionate amount of American troop casualties, as much as 30 percent, even though they only made up 11 percent of the U.S. population and 22 percent of the soldiers.

In answering another reporter, who asked whether he was prepared to go to jail for his beliefs, Ali revealed that he had been visiting prisons to get accustomed to them. "They say you're all right in them federal places. You can pay for your own food. You get TV. Only thing you don't get is your girlfriends."

Somebody at the table volunteered how it was sad that such a handsome and gifted young man should have to even contemplate death and imprisonment. One of those present, describing his reaction to this lament, noted that "his eyes became bright again like a martyr's flames." Ali responded philosophically: "Allah okays the adversary to try us. That's how He sees if you're a true believer. All a man has to show for his time here on earth is what kind of a name he had. Jesus. Columbus. Daniel Boone. Now, take Wyatt Earp. Who would have told him when he was fighting crooks and standing up for principles that there'd be a television show about him? That kids on the street would say, 'I'm Wyatt Earp. Reach.'" At this, he recited one of his trademark poems, seemingly composed on the spot:

> Two thousands years from now,
> Muhammad Ali, Muhammad Ali,
> He roamed the Western Hemisphere,
> He was courageous and strong,
> He called the round when the clown hit the ground.
> Tell little children whatever they believe,
> Stand up like Muhammad Ali.

With that, he retired to his room, leaving no one present with any doubt as to what he would do the next day when his name was called at the induction center.

Although he had left his companions with the impression that he was very calm with his impending decision, Bundini Brown later recalled that Ali couldn't get to sleep; he had too many things on his mind, and the two stayed up talking until 2 A.M.

"It was like the night before a fight," Brown later said. "The champ has got to talk and talk until he can fall asleep without tossing and turning."

By morning, when his lawyers came by to fetch him, he seemed to have slept off his jitters. "He was a lot cooler than we were," recalled his lawyer Quinnon Hodges.

His coolness quickly turned to fury as he read the *New York Times* over breakfast. Sportswriter Arthur Daley had written a patronizing column about Ali's decision. Daley, like most journalists, still refused to call him Muhammad Ali, writing:

> People change in seven years and few have changed more than Clay. The delightful boy of 1960 has become a mixed-up man. If there was skepticism about the sincerity of his motives when he first fell under the sway of the Black Muslims, it exists no longer. He has been so thoroughly brainwashed that he now believes what he says even if the words are put into his mouth by the Muslims . . . .
>
> The Muslims, who direct his every move, have gained a meal ticket and lost a martyr. The shrewd men at the head of the movement must think that sacrificing him is worth the price . . . . As a fist-fighter, Cassius might very well have become the greatest. But we'll never know. Instead, he seems fated to bring about his own destruction.

Daley's sentiments were almost universally shared by the American media, which was still a long way from turning against the war in Vietnam. A reporter defended Ali at his own peril—as syndicated sports columnist Jerry Izenberg discovered when he took up Ali's cause. "The backlash was unbelievable," he recalls. "The first time I defended him, my column was being carried by twenty-six newspapers. That night, half of them cancelled. I received death threats, many of them with an anti-Semitic element, telling me they wished I had died in the concentration camps. I used to drive a gray Monte Carlo. One day, I pulled up at a light at the same time another gray Monte Carlo pulled up in the opposite direction. A couple of guys got out of a car, ran up to the other Monte Carlo, and smashed its windshield with a sledgehammer. They thought it was me."

As Ali finished breakfast, a reporter asked him about the prospect of losing his title if he refused to take the step that morning.

"They can strip me of it at the boxing commission but not in the eyes of the people," he responded. "The people know the only way I can lose my title is in the ring. My title goes where I go. But if they won't let me fight, it could cost me $10 million. Does that sound like I'm serious about my religion?"

His lawyer Hayden Covington interrupted. "Come on, champ, come on. We've got twenty-five minutes."

"If we're one minute late, they're liable to shove you behind bars," Hodges pleaded.

They jumped in a taxi and rode to the municipal courthouse where the induction was scheduled for 8 A.M. They passed Muhammad Ali Street, named for the champ with much fanfare five months earlier, after he fought Cleveland Williams in Houston. The next day it would be quietly changed back to its old name, Thomas Jefferson Street. When they arrived at the courthouse, about a dozen demonstrators were waiting with a banner reading, STAY HOME, MUHAMMAD ALI, and shouting, "Don't go! Don't go!" —a far cry from the mass demonstrations Ali had predicted. Black Panther H. Rap Brown led a group of black protesters in a chant of "Hep! Hep! Don't take that step."

Robert Lipsyte, who covered the induction for the *New York Times*, reveals that the scene was actually a media charade. "You have to understand that Ali still didn't have a lot of support," he recalls. "Other than some students and black militants, the country was still solidly against him and for the war. They were expecting thousands of demonstrators at the courthouse and it just didn't happen. So the TV guys rounded up a bunch of secretaries and curious bystanders and promised them exposure on the evening news if they would carry signs and whip up a pro-Ali demonstration. It was actually a big scam."

Not everybody was a prop, however. An elderly woman ran across the street as Ali emerged from the cab, grabbing his hand and whispering, "Stand up, brother. We're with you. Stand up, fight for us. Don't let us down!"

Reporters cried out, "Muhammad, give us the answer! . . . Are you going in? . . . What will your stand be?"

Across the street, FBI agents with walkie-talkies surveyed the scene. Ali's lawyers pointed them out to him, whispering, "G-Men."

Forty-six recruits were scheduled to be inducted that morning. One of them, a white twenty-two-year-old named John McCullough, was asked by reporters what he thought of Ali's impending action. "It's his prerogative if he's sincere in his religion," he said, "but it's his duty as a citizen to go in. I'm a coward, too."

Howard Cosell stood in front of the courthouse with an ABC television crew. As Ali passed, he yelled out, "Are you going to take the step, Muhammad? Are you going to take the step?"

Ali grinned and said, "Howard Cosell—why don't you take the step?"

"I did," Cosell snapped back. "In 1942."

As Ali entered the building, he was led into a large room along with the other recruits, each carrying a canvas overnight bag—all except Ali, who knew he wouldn't be leaving with them on the 6 P.M. bus to Fort Polk, Louisiana.

"It was great the way he came in," inductee Ron Holland later told reporters. "He told us we all looked very dejected and said he was going to tell us some jokes. He was very cheerful. He cheered us all up. He told us his mind was made up. He said if he went into the army and some Vietcong didn't get him, some redneck from Georgia would. He was in good spirits. I got his autograph."

Ali describes his own thoughts as he entered the courthouse: "That day in Houston when I went into the induction center, I felt happy, because people didn't think I had the nerve or they don't have the nerve to buck the draft board or the government. And I almost ran there, hurried. I couldn't wait to not take the step. The world was watching, the blacks mainly, looking to see if I had the nerve to buck

Uncle Sam, and I just couldn't wait for the man to call my name."

After a long wait, an Army officer came out and took roll call, then dispersed the recruits in groups of ten to take a physical. When Ali's group was called, they were brought to another large room furnished with eight canvas-covered cubicles, each one manned by a doctor.

"Strip down to shorts," barked an officer.

Ali complied and was led to a booth, where one of the doctors stood by a table. "His eyes lit up when he saw me, as though that's why he came to work that day," Ali later recalled.

The doctor got right to business. "What's your name?" he asked.

"Muhammad Ali."

The doctor frowned. "It's Cassius Clay," he said emphatically.

Ali kept quiet.

"It's Cassius Clay," he repeated. "Isn't it?"

"Well, it used to be, but—"

"It's still Cassius Clay," he said angrily. "That's who you're registered as." The doctor turned to his assistant. "Put down Cassius Clay," he said.

As this episode was unfolding, Ali flashed back to an incident that took place when he collapsed shortly before he was scheduled to fight the rematch against Sonny Liston in 1964. He was diagnosed with a hernia and told that he needed an operation immediately.

"What's your name?" one of the doctors asked on that occasion.

"Muhammad Ali."

"No, that's not your real name," he said in an irritated tone. "What's your real name?"

"Muhammad Ali is my real name."

"Listen, I'm not going to send you up to the operating room until you tell me your legal name."

"I don't care what you do," Ali responded as the pain ripped through him like hot knives. "My name is Muhammad Ali and I'll die right here before I answer to any other name."

Finally, another doctor ordered that he be rushed to the operating room.

While Ali proceeded through pre-induction in Houston, Congress continued to agonize over the merits of the escalating Vietnam War. In Washington that morning, General William Westmoreland, the commander of the U.S. Forces in Vietnam, addressed the Senate, vowing that "American forces will prevail in Vietnam over the Communist aggressor." A day earlier he had told a convention of newspaper publishers that "unpatriotic acts at home" were encouraging Hanoi and the Vietcong to continue fighting.

As the medical checkup progressed, Ali moved from cubicle to cubicle, each doctor conducting his own routine exam. As he was ushered into the last stall, the doctor snapped, "Gimme your papers," in a strong Southern drawl. Then he ordered Ali to remove his shorts so he could check for a hernia. The doctor jabbed his hand into Ali's testicles and told him to cough. As he pressed harder, he sneered, "So you don't want to go and fight for your country?" As this was happening, Ali later recalled, he thought back to the days when castration and lynchings were common in the South.

When the checkup was finished, the recruits were given a short break and handed a box lunch. Ali ate almost everything but tossed aside the ham sandwich in deference to Muslim dietary laws.

Meanwhile, outside the courthouse, some genuine protesters had arrived from the nearby Southern Texas University. Five black students burned their draft cards while others marched in a circle carrying placards and a Black Power flag. They read from the writings of Malcolm X and shouted, "America is a house on fire. Let it burn, let it burn."

Back inside, the inductees were ordered to assemble in Room 1B. When they arrived in the small room, which had been used as a judge's chambers years earlier, a young officer, Lieutenant Steven S. Dunkley, stood behind an oakwood rostrum with American flags on both sides. A number of official-looking but out-of-place civilians, later revealed to be FBI agents, had gathered to witness the unfolding drama.

Dunkley later recalled the scene. "The way I felt the day that Muhammad Ali was coming up was that it was definitely going to be a different day at work that day . . . . We knew that the whole thing was going to be monitored from the Pentagon on a direct phone line the whole day, all of his activities. A lot of the guys who worked at the center were fans of Ali. You know, he was the heavyweight champion of the world and it's not every day you get somebody like that come through the induction center, so they were excited about that."

As the inductees assembled, Dunkley cleared his throat and barked, "Attention." Then he read the prepared statement that had been heard thousands of times before by scared young men about to be ripped away from their old lives. "You are about to be inducted into the Armed Forces of the United States, in the Army, the Navy, the Air Force or the Marine Corps, as indicated by the service announced following your name when called. You will take one step forward as your name and service are called and such step will constitute your induction into the Armed Forces indicated."

All eyes appeared to be on Ali as the induction began.

"Jason Adams—Army."

The first man stepped forward.

The roll continued until the last man before Ali on the list.

"Luis Cerrato—Army."

He had been anticipating the next words for a long time but now Ali's hands were sweating as he wrestled with the decision which would alter his life.

Years later, in his autobiography, Ali would recall his emotions: "For months I drilled myself for this moment, but I still felt nervous. . . . What did I fear? Is it what I'd lose if they take my title? If I'm jailed or barred from the ring? Was it fear of losing the good, plush life of a world champion? Why was I resisting? My religion, of course, but what the politician told me in Chicago was true. I won't be barred from the Nation of Islam if I go into the army . . . I recalled the words of the Messenger: 'If you feel what you have decided to do is right, then be a man and stand up for it. . . . Declare the truth and die for it.'"

Finally, as Ali stared impassively into Dunkley's eyes, the officer called out,

"Cassius Clay—Army."

Silence. Ali stood straight, unmoving. One of the recruits snickered and Dunkley turned beet red, ordering all the draftees out of the room. They filed out, leaving Ali standing there.

"Cassius Clay, will you please step forward and be inducted into the Armed Forces of the United States."

Still nothing. Another officer, Navy Lieutenant Clarence Hartman, came forward to confer with Dunkley, then walked over to the man whose action was about to shake the world. "Mr. Clay," he began. "Or Mr. Ali, as you prefer to be called."

"Yes, sir?"

"Would you please follow me to my office?" he asked politely. "I would like to speak privately to you, if you don't mind."

When they repaired to a small green room, its walls covered with pictures of Army generals, Hartman's tone suddenly became brusque. "Perhaps you don't realize the gravity of the act you've just committed. Or maybe you do, but it's my duty to point out that if this should be your final decision, you will face criminal charges and your penalty could be five years in prison and ten thousand dollars fine." He offered Ali a second chance to reconsider his decision.

"Thank you, sir, but I don't need it."

He was told he would have to go back out, stand before the podium, and face the call again.

When he returned to the room, a private handed Ali a note, saying "This is from your lawyer." It was written by U.S. Attorney Mort Susman:

> I am authorized to advise you that we are willing to enter into an agreement. If you will submit your client for induction, we will be willing to keep him here in the Houston area until all of your civil remedies are exhausted. Otherwise, he will be under criminal indictment.

Ali was unimpressed by the offer and crumpled up the note. Dunkley waited with the induction statement in his hand. "Mr. Cassius Clay," he began again, "you will please step forward and be inducted into the United States Army."

Again Ali refused to move. Finally, realizing that further attempts would be futile, Lieutenant Hartman asked him for a written statement regarding the reason for his refusal. Ali took a piece of paper and wrote, "I refuse to be inducted into the armed forces of the United States because I claim to be exempt as a minister of the religion of Islam."

The station commander, Colonel Edwin McKee, proceeded outside to issue a statement to the hundreds of waiting journalists: "Ladies and gentlemen; Cassius Clay has just refused to be inducted into the United States Armed Forces. Notification of his refusal is being made to the

United States Attorney, the State Director of the Selective Service system, and the local Selective Service Board for whatever action is deemed appropriate. Further questions regarding the status of Mr. Clay should be directed to Selective Service." In McKee's pocket was a copy of an alternative statement to be read if Ali had been inducted, informing the media that he was being transported to Fort Polk.

Then, Ali appeared in the press room and handed out copies of a four-page statement he had prepared in advance, thanking numerous individuals and organizations for their support. It read, in part:

> It is in the light of my consciousness as a Muslim minister and my own personal convictions that I take my stand in rejecting the call to be inducted in the armed services. I do so with the full realization of its implications and possible consequences. I have searched my conscience and I find I cannot be true to my belief in my religion by accepting such a call.

> My decision is a private and individual one and I realize that this is a most crucial decision. In taking it I am dependent solely on Allah as the final judge of these actions brought upon by my own conscience.

> I strongly object to the fact that so many newspapers have given the American public and the world the impression that I have only two alternatives in taking this stand: either I go to jail or go into the Army. There is another alternative and that alternative is justice. If justice prevails, if my Constitutional rights are upheld, I will be forced to go neither to the Army nor jail. In the end, I am confident that justice will come my way for the truth must eventually prevail.

> I am looking forward to immediately continuing my profession.

> As to the threat voiced by certain elements to strip me of my title, this is merely a continuation of the same artificially induced prejudice and discrimination.

> Regardless of the difference in my outlook, I insist upon my right to pursue my livelihood in accordance

with the same rights granted to other men and women who have disagreed with the policies of whatever Administration was in power at the time.

I have the world heavyweight title not because it was "given" to me, not because of my race or religion, but because I won it in the ring through my own boxing ability.

Those who want to "take" it and hold a series of auction-type bouts not only do me a disservice but actually disgrace themselves. I am certain that the sports fans and fair-minded people throughout America would never accept such a title-holder.

Lieutenant Dunkley looks back on that day and recalls, "As Muhammad Ali walked out of the center, my thoughts were that he had done the wrong thing. I felt that if he would have taken induction they would have put him in Special Services. He probably would have ended up coaching the boxing team or something like that. Or, like Elvis Presley was assigned to a special unit in Germany or something like that. I believe, I'm not positive, but I think Elvis made two movies while he was in the service, and so I think for Ali probably a couple of fights could have been arranged and also he wouldn't have been stripped of his title as heavyweight champion of the world. So, I felt that he should have taken induction and he should have served his country and that he would have been treated fairly by the U.S. Army, I really do. I think he made a mistake."

As Ali left the courthouse with his lawyers and stepped into a cab, an elderly white woman approached waving a miniature flag and yelling, "You heading straight for jail! You ain't no champ no more. You ain't never gonna be champ no more. You get down on your knees and beg forgiveness from God!" Ali started to answer, but Covington pushed him into the cab. The woman leaned into the window and said, "My son's in Vietnam, and you no better than he is. He's there fighting and you here safe. I hope you rot in jail."

The reverberations of Ali's decision were swift and decisive. Between the time they left the courthouse and the time they returned to the hotel, less than an hour after his refusal to take the step, the New York

State Athletic Commission announced that it had "unanimously decided to suspend Clay's boxing license indefinitely and to withdraw recognition of him as World Heavyweight champion."

Columnist Jerry Izenberg recalls the scene. "I didn't go to Houston to cover the induction, I knew it would be a circus," he says. "I thought it would be more interesting to station myself at the New York Athletic Commission to see how many seconds it would take them to strip Ali of his title. As it turned out, they did it even faster than I anticipated. It was sickening."

In fact, the commission had prepared four press releases, anticipating a number of possible scenarios. The one that would have been released had Ali accepted induction praised the boxer for his "patriotism." The three-member commission had met the previous day and made the decision to strip Ali of his title if he failed to take the step.

Inside the Houston induction center had been two open lines monitoring the events. One led to the Justice Department in Washington, the other to the athletic commission in New York. When Ali emerged from the induction center and announced his decision, the commission wasted little time in issuing the appropriate release.

NYAC chairperson Edwin Dooley, a former Republican congressperson and college football hero, told reporters, "His refusal to enter the service is regarded by the Commission to be detrimental to the best interests of boxing."

The World Boxing Association, as well as the Texas and California athletic commissions, immediately followed suit, making it virtually impossible for Ali to fight in the United States. In England, the British board of boxing declared the title vacant. The only dissent from what Ali later called a "legal lynching" was from a number of Muslim countries who continued to recognize Ali as the world champion.

It seemed obvious that Ali would have to stand alone for the time being. But the news of the commission's decision didn't seem to faze him. He had other things on his mind as he returned to the hotel. He went up to his room and placed a call to Louisville.

"Mama," he said into the phone. "I'm all right. I did what I had to do. I sure am looking forward to coming home to eat some of your cooking."

CHAPTER SEVEN:
Backlash

THE PUBLIC AND MEDIA REACTION had been overwhelmingly hostile after Ali declared he was a Muslim. When he made his first comments about the Vietcong, it had turned vicious. Both responses, however, seemed positively restrained compared to the torrent of abuse unleashed after he refused induction.

The sports editor of his hometown paper, the *Louisville Courier-Journal*—looking forward to the expected jail term—wrote, "Cassius Clay had a responsibility to himself and the boxing game that has given him so much, but Clay is a slick opportunist who clowned his way to the top. Hail to Cassius Clay, the best fighter pound for pound that Leavenworth prison will ever receive."

Gene Ward warned in the *New York Daily News*, "I do not want my three boys to grow into their teens holding the belief that Cassius Clay is any kind of hero. I'll do anything to prevent it."

Milton Gross of the *Post* raged, "Clay seems to have gone past the borders of faith. He has reached the boundaries of fanaticism."

In an editorial, the *New York Times* indignantly declared, "Citizens cannot pick and choose which wars they wish to fight any more than they can pick and choose which laws they wish to obey."

The black press, generally supportive of the war, was no more sympathetic; but there, at least, some reporters questioned the government's motives in drafting Ali. "Clay should serve his time in the Army just like any other young, healthy, all-American boy," wrote James Hicks in Louisville's black newspaper, the *Defender.* "But what better vehicle to use to put an uppity Negro back in his place than the United States Army."

In Congress, reaction to Ali's action was equally fierce. Republican Congressman Robert Michel was incensed that Ali was not thrown in jail immediately after his induction refusal:

> It seems totally unfair to me that merely because Clay has made a lot of money, he should be able to stay out of the draft while lawyers prepare a barrage of appeals.

As African-American historian Jeffrey Sammons has observed, "For Ali to score victories in the ring, a circumscribed arena with its own rules, seemed tolerable, but when he took his fight beyond that arena, as his gladiatorial ancestor Spartacus had done, the forces of an ordered white-dominated society responded to the perceived threat."

But, if scarce, there were a number of liberal writers and intellectuals who supported Ali's action, particularly in New York, and several of them bonded together to form an ad-hoc committee to push for the boxer's reinstatement. Among the most prominent members of the committee were Norman Mailer, Pete Hammill, and George Plimpton.

"We all got together and decided to do something because we were outraged by the boxing commission's action," recalls Plimpton, at the time a writer for *Sports Illustrated.* "Not because we opposed the Vietnam War—most of us did—but because it was so clearly wrong what they were doing to Ali just because he had the courage to take a stand."

One of the names most conspicuously absent from the committee, however, was ABC boxing commentator Howard Cosell. For almost two years, Cosell had become inextricably linked in the public's mind with Muhammad Ali. Their association, in fact, came about as a direct result of Ali's pariah status.

After Ali made his infamous remark about the Vietcong in 1966, the economics of boxing changed dramatically. Before this incident, fight promoters made most of their money selling closed-circuit rights to

With long time friend and Nemesis, Howard Cosell, who was first unwilling to support Ail's stand.

theaters, where the public would pay to watch the fights. Ali's anti-war stand, however, prompted veterans groups to threaten theaters with massive boycotts if they dared to show an Ali fight.

In response, ABC television stepped in and signed an exclusive contract to televise Ali's fights, beginning a new era of televised boxing. Moderating these fights for ABC was a loud-mouthed, nasal-voiced sports radio personality, whose televised exchanges with Ali became the stuff of legend. Each fed off the other's personality to create a series of classic—and often comical—confrontations. In May 1966, Cosell was in London to cover the Ali fight against Henry Cooper. He started an interview with the champion, announcing to the camera, "I am with Cassius Clay, also known as Muhammad Ali." His subject turned to him with a glare, saying, "Are you going to do that to me, too?" Cosell responded, "No, I won't ever do that again as long as I live, I promise. Your name is Muhammad Ali. You're entitled to that." From that point, Cosell became known as one of Ali's most passionate defenders. He later recalled the consequences of this support. "I got thousands of nasty letters and death threats for supporting Ali," he said, "most of them starting 'Cosell, you nigger-loving Jew bastard'!"

Years later, Cosell would express his outrage over the athletic commission's decision to strip Ali of his title. "It was an outrage," he told Thomas Hauser shortly before his death, "an absolute disgrace. You know the truth about boxing commissions. They're nothing but a bunch of politically appointed hacks. Almost without exception, they're men of such meager talent that the only time you hear anything at all about them is when they're party to a mismatch that results in a fighter being maimed or killed. And what did they do to Ali! Why? There'd been no grand jury impanelment, no arraignment. Due process of the law hadn't even begun, yet they took away his livelihood because he failed the test of political and social conformity. Muhammad Ali was stripped of his title and forbidden to fight by all fifty states, and that piece of scum Don King hasn't been barred by one."

As Ali's most high-profile supporter, Cosell seemed a natural member for the committee, and Plimpton was dispatched to enlist his support. But when he got to the TV personality's ABC office and announced his mission, Cosell quickly cut him off.

"Georgie boy, I'd be shot, sitting right here in this armchair, by some crazed redneck sharpshooter over there in that building," Plimpton recalls him saying. "If I deigned to say over the airwaves that Muhammad Ali should be completely absolved and allowed to return to the ring, I'd be shot, right through that window.

"My sympathies are obviously with Muhammad. He has no greater friend among the whites, but the time, at this stage in this country's popular feeling, is not correct for such an act on my part. There is a time and place for everything and this is not it."

Years later, reviewing Plimpton's book *Shadowbox*, a *New York Times* reviewer mentioned Plimpton's assertion that Cosell refused to join the committee.

"I remember Cosell's wife called me up after the review came out, extremely upset," Plimpton says. "Cosell himself never said anything about this but his wife got extremely upset and told me Howard had been involved from the very beginning in all this, he's always been a champion of Muhammad Ali and tried to get me to write a letter of apology, which I did because of my respect for Howard, and to be fair he later came out on Ali's side. But I remember the incident clearly, Howard would not join us."

If Plimpton's recollection doesn't prove Cosell's early reluctance to support Ali's stand against the draft, a column by Jackie Robinson written a month *before* the induction refusal provides good testimony. He refers to an interview with Ali on an episode of ABC's *Wide World of Sports* in which Cosell seemed to be badgering the boxer about his upcoming induction.

In his syndicated column, Robinson—an Army veteran who supported the Vietnam War and was himself later critical of Ali's failure to serve—wrote, "I think it is most significant that some of the writers, even the so-called liberals, do not want to grant this young champion his due. One of the sports-writing fraternity whom I have considered a liberal for a long time is Howard Cosell. And Cosell has seemed to be in Clay's corner for several years. Yet, in a recent television interview with Clay, it struck me that Howard was being quite vicious in the way he tried to sway public opinion to his anti-Clay way of thinking."

HBO boxing commentator Larry Merchant, who knew Cosell and was an early supporter of Ali, believes the controversial TV personality may have been afraid of jeopardizing his position at ABC. "At the time, Cosell still wasn't the star he would later become and he may not have been secure enough at ABC in rocking the boat by supporting Ali's draft stand. It was a very conservative network and they were supporting the war. It was one thing to call him by his Muslim name but this was a much more serious issue," he explains. "But let's face it, Howard definitely supported Ali later on, and very publicly. You have to give him credit."

Cosell seemed to confirm his insecurity in a later interview, although he never acknowledged his early failure to support Ali. "The powers he fought! The forces that lined up against him! Even I wasn't immune to fear," he explained. "I supported him, but I often wondered how long ABC would back me. I'd come into the business at a very late age, and could have been snuffed out like that."

Plimpton and the committee continued their efforts to have Ali reinstated but to no avail. "I was playing in a touch football game at Hickory Hill, Robert Kennedy's estate," Plimpton recalls. "And playing with us was Justice Byron White, who was on the Supreme Court. I said, 'Mr. Justice, isn't there something very wrong about the Muhammad Ali business, the boxing commission depriving him of his livelihood?' and he said to me very solemnly that he wasn't allowed to discuss it because it might come before the Supreme Court."

Two days after the induction refusal, Martin Luther King Jr. took his support for Ali's draft stand public for the first time. In a sermon from the pulpit of Ebenezer Baptist Church in Atlanta, King praised Ali's courage: "He is giving up even fame. He is giving up millions of dollars in order to stand up for what his conscience tells him is right. No matter what you think of Muhammad Ali's religion, you have to admire his courage."

Then, in his most controversial statement about the war to date, King used Ali as an example for others who oppose the war. "Every young man in this country who believes that this war is abominable and unjust should file as a conscientious objector," said the Nobel Peace Prize winner.

Referring to the accusations of treason against Ali that had filled the media since the day before, he said, "There is a very dangerous development in the nation now to equate dissent with disloyalty. I don't know about you but I ain't going to study war no more."

King's top lieutenant, Andrew Young, remembers the events of that week.

"Dr. King appreciated his stand and knew how much he had suffered from what he had done," says Young. "He wasn't the kind of man to let Ali go through it alone."

As King spoke, Stokely Carmichael sat in the congregation leading the applause. After the sermon, he called Ali "my hero" and praised his decision to defy the army.

"Here is a black man who can't live where he wants to live," Carmichael told reporters afterwards. "And they want to send him to Vietnam. It's about time we're going to tell him [the white man], hell no, we won't go."

Referring to the athletic commission's decision to strip the heavyweight crown from Ali, Carmichael said, "A bunch of honkies took the title away from him as if they gave it to him. He beat every white man who got into the ring with him. Tell them boxing officials to get in the ring and get his title."

The Johnson Administration was so worried about King's remarks supporting Ali that they commissioned a Gallup poll to determine their impact. The results confirmed what most objective observers had

Houston, 1967. Ali and his legal team meet with prosecutor Mort Susman (right) on the day of his induction refusal.

already sensed. J. Edgar Hoover and the White House had completely overestimated the influence of Ali. Most Americans, white *and* black, had no sympathy for Ali's stand, even with the endorsement of Dr. King. And the antipathy for the reluctant draftee was especially strong in the armed forces.

Clide Brown, a black Marine sergeant serving in Vietnam, told *Time* magazine, "Clay gave up being a man when he decided against getting inducted. And I don't want him as no Negro either. They're separatists and there's nothing separate about this war."

Many of the black soldiers in Vietnam had marched for civil rights and admired Martin Luther King Jr. before they entered the army. His anti-war statements caused considerable consternation.

"I don't think any American leader, black or white, can assist the cause of freedom by preaching the cause of sedition," said Lieutenant Colonel Warren Kynard at the time. "I don't believe Martin Luther King is qualified enough in international relations to open his mouth on American policy on Vietnam." These words were especially harsh considering Kynard, who is black, was once engaged to Coretta Scott King and was still a close friend of the couple.

Houston, 1967. "I will not be what you want me to be."

On the battlefields of Vietnam, Ali's actions were as controversial as they were back home. Wayne Smith was a combat medic in Vietnam for eighteen months. Today he recalls his emotions when Ali refused induction: "I had very mixed feelings. My family raised me to believe that as a black American, I had a duty to convince white Americans that blacks were just as patriotic as they were. But I was very aware of the inequities. I think at first when Ali came out against the war, I disagreed with him."

Smith, who is now on the board of the National Veterans' Legal Services Project, recalls that Ali was a hot topic of conversation at the time in Vietnam: "The Viet Cong used to leave propaganda leaflets on the side of the road for us to find saying, BLACK SOLDIERS: NO VIETNAMESE EVER CALLED YOU NIGGER! The white soldiers would constantly denigrate him, the conversations would be pretty nasty. After a while, I began to realize that the war was largely a sham. In retrospect, I have greater respect for Ali. It took a lot of courage for him to take that stand."

In Vietnam in April 1967, there were 380 combat battalions. Only two were headed by blacks. Out of 11,000 officers serving in Southeast Asia, fewer than 600 were black. "White officers," noted *Time* magazine in an article about blacks in Vietnam, "stubbornly kept Negroes out of top command positions."

According to Robert Lipsyte, there was a prevailing myth about racial attitudes towards the war at the time Ali took his stand. "A lot of people believe whites supported the war and blacks opposed it at that time," he says. "In fact, most white *and* black Americans supported the war and opposed Ali in April 1967."

This seems to be borne out by Wallace Terry, who covered the war for *Time.* "In 1967, only thirty-five percent of Blacks and less than twenty percent of whites opposed the war," he says. "I did a survey of Blacks in the armed forces and they were still overwhelmingly supportive of the war. That was about to change but at the time Ali took his stand, he didn't have a whole lot of sympathy from black soldiers."

Three days after he refused to take the step, Ali's legal team filed an appeal in federal court, arguing that his draft call was unconstitutional because Blacks were significantly under-represented on draft boards. In Kentucky, where Ali was first drafted, only one of 641 draft board members was black, or 0.16 percent, even though Blacks comprised 7.1 percent of the Kentucky population. Ali's lawyer, Charles Morgan Jr., had already filed a lawsuit on behalf of the American Civil Liberties Union in South Carolina and Georgia—another state where only one black sat on a draft board.

The appeal filed on behalf of Ali charged that his Selective Service file was jammed with "reams of letters and newspaper clippings of a prejudicial nature" that deprived the former champion of a fair process.

"From big cities to small towns across America came the cry 'Get him,'" the appeal asserted, citing one letter to Ali's Louisville draft board that said, "You are still cowards, eh? Send that nigger away."

Ali's lawyer asked that induction of *all* blacks be halted until the draft system inducting them was integrated.

"These suits were more political than anything else," admits Morgan today. "They were designed to point out the unfairness of the draft system, where blacks were being sent to Vietnam in disproportionate numbers by white boards."

In fact, during the war, 31 percent of eligible black males were drafted, but only 18 percent of whites, who were more likely to receive student deferments or be declared ineligible on a technicality—usually arranged by a high-priced lawyer.

On May 8, Ali was indicted as expected by a federal grand jury in Houston—the first step leading to what was assumed would be his conviction and incarceration. Only one of the twenty-one grand jurors was black. A trial date was set for June and he was photographed, fingerprinted, and released on $5,000 bail. If the indicted champion was having second thoughts about his decision, it didn't show two days later when he addressed a crowd of sixteen hundred students at the University of Chicago stadium.

"My intention is to box to win a clean fight but in war the intention is to kill, kill, kill and continue killing innocent people," he told the mostly white crowd. "It has been said that I have two alternatives—go to jail or the army. But there is another—justice! If justice prevails, I will neither go to jail or to the army."

Yet privately, Ali held out little hope for justice. He was already making plans to go to prison and sorting out his financial affairs. His first stop was to Dibble's Garage in Chicago to store his bus. Then off to close up his long-term room at the 50th-on-the-Lake Motel where he had stayed in Chicago since his apartment was firebombed following the assassination of Malcolm X two years earlier.

"I don't want to go to jail," he said as he took care of business, "but I've got to live the life my conscience and my God tell me to. What does it profit me to be the wellest-liked man in America who sold out everybody?"

Still, despite the indictment, prison was not an inevitability. The head of the Houston U.S. Attorney's office, Mort Susman, signaled to Ali's legal team that it wasn't too late to work out a deal. Calling together Ali, his lawyers, and selected advisers, Susman arranged a series of meetings at the Houston federal building. "They tried to convince me that we didn't have a case, that Ali would almost surely win on appeal, and that I should drop the charges against him," Susman recalls. "That wasn't going to happen. First of all, this was a high-profile case and we couldn't just let him get away with refusing induction. That would have sent a very negative signal at the time when the war was heating up. But I had been talking to the Army and the Justice Department and I had been given a very strong assurance that if Ali accepted induction, he would be able to enter Special Services. He could fight exhibitions, that sort of thing. If he went to Vietnam, it would only be to entertain the troops, not to fight. I wouldn't call it a deal exactly. I wasn't authorized to promise him anything but they knew what was being offered.

"We met more than once and I can tell you that they were very close to accepting, very close. But in the end, they called and said no. I don't know what happened exactly, I think he almost changed his mind but his people wanted to make a martyr of him."

Susman's assessment of the situation is only partially correct. A deal was almost struck, but it was Ali, not his advisers, who rejected the government's offer.

A year before, Ali's original contract with the Louisville Sponsoring Group had expired. Sensing the potential for immense revenues, the Nation of Islam stepped in to fill the void. Elijah Muhammad's son, Herbert, and John Ali—national secretary of the Nation and its second most powerful official—formed a promotional company called Main Bout, Inc. to market the ancillary rights to Ali's fights. The two prominent Muslims controlled 50 percent of Main Bout stock; the rest was split among Bob Arum, a former New York City prosecutor; Mike Malitz, son of closed-circuit pioneer Lester Malitz; and football star Jim Brown, who had retired from professional sports in 1965 and had become very close to Ali.

With revenues set to dry up if Ali went to prison, the new firm stood to lose millions of dollars. It was this financial consideration, reveals Brown, that hung over the negotiations to have Ali accept induction.

"I received a call from Herbert Muhammad," he later recalled. "He said he had reason to believe that the United States government would make a deal with Ali, allow him to enter the Special Services, where he wouldn't have to go to war, could perhaps retain his title, continue boxing. Herbert wanted me to broach the idea to Ali. But he wanted me to do it without telling Ali who I received my information from . . . . I'll tell you the truth, Herbert would not have minded Ali going into the Army, because they were starting to make good money together."

Brown—who admits that he didn't necessarily oppose the deal—called together ten of the most prominent black athletes in the country to meet Ali and discuss his options. Among the athletes who met with Ali at Brown's Cleveland office were Bill Russell, the Boston Celtics basketball star; All-American UCLA basketball player Lew

Alcindor (who later converted to Islam and changed his name to Kareem Abdul-Jabbar); Bobby Mitchell and Jim Shorter of the Washington Redskins; Willie Davis of the Green Bay Packers; John Wooten, Sid Williams, and Walter Beach of the Cleveland Browns; and Curtis McClinton of the Kansas City Chiefs. Some of them tried hard to dissuade Ali from his decision to defy the draft.

Brown already knew their arguments would fail to change the indicted champion's mind. The night before the meeting, he met privately with Ali and, as promised, broached the subject of the government deal. He recalls his friend's unequivocal response.

"Man, you know I believe in my religion," Ali said, unaware that the son of his spiritual leader was hoping he would accept the deal. "My religion says I'm not supposed to get in any wars and fight. I don't want any deals. I don't plan to fight nobody that hasn't done nothing to me, and I'm not going in any damn service."

Now, surrounded by the group of famous athletes, Ali told them

Cleveland, 1967. America's top black athletes hold a press conference to support Ali's decision to refuse induction. (Front row) with Bill Russell, Jim Brown and Lew Alcindor (Kareem Abdul Jabbar); (back row, left to right) Cleveland Mayor Carl Stokes, Walter Beach, Bobby Mitchell, Lorenzo Ashley, Sidney Williams, Curtis McClinton, Willie Davis, Jim Shorter and John Wooten.

roughly the same thing. "I'm doing what I have to do," he said. "I appreciate you fellows wanting to help and your friendship. But I have had the best legal minds in the country working for me, and they have shown me all the options and alternatives I could use if I wanted to go in. Things like going in to be an ambulance driver, or a chaplain, or a truck driver. Or joining and saying I would not kill. I could do any of these things, or I can go to jail. Well, I *know* what I must do. My fate is in the hands of Allah, and Allah will take care of me. If I walk out of this room and get killed today, it will be Allah's doing and I will accept it. I'm not worried. In my first teachings I was told we would all be tested by Allah. This may be my test." Then he launched into one of his trademark sermons about the Nation of Islam, the mothership, and Elijah Muhammad. "He was such a dazzling speaker, he damn near converted a few in that room," Brown recalled. Each left the room convinced of Ali's sincerity.

Bill Russell later wrote about the meeting for *Sports Illustrated*, revealing that he envied Ali's absolute and sincere faith. "One of the great misconceptions about Ali is that he is dumb and has fallen into the wrong hands and does not know what he is doing," he wrote. "On the contrary, he has one of the quickest minds I have ever known. At the meeting in Cleveland, all of us found out thoroughly that he knew a great deal more about the situation than we did. If he were being led blindfolded by the Muslims, I doubt very much that he would be taking the stand he is. What good will he do the Muslims in jail? Right now he is the best recruiter they have."

Ali's longtime friend Lloyd Wells lived in Houston and recalls the boxer's reaction to all the pressure to accept a deal and fight exhibitions.

"He could have easily been like Joe Louis and had an easy time in the army. They promised him he wouldn't have to fight," Wells says. "But he never considered it for a moment. He kept saying, 'I'd be just as guilty as the ones who did.'"

As Ali was being indicted in Houston, the British philosopher Bertrand Russell had convened an International War Crimes Tribunal in Stockholm to hear evidence on the American government's conduct in the Vietnam War and "to prevent the crime of silence." Russell had followed Ali's draft case quite closely and had recently sent him a letter supporting his stand:

In the coming months there is no doubt that the men
who rule Washington will try to damage you in every
way open to them, but I am sure you know that you
spoke for your people and for the oppressed everywhere in the courageous defiance of American power.
They will try to break you because you are a symbol
of a force they are unable to destroy, namely, the
aroused consciousness of a whole people determined
no longer to be butchered and debased with fear and
oppression. You have my wholehearted support.

The principled stands of Martin Luther King Jr. and Muhammad Ali
were at least partly responsible for a perceptible shift in black American
attitudes toward the war. At the Stockholm tribunal, the African-
American novelist James Baldwin expanded on their message: "I speak
as an American Negro. I challenge anyone alive to tell me why any
black American should go into those jungles to kill people who are not
white and who have never done him any harm, in defense of a people
who have made that foreign jungle, or any jungle anywhere in the
world, a more desirable jungle than that in which he was born, and to
which, supposing that he lives, he will inevitably return."

As black and white protest against the war stepped up, a dispropor-
tionately large number of high-profile protesters were, it appeared,
being inducted into the Army, which was supposed to rely on a random lottery to select its draftees. Within a year of its decision to turn its
efforts to protesting the Vietnam War, SNCC's ranks rapidly dwindled
as its leaders were drafted one after another. In the three months pre-
ceding Ali's induction, sixteen members of the organization were called
into the armed forces—a suspiciously high rate to many onlookers. A
month before Ali's induction, a SNCC field secretary named Cleveland
Sellers had been ordered to report for induction at the Atlanta Armed
Forces Examining and Entrance Station. When he arrived, three
Counterintelligence Corps agents took him into a room to question
him. He later denounced his interrogation as "intimidation" and
charged the government with "a conspiracy to induct the whole SNCC
organization." After the ACLU took his case, it was revealed that
Sellers's draft board files contained references to his SNCC employ-

ment, an FBI agent's visit to the draft board, and an interesting observation by the psychiatrist who had interviewed him at his physical examination, describing him as a "semiprofessional race agitator."

Cases like Sellers's were fuelling suspicions that the draft system was being used to target war protesters. Comments from some prominent Washington politicians did little to dampen such speculation. The second highest ranking member of the House Armed Services Committee, F. Edward Hebert, had recently urged his congressional colleagues to "forget the First Amendment." Agreeing with Hebert, the committee chairperson L. Mendel Rivers urged the speeding up of the prosecution of draft cases and bringing charges against the "Carmichaels and Kings." For some time, many had speculated that Ali's suspicious reclassification—the result of a lowering of standards by the Selective Service—was a political act. Without proof, however, it was impossible to make this case stick.

Thirty years later, however, former Attorney General Ramsey Clark reveals a remarkable feud he was engaged in around the time of the Ali prosecution with the head of the Selective Service, General Lewis Hershey. "Hershey wanted to accelerate the inductions of anti-war protesters and I thought that violated the Constitution because it went against the First Amendment," recalls Clark, who served as attorney general in the Johnson Administration from 1966 to 1969. "As Director of the Selective Service, he had a lot of power in this area, of course. Hershey wanted to use the system to crush the protests. I was personally opposed to the war right from the beginning so needless to say I wasn't very sympathetic to his aims. I remember I opposed him all the way on this but the White House didn't want to get directly involved. They told us to sit in a room together and work it out. I could have resigned to express my opposition but if I had done that, I'm convinced there would have been mass targeting of young protesters on a much larger scale. My conscience couldn't allow that to happen."

As attorney general, Clark ended up personally approving Ali's prosecution, an unusual role for the head of the Justice Department. He says his feud with Hershey was partly responsible.

"I had a policy of not getting involved in individual cases but I ended up looking at the Ali case because of all the controversy over the draft issues. I was always a strong supporter of the right to conscientious

Houston, 1967. Ali outside the court room moments after being convicted of draft evasion.

objection. I enlisted in the Marines during the Korean War but some of the best people I knew were conscientious objectors. Thoreau had always been a hero of mine, I had read his essay on civil disobedience and I always admired his statement, 'I was not born to be forced.'

"Here I was the Attorney General of the United States and the Ali case was going down. It presented a real conflict. Although I supported the right to conscientious objection, I took a look at his case and realized there was not an objection to war per se but rather this war in particular. To me, it wasn't moral resistance, it was a political choice. Although I respected his choice, I didn't think the law permitted this form of objection. Society would break down if each individual was permitted to choose which laws they obeyed based on their political views."

Ironically, Ramsey Clark now represents Ali as a private attorney.

On June 20, Ali appeared in federal court to face trial for refusing induction. Carl Walker, a black assistant U.S. Attorney, prosecuted the case for the government.

"I would say it became a political case. I think politics got into it more than anything else," Walker later claimed. "Back in those days, I was responsible for prosecuting all of what we called the 'draft evaders'

. . . . Muhammad had joined the Muslims, who were a very unpopular religious group. In fact, to some people they weren't a religious group at all. They were looked upon like the Black Panthers or something along those lines, and there was a feeling that if Ali were allowed to escape the draft, it would encourage other young men to join the Muslims. But under our Constitution, every religion has to be recognized, and I always felt it was a case the government would lose in the end. I knew we'd win at trial. At that time, any jury in the United States would have convicted him."

According to Walker, a rumor was circulating that thirty thousand black Muslims from all over the United States were planning to descend on Houston and stage a mass demonstration outside the courthouse. Racial tensions were already high in the city. At the black Houston university, Texas Southern, eight weeks earlier, a student protest resulted in two buildings being burned to the ground and four students killed. Officials were terrified that the Muslim protest would lead to a race riot. At a pre-trial meeting, U.S. Attorney Mort Susman asked Ali to call the demonstration off.

"He was wonderful about that," said Walker. "Even with his own problems, he was concerned about someone else getting hurt."

The outcome of the trial was never in doubt. After a routine presentation of evidence by the government, the defense attempted to prove that the Louisville board that drafted Ali was racially biased because there were no blacks. Ali sat subdued, doodling on a legal pad, as Federal District Court judge Joe Ingraham read his charge to the all-white jury. The only question, said the judge, was whether the defendant knowingly and unlawfully refused to be inducted into military service. The jurors took only twenty-one minutes to find the defendant guilty as charged. On his yellow pad, Ali had drawn a picture of a plane crashing into a mountain.

When the jury returned with its verdict, Ali told the judge, "I'd appreciate it if the court would give me my sentence now instead of waiting and stalling."

U.S. Attorney Mort Susman, grateful for Ali's cooperation in calling off the Muslim demonstration, told the Court the government would have no objection if Ali received less than the five-year maximum sentence allowed by law.

"The only record he has is a minor traffic offense," Susman explained. "He became a Muslim in 1964 after defeating Sonny Liston for the title. This tragedy and the loss of his title can be traced to that." Susman observed that he had studied the Muslim religion and found it "as much political as it is religious."

At these words, Ali leaped to his feet and displayed his first emotions since the trial began.

"If I can say so, sir, my religion is not political in any way," he said.

The judge quickly rebuked him, saying, "You'll be heard in due order."

He then imposed the sentence: five years in prison and a $10,000 fine. At this point, Judge Ingraham issued the directive that some believed was worse than the prison sentence. He ordered Ali's passport confiscated. For the time being, the convicted felon would stay out of prison pending appeal, but the revocation of his passport meant that his boxing career was over. He was already prohibited from fighting in the United States by the actions of state boxing commissions. Now he could not travel to the few countries which still recognized him as world champion.

But if he was worried about what lay ahead, it didn't show. "I'm giving up my title, my wealth, maybe my future," he said outside the courtroom. "Many great men have been tested for their religious belief. If I pass this test, I'll come out stronger than ever."

The World Boxing Association immediately announced an elimination bout to crown a new champion. Ali reflected the sentiments of many boxing aficionados—even his detractors—when he declared, "Let them have the elimination bouts. Let the man that wins go to the backwoods of Georgia and Alabama or to Sweden or Africa. Let him walk down a back alley at night. Let him stop under a street lamp where some small boys are playing and see what they say. Everybody knows I'm the champion. My ghost will haunt all the arenas. I'll be there, wearing a sheet and whispering, "Ali-e-e-e! Ali-e-e-e!"

When Ali was convicted, many Americans believed he had got what was coming to him and looked forward to his five-year prison sentence. When it was reported that the convicted boxer would remain free on appeal, his attackers seemed to feel cheated. They took out their hostility on his local draft board, which received an avalanche of mail demanding Ali be jailed immediately.

"Dear Skunks: You yellow-bellied scum—you are as bad as those picketing against the U.S. and those burning their draft cards," read one angry missive. Another letter writer smelled "a rat—or maybe a payoff! That Black Bastard Cassius Clay should be in Vietnam right now with our fighting men instead of hiding behind some phony heathen religion. He is a disgrace to the sports world—his race—and his country—and so are you for letting him get away with such crap."

President Johnson was also inundated with a new round of letters from outraged Americans. "Dear Mr. President," wrote one Texas citizen. "It amazes me and so many, many others that three hours after Cassius Clay's refusal to take the oath and be inducted into the Army, that you have not ordered his immediate arrest, without bond and a trial in the morning to send him and his Black Muslim pals to jail for treasonable acts, because what they and his attorneys are advising is treasonable. If you want to close your credibility gap a little, do the incredible thing and see this case is disposed of."

Three days after his conviction, Ali appeared for the first time at one of the increasingly frequent anti-war demonstrations sweeping the country. This one was in Los Angeles, where President Johnson was attending a fundraiser. Despite Elijah Muhammad's edict that members of the Nation must divorce themselves from white politics, Ali—who had become the most visible symbol of resistance to the increasingly unpopular war—stood on top of a garbage can and addressed the crowd of thirty thousand protesters.

"I'm with you," he shouted. "Anything designed for peace and to stop the killing I'm for one hundred percent. I'm not a leader. I'm not here to advise you. But I encourage you to express yourself and to stop this war."

After Ali left, the mayor of Los Angeles unleashed more than a thousand LAPD officers on the demonstrators, attacking them with police batons after they staged a nonviolent sit-in in front of the Century Plaza Hotel where L.B.J. was speaking. Some 275 demonstrators were injured in the police riot. California's right-wing governor, Ronald Reagan, who had placed the National Guard on alert, made it clear how he thought the protesters should be handled. "If it takes a bloodbath, let's get it over with. No more appeasement," he declared.

As Ali watched the brutality on television that night, he vowed to himself not to participate in any more anti-war demonstrations. But his stepped-up rhetoric against the war infuriated J. Edgar Hoover, who ordered continued surveillance of the boxer. In a July 25 memo to the director, an FBI agent reported:

> Cassius Clay, alias Muhammad Ali, is an admitted active member of the Nation of Islam, which is a highly secretive organization whose membership is made up entirely of selected Negroes who advocate and believe in the ultimate destruction of the white race and complete control of the civilized world by the Negro cult. The Muslims, as members of this organization are referred to, hold highly secretive meetings which exclude all persons not Negro, which exclude all non-Muslims. The Muslims promote segregation, and they advocate that their members not serve in the military service of our country. Within their organization, however, they train their members in military tactics, conduct classes in physical conditioning and karate, and utilize the paramilitary training normally used by secret militant type groups. Clay, who purports to be a minister in this organization, has utilized his position as a nationally known figure in the sports world to promote through appearances at various gatherings an ideology completely foreign to the basic American ideals of equality and justice for all, love of God and country.

As attorney general, Ramsey Clark was technically Hoover's boss. He explains why the FBI chief considered Ali a threat.

"He was totally out of touch with the reality of Muhammad's influence," Clark says. "He thought Ali was some sort of a pied piper leading all these soldiers not to go to Vietnam. It was a fantasy. He was never able to contain himself about his hatred for Dr. King but he also had this thing about black leaders in general. This is a guy who grew up in the South in another era. I remember I was with Bob Kennedy when we met with Hoover and asked him why there were no blacks in the FBI. Basically, he was an anachronism."

Two weeks later, Hoover's paranoia toward black activists prompted the FBI to launch the COINTELPRO program, which was designed to "neutralize militant black nationalists." The agency recruited thousands of informants to infiltrate and disrupt these organizations—an operation so successful the Bureau extended the program to destabilize the anti-war movement as well.

Things were heating up. Dr. King's message of nonviolence was being usurped by the late Malcolm X's calls for confrontation. The Black Power movement intensified its rhetoric, and urban unrest increased in every American ghetto.

Ali, however, conscious of his growing influence and wary of inciting violence, distanced himself from it all as he prayed toward Mecca five times a day and mentally prepared himself for a long prison sentence.

The Black Panthers had adopted the slogan "We're the Greatest." Whether or not this was in tribute to Ali is open to speculation, but Panther leader Stokely Carmichael had recently called Ali "my hero." Panther Minister of Defense H. Rap Brown—anxious to capitalize on the boxer's popularity with ghetto youth—had organized a demonstration outside the Houston induction center to show support for Ali. But Ali, in Houston to appeal the confiscation of his passport, told a reporter, "Rap Brown and these boys can say what they like because they're nobody. Nobody gives a damn. With me it's different. If I went to a Negro district they'd come running. It would just take some young fool to throw something and that would be it. He don't care anything about race. He wants publicity. He wants to see a nice fire. I want to keep away from that stuff."

Ali's restraint failed to impress Jackie Robinson, who had been a frequent defender of the boxer's religious freedom. The increasingly conservative black baseball pioneer told the media, "He's hurting the morale of a lot of young soldiers in Vietnam. The tragedy is that he's made millions of dollars off the American public and now he's not willing to show his appreciation to a country that's giving him a great opportunity. This hurts a great number of people."

At the Houston appeal hearing to get back his passport, Ali's lawyer Hayden Covington played recordings of his client's appearances on the *Tonight* Show and other public events to demonstrate that Ali had said nothing anti-American. But his appearance at the Los Angeles anti-war rally the month before seemed to undermine this argument. The judge ruled that this event "proves Mr. Clay demonstrates a ready willingness to participate in anti-government and anti-war activities." The appeal was rejected.

By the fall of 1967, the war had escalated significantly. Five hundred thousand U.S. troops were now stationed in Vietnam; 9,353 Americans were killed in combat that year. Tens of thousands of Vietnamese civilians suffered a similar fate. Ali's uncharacteristically quiet dignity and principled stand were beginning to resonate in marked contrast to the graphic images beamed into American living rooms each evening.

While the majority of the media continued to support the war and attack Ali, *Freedomways* magazine ran an editorial expressing a sentiment which would one day be echoed by many. At the end of 1967, however, it was still a lonely, almost heretical, voice:

> *"I won't wear the uniform,"* declared the world heavyweight champion. Of all the rhetoric used to express opposition to the Vietnam War, these words may prove to be the most eloquent as a statement of personal commitment. They are words which should echo among the youth in every ghetto across this land. In taking his stand as a matter of conscience, the world heavyweight champion may be giving up a small fortune, but he has undoubtedly gained the respect and admiration of a very large part of humanity. That, after all, is the measure of a Man.

CHAPTER EIGHT:
Exile

IN 1967, THE ERA OF MULTI-MILLION-DOLLAR boxing purses was still in the future. Nevertheless, the heavyweight crown had always brought its bearer vast sums of money, and Muhammad Ali was no exception. Millions of dollars had passed through his hands since 1964 —$3.8 million from the ring, to be exact, and almost as much in endorsements and ancillary income. Yet at the time he refused induction in April 1967, virtually every penny had already disappeared.

Taxes and alimony payments to Sonji accounted for some of this financial attrition, but what happened to the rest has always been a matter of speculation. Cassius Clay Sr. and others believed that the coffers of the Nation of Islam were being filled with the earnings of its celebrity cash cow. Like all members of the Nation, Ali was expected to contribute a 10-percent tithe of his income. But Ali has always insisted that the Nation never asked him for money and, on the contrary, twice loaned him $25,000 when he was short of funds. Where, then, did all the money go?

To the dismay of many of his friends and supporters, Ali has a reputation for being extraordinarily trusting of those around him. He cares so little for money and is so generous with what he does have that he has always been known as a soft touch and an easy mark. As a result, he was a constant target for con men, hustlers, and outright thieves. And his entourage had always been filled with plenty of each.

"Life around Ali was a constant hustle," fight publicist John Condon recalled. "A lot of people in the entourage were only there to serve their own needs, and too often Ali's interests took a back seat."

There were any number of ways to feed from the Ali trough. Somebody would pick up a training camp expense and ask to be reimbursed by the boxer. Then they would send the receipt to the Nation of Islam head-quarters in Chicago to be reimbursed again. This kind of fraud, only one of many everyday scams, was greatly troubling to the honest members of his entourage, some of whom say they were regularly driven to tears of frustration by what they saw. And when Ali wasn't being robbed blind by those around him, he was as likely as not falling prey to a sob story by a con man whose "wife needs an operation."

Not all his generosity resulted in being taken advantage of, however. Once in Los Angeles, a returning Vietnam veteran was on the balcony of the ninth floor of a building threatening to jump. Ali walked out on the balcony, put his arms around the distraught man, brought him inside, and comforted him. Then he spent $1,800 on clothes and rent so the man could get his life back on track.

His friend Lloyd Wells recalls another incident, when he accompanied Ali to the Western Union office where $1,000 in emergency funds had been wired to the boxer.

"After he picked up the money, we went outside and there were a bunch of bums on the sidewalk looking pretty hard up. They would congregate outside the Western Union office because they knew people went in there for money. The cash had been paid to him in hundreds and he went up to each of them and gave them a hundred dollar bill. He badly needed the money himself, that's why it had been wired to him, but that's the kind of person he was."

Ali summed up his philosophy when he said, "service to others is the rent you pay for room here on earth."

Wherever the money went, the fact is that at the time he refused induction, Ali was broke. And, facing the loss of his professional liveli-hood, he had few financial prospects.

Then, just when things looked like they could get no bleaker, they did. Ali's lawyer Hayden Covington filed a lawsuit against his former client for $247,000 in unpaid legal bills, forcing him to sell many of his assets, including his bus.

Eugene Dibble was a Chicago businessman and investment counselor who owned a South Side garage. He had been friends with Ali since 1965. When Ali returned to Chicago following his indictment, he pulled up at Dibble's garage one day in his Cadillac.

"I was amazed," Dibble recalls. "He didn't have a dollar to buy gasoline. He was absolutely broke. He had been robbed blind by his so-called friends and then, when his earning power dried up, all the vultures suddenly disappeared. They jumped off the ship and abandoned him."

For the next three years, Dibble's garage became Ali's unofficial headquarters in exile.

"He would take money out of the cash register whenever he needed some cash, sometimes he would even pump gas, and he'd often ask, almost to himself, 'where did all the money go?'" says Dibble. "He was a little depressed for a while but never bitter. And he would never blame anyone. It was obvious that he'd been used, taken advantage of and exploited by almost everybody around him but his attitude was that he was helping his friends, they must have needed the money. I remember he came to me one day and told me his electricity was about to be cut off because he couldn't pay the bill so I wrote a check to the electric company. "

In July, the twenty-five-year-old Ali announced he was engaged to marry a seventeen-year-old Muslim woman named Belinda Boyd. The two had met for the first time in 1961, when she was only eleven and the young Cassius Clay had visited her Nation of Islam elementary school, announcing to the students that he would be heavyweight champion of the world before he was twenty-one.

Belinda's mother, Aminah, was a devout Muslim and had no qualms about letting her young daughter marry an older man who was facing a long prison term. On the contrary, his political problems were what most impressed her.

"Muhammad was always a nice person," she later explained. "He loved children, he was truly generous. But what touched me most was when they wanted him to go into the service and he refused. I have great respect for anyone, regardless of what they believe, if they stand on conscience and don't let themselves be dissuaded."

On August 17, with the nation's youth caught up in the Summer of Love, the two were wed at a Chicago mosque. Eugene Dibble paid for the minister and the caterer.

For his part, Ali's seemingly imminent prison term may have been a factor in his surprise engagement and marriage. After Belinda became pregnant soon after their wedding, he pointed out his new wife to an interviewer and said, "I'm prepared, I'm thinking ahead. You see that pretty young wife. I'll have one child, maybe two before I go to jail. Then, during the years when I'm in jail, they'll be getting bigger, so when I get out I'll already have them and I won't be starting at thirty. And my wife will still be young."

Soon after, Ali was so hard up for money that he took a job as a sparring partner to British boxer Joe Bugner, who was training in the United States.

"We paid him $1,000," Bugner later recalled. "He seemed glad to oblige. I know he was broke because he tried to sell me a portable radio gadget for $1,200. He said, 'It's just what you need, Joe.'"

At dawn each day, Ali and his new wife would rise, wrap themselves in shawls, and pray to Allah. Then, for three hours, the exiled boxer sat at his desk studying the Koran, the Bible, and the dictionary.

"I've got a lot of lost education to make up for," he would explain.

Ali's stand had made him an even greater hero to the nation's Muslims, and he continued preaching at mosques around the country. It has often been said that what sustained Ali during this dark period was his absolute faith in Allah and devotion to Elijah Muhammad. But his longtime friend Lloyd Wells insists that it went beyond religion.

"His faith was important to him, of course," says Wells. "But it is something else which kept him going, something he had long before he discovered Allah. It was his personal inner being, a confidence, a quality which he was born with, which drove him. People who knew him when he was a child talk about it. It had nothing to do with religion. You have to experience it to understand it."

Despite his preaching, Ali was as bored and frustrated during this period as he had ever been. It seemed as if neither the prospect of jail nor being forced to stop boxing troubled him as much as the idea of giving up his place on the national stage. Ali craved attention, not so much out of vanity but because it served to fuel his remarkable, gregarious personality.

During these days, passersby on the sidewalks of Chicago were frequently startled to see the undefeated heavyweight champion of the world come towards them, raise his arms above his head, and shout good-naturedly, "Who's the greatest around here? I'm looking for a fight."

Gene Dibble correctly sensed that his friend needed an audience and arranged to take him around to a number of local high schools and colleges to speak to the students.

"He was in his element with those students," Dibble recalls. "He just came alive and I saw a spark in him for the first time in months. It's exactly what he needed. He had preached all those sermons for the Muslims so he was a natural speaker."

Word quickly spread of Ali's new calling, and he was approached by two professional speakers' bureaus who offered to book him on the college lecture circuit.

Robert Walker ran the American Program Bureau, which booked many of the nation's most notorious radicals, including Dick Gregory, Abbie Hoffman, and Dave Dellinger as well as Martin Luther King Jr. and Jane Fonda.

"A mutual friend told me that Ali was in dire straits, completely broke," Walker recalls. "He suggested I book a speaking tour with him. I thought it was a great idea, there would be huge demand on college campuses. So I met with Ali a couple of times and I thought we had a deal. Then one night I was watching TV, Dick Cavett or Johnny Carson, and there was Ali announcing that he had just signed to do a college lecture tour with Richard Fulton, one of my rivals. I couldn't believe it. I don't know what happened."

For $1,500 a speech, hardly enough to put a dent in his huge legal bills, Ali invaded the nation's campuses. But not before assiduous preparation. He approached his speaking tour with the same intensity as he trained for a big fight. For eight weeks he composed a series of six different lectures, putting down his ideas on little note cards and then practicing again and again in front of a mirror until he memorized each one. "Talking is easier than fighting," he would say. Each lecture had a different theme. Students attended, expecting him to talk about boxing or express his views on Vietnam; instead they were surprised to hear him extol the importance of early childhood education or launch a diatribe against social selfishness:

Nashville, 1964. Black University students welcome Ali to campus.

On the art of personality: "Personality is not something you're born with. We're born as individuals. What I'm trying to say is that personality is the development of individuality."

On the education of the infant: "Children go through three or four or five different colleges within themselves, even before they're three years old."

On the power of suggestion: "If you suggest failure to yourself, then you'll be a failure. Some people say 'I'm timid' or 'I'm forgetful' or 'I'm stupid.' And once you repeat it two or three times, it deepens your stupidity or forgetfulness."

On friendship: "Whenever the thought of self-interest creeps in, that means a destruction of friendship. Every little thought of profiting by it means destruction. This is what I am doing, things I am doing today. It can never develop into a real friendship, it can only develop into a business relationship. It will last as long as the business relationship lasts. Like me and Cosell. If I lose, he goes to somebody else."

Ali's longtime supporter Jerry Izenberg attended a number of his lectures. "The students went wild when he talked about these things," he recalls. "It was a little surreal."

Yet if each lecture was different, they all ended alike, with the fighter-turned-speaker shouting, "Can my title be taken away without me being whupped?"

"No!"

"One more time."

"No!"

"Now I'd like to hear this from you, and I want the world to hear. Who's the heavyweight champion of the world?"

"You are!"

"One more time. We don't want no excuses. They might say the film was bad or the camera was broke. Who's the champ of the world?"

"You are!"

Finally came the question-and-answer-period—usually the point where things really got interesting. "It was amazing," recalls Lloyd Wells. "Here was this guy who just barely graduated high school matching wits with Harvard students and always getting the better of them."

Not all the questioners were friendly. At one stop Ali was asked, "How can you condone fighting in the ring and yet refusing to fight for your country?"

Ali was unfazed. "It's *my* country at *draft-time*," he responded. "But not when I come back. Best think before you ask a question: you can lose a debate just like you can lose a fight. White boys go to Canada. George Hamilton can't be drafted because he has to support a millionaire mother. White men tear up a whole draft board in protest and maybe get a two-year sentence. I've never burned a draft card, never sat on the Pentagon steps, and I get five years and a $10,000 fine. You know good and well you're not as dumb as you look."

At a Christian college, he was asked about his religious background.

"I used to be a Baptist. I used to wait for pie in the sky by and by. Now I want something sound on the ground while I'm around."

At all times, Ali appeared to have his eyes cast forward, intent on how he would be portrayed by history, how future generations would look back on him. Asked how he could give up all the money that goes with being the heavyweight champion, he replied, "Money ain't worth a damn thing when it comes to being a black man. What do I need money for? Don't drink, don't smoke, don't go nowhere, don't go running with women. I take my wife out and we eat ice cream. I've looked the white man in the eye. I go to sleep happy, I wake up happy. I'll go to jail for ten years happy. When they talk about me, it'll always be said 'there is one who didn't compromise.' There are only two kinds of men, those who compromise and those who take a stand. That's who they write history about, who they make movies about. I turned down ten million dollars in commercial royalties. They have to look at me now greater than just in the boxing ring."

At almost every stop, he was asked if he hated whites.

"I don't hate nobody and I ain't lynched nobody," he would reply. "We Muslims don't hate the white man. It's like we don't hate a tiger; but we know that a tiger's nature is not compatible with people's nature since tigers love to eat people. So we don't want to live with tigers. It's the same with the white man."

For Jerry Izenberg, the most memorable moment he witnessed on the lecture tour concerned Ali's imminent jail term. "A guy in the audience told Ali he'd serve his prison term for him in exchange for ten thousand dollars. Muhammad just shook his head and said, 'Brother, your life's worth more than ten thousand dollars.'"

Many questioners seemed obsessed with the amount of money Ali was giving up for his principles. He always sounded the same theme: "I could make millions if I led my people the wrong way, to something I know is wrong. So now I have to make a decision. Step into a billion dollars and denounce my people or step into poverty and teach them the truth. Damn the money. Damn the heavyweight championship. I will die before I sell out my people for the white man's money. The wealth of America and the friendship of all the people who support the war would be nothing if I'm not content internally and if I'm not in accord with the will of Almighty Allah."

Invoking the name of Allah always seemed to send Ali back to his role as minister. Occasionally, he would launch into a sermon about the strict moral code of the Nation of Islam. This struck reporter Robert Lipsyte as ironic:

"Here was Ali preaching against pre-marital sex and drugs to all these free love, pot-smoking hippies. But they loved him. The only problem came when he denounced interracial dating. Occasionally, a mixed couple would boo him and walk out." After each lecture, he would collect his check, hop on a bus, and head for the next campus. It was a far cry from his boxing days, when he traveled first-class, surrounded by a large entourage. Nevertheless, he remembers this period fondly.

"During all the years I was away," he said. "I was never lonely. Oh, I had a ball, driving to colleges, staying at the inns, and meeting students and Black Power groups and all the white hippies. We'd all have sessions over dinner on what we was gonna talk about and then we'd go to the student union building and have the meeting and they'd ask me questions—all the boys and girls, black and white. Like 'What should we do?' or 'What do you think was going to happen here?' you know, as if I was one of those sleepy-eyed Senators up in the Capitol."

And wherever Ali went, he was never alone. Since his conviction, responsibility for surveillance activities against him had been transferred from the FBI to the U.S. Army Intelligence and Security Command, which kept a constant eye on his activities. One report read:

> At 1555 hours 21 May 1968, Cassius Clay arrived at Lambert Field, Missouri. He proceeded to the Carousel Motel, North Kings Highway, St. Louis, Missouri, to change clothing. At 1900 hours 21 May 1968, he arrived at the Riviera Civic Center (a nightclub in an all-Negro area), 4460 Delmar Ave, St. Louis, to attend a Black Muslim convention sponsored by the Moslem mosque #28 of St. Louis, Missouri. About 600 persons were in attendance. Clay spoke for about 45 minutes, mostly about himself and about his cause, which is to avoid being placed in a white man's army. He stayed at the

Riviera from 1900 hours to 2200 hours. He departed
for the Carousel Motel at 2200 hours. Shortly thereafter, he left for Lambert Air Field, and departed for
Chicago at 2350 hours, 21 May 1968.

For *Miami Herald* sportswriter Pat Putnam, one thing stood out about
this period. "The thing that struck me," he recalls, "is that never once
during those years did I ever hear Ali complain about what was happening to him. He was going through a bad time but he never seemed
bitter. God knows, he had a right to complain but I never saw it."

▶ ▶ ▶

On the morning of January 30, 1968, nine months into his internal
exile, Ali boarded a bus to New Haven where he was to give the thirty-
sixth speech of his campus tour. Meanwhile, half the world away, on the
first day of the Vietnamese New Year (Tet), the Vietcong launched their
biggest offensive of the war. One thousand Vietcong troops infiltrated
the South Vietnamese capital of Saigon. The enemy guerrillas captured
the Citadel at Hue and seized part of the U.S. Embassy in Saigon. It took
nearly two weeks for the American army to completely rout the
Vietcong troops. On the face of it, the attack proved a military disaster
for the Communists: they lost over ten thousand men and failed to hold
any of their objectives. Nevertheless, the Tet Offensive constituted an
important symbolic victory for the Vietcong. For many Americans who
had believed that the war was being won, the sight of Vietcong troops
holding the U.S. Embassy proved a rude awakening, forcing them to
question the truth about the American military presence. President
Johnson's approval rating plunged to 24 percent.

The Tet Offensive also marked a pivotal moment in America's rapidly evolving social climate and, ultimately, would have a profound
impact on how the country viewed Muhammad Ali. It was only the first
significant event in a year that would divide a nation and shake it to its
very foundations, forcing its people to question their core beliefs while
robbing them of some of their brightest hopes and luminaries. And,
some would say, of its ignorance and innocence.

But meanwhile, the boxing establishment, as impervious as any to what was happening all around it, was trying to figure out a credible way to fill Ali's vacant title. In October 1967, Robert Lipsyte wrote in the *New York Times*, "No matter who a cabal of television executives, Texas showmen, fools, and sly-fingers offer us, Muhammad Ali is the heavyweight champion of the world."

The New York, Massachusetts, and Illinois boxing commissions met and decided they would stage a series of elimination bouts between the leading contenders, starting with Buster Mathis and Joe Frazier on March 4. The winner of the series would be awarded the heavyweight crown stripped from Ali ten months earlier.

On March 1, a coalition of black organizations held a press conference to announce their opposition to the Mathis-Frazier fight, scheduled three days later at Madison Square Garden.

"To us and to millions of other blacks at home and throughout the world, Muhammad Ali is the world's heavyweight champion," declared Lincoln Lynch of the United Black Front. "He is still the greatest."

Prominent black activist LeRoi Jones echoed the sentiments, pronouncing the fight a mirage: "Even though Buster Mathis and Joe Frazier might tell white people that they are the heavyweight champion after this fight, they will never come in the black community claiming that they are the heavyweight champion. They know that little kids would laugh them out of the streets."

At the fight, while Frazier was knocking out Mathis, a persistent chant floated down from the rafters: "Ah-lee, Ah-lee." Real fight fans knew who the true champion was. "The only way you can take my title is by whupping me in the ring," Ali repeated after his former sparring partner Jimmy Ellis eventually won the questionable title.

Two weeks later, on March 16, a U.S. Army lieutenant named William Calley ordered his battalion to slaughter five hundred unarmed Vietnamese villagers, including two hundred children, at the hamlet of My Lai.

Hundreds of thousands of students all over America stepped up their tactics against what they called an immoral war. For the first time, average Americans were beginning to agree. Each new poll showed increasing opposition to the American presence in Vietnam, especially in the black community, where for the first time a majority—56 percent—opposed the war, according to a *Newsweek* poll.

Bemused by the unprecedented social turmoil, the establishment looked for a scapegoat. Congressman Claude Pepper took to the floor of the House of Representatives and bellowed, "If any one individual contributed to the contagious disrespect for law and love of country, then it would have to be our disposed fighting king."

The seismic shifts in public opinion were beginning to have their effect in Washington. On March 31, President Johnson went on national television to announce a unilateral bombing halt. At the end of the speech, Johnson stunned the nation by announcing that he would not run for a second term.

Four days later, Martin Luther King Jr. was gunned down in Memphis on the balcony of his motel by a white assassin, sparking the worst race riots America had seen since Jack Johnson won the heavyweight title fifty-eight years earlier.

Suddenly, it wasn't just Muhammad Ali who was under siege—it was the whole country.

▶▶▶

Sports columnist Jerry Izenberg likes to point out a rarely discussed irony of the growing anti-war movement. "You have to remember that all those kids protesting the war were basically acting out of self-interest. They didn't want to go to Vietnam so they did everything they could to stay out of the army. They got themselves student deferments, they fled to Canada, very few of them actually took a real stand. Compare that to Ali who put everything he had on the line and was willing to go to jail for what he believed in. I always thought about that when I watched the demonstrations on TV. And remember Ali was first. When he made his comment about the Vietcong, nobody was protesting yet. He paved the way, but they never gave him credit for that; the Abbie Hoffmans and Jerry Rubins were too busy taking credit themselves. You never saw them carry signs asking for his reinstatement. They were only looking out for themselves."

Stokely Carmichael, one of the highest profile of these protesters, seemed to echo Izenberg's attitude when he said, "No one risked or suffered like Muhammad Ali. I didn't risk anything. I just told people not to go."

Indeed, the statistics seem to confirm that this generation was less likely to take a genuine risk, compared to the generation before. In 1966, only 353 out of 1,100,000 eligible American men were convicted as draft dodgers, although this figure would climb significantly before the end of the war. This compares to one-year totals of 8,422 during World War I, 4,609 during World War II; and 432 during the Korean War.

But if the hippies never acknowledged Ali's influence, there was at least one group determined to pay the deposed boxer his due.

By the late 1960s, black athletes in America had failed to cash in on the progress of the civil rights movement. They were no longer excluded from the major sports leagues as they had been thirty years before. But in some ways, a uniquely American form of sports apartheid continued to plague many of the country's sports institutions.

Virtually every major athletic and country club in the country—North and South—was segregated, making it virtually impossible for blacks to break into sports such as golf and tennis.

As late as 1968, black athletes in the South and even in northern cities such as Chicago, Buffalo, and Montreal were refused service in many restaurants and were forced to stay in different hotels than their white teammates. Until only a few years before, when Northern universities played Southern colleges, they were expected to sit out their black players in deference to Southern tradition. Even when the Southern teams came north, many teams considered it a form of gracious hospitality to keep their black players out of the game.

By the 1960s, a few Southern colleges had taken to recruiting black athletes but many teams were still segregated. In 1965, the University of Texas at El Paso (UTEP) became the first Southern university to field a black player. Still, UTEP athletic director George McCarty made it abundantly clear that his liberal attitudes on race only went so far when he explained his rationale. "In general, the nigger athlete is a little hungrier, and we have been blessed with having some real outstanding ones," he said. "We think they've done a lot for us, and we think we've done a lot for them."

In 1967, black athletes finally decided that they wanted a share of the racial progress sweeping the rest of society. The Revolt of the Black Athlete was born. Its architect was a former college basketball and track star named Harry Edwards.

Standing six-foot-eight and weighing 240 pounds, Edwards was a formidable presence. Five years earlier, he had rejected a number of pro football offers in favor of an academic career at Cornell. In 1967, at the age of twenty-five, he was teaching sociology at San Jose State University (SJSU), where he ignited the first spark of the revolt.

Edwards had demanded a meeting with SJSU president Robert Clark to discuss grievances about racism at the university. When he was rebuffed, he organized a rally setting out the conditions for eradicating injustice at the institution. If the conditions were not met, he threatened, the upcoming football game between SJSU and the University of Texas at El Paso would be disrupted. Refusing to cave into the demands, the president cancelled the football game, infuriating California Governor Ronald Reagan, who publicly castigated Clark for allowing himself to be coerced by Edwards.

Before long, the movement had spread to universities throughout the country, and black athletes nationwide began to demand a better deal. In December 1967, at a black youth conference in Los Angeles, Edwards gathered a number of top-ranking black athletes and formed an organization calling itself the Olympic Project for Human Rights (OPHR).

The OPHR threatened a black boycott of the 1968 Mexico City Olympics unless a series of demands were met. Among these:

- The appointment of another black to the nearly all-white U.S. Olympic Committee.
- The resignation of the controversial International Olympic Committee (IOC) chairperson Avery Brundage, who had made a number of controversial racial comments in the past. Asked by a reporter, for example, why he thought black athletes had dominated the track and field events, he replied, "This is nothing new. Even as far back as 1936, one could see, particularly with Jesse Owens, how the Negroes could excel in athletics. Their muscle structure lends itself to this sort of competition about which we are all delighted."
- The expulsion of South Africa and Rhodesia from the games because of their apartheid systems. South Africa, in fact, had already been banned, but it was on the verge of reinstatement by the IOC.

But number one on the OPHR list of demands was the reinstatement of Muhammad Ali as heavyweight champion and the restoration of his boxing license. The inclusion of Ali on the list was puzzling to many, because the IOC had nothing to do with boxing licenses.

"We put Ali on the list as a symbolic gesture to express our gratitude for the stand he took," explains Edwards, who is today a sociology professor at Berkeley University. "We had no illusions of getting his license back. Boxing commissions are the most corrupt and contemptible institutions in sports. But we were saying thank you to Ali for what he did. When he refused to be inducted, it heightened the consciousness of all black athletes. Before Ali, the Jesse Owenses, the Jackie Robinsons, the Joe Louises had to turn the other cheek in terms of their dignity to gain access. They had to make sure they didn't do anything to alienate white folks or to hurt black folks. I'm not faulting them. It was part of the tradition of being twentieth-century gladiators in the service of white society. Ali broke with all that. He was the forerunner in the movement to demonstrate that blacks had a responsibility to be a different kind of athlete, in terms of not buying into white society's expectations. He had an enormous impact and we were just acknowledging that. In many ways, Muhammad Ali was the father of the Revolt of the Black Athlete."

In January 1968, the New York Athletic Club scheduled its annual indoor track and field meet at Madison Square Garden to commemorate the club's 100th anniversary. The meet would have been a showcase for some of the premier black athletes in the country. Edwards saw his chance to show he meant business. The NYAC, like most elite clubs, still had an all-white membership policy and the OPHR called for blacks to boycott the meet as a signal that their threat of an Olympic boycott was serious. On the day of the event, there was hardly a black face to be seen. The boycott was a resounding success, and the IOC started to get nervous.

"You can no longer count on the successors of Jesse Owens to join in a fun-and-games fête propagandized as the epitome of equal rights so long as we are refused those rights in a white society," Edwards warned.

American track and field stars Lee Evans and Tommie Smith were the first athletes to publicly declare their intention to boycott the games as part of Edwards's movement. *Track & Field* magazine printed a sampling of the letters the two black athletes received in response to their threat.

One letter from San Francisco read, "Smith: Thanks for pulling out. I quit being interested in watching a bunch of animals like Negroes go through their paces. Please see what you can do about withdrawing Negroes from boxing, baseball, and football." Another Californian wrote, "How much are the communists paying you to make fools out of your fellow Americans?"

IOC Chairperson Avery Brundage huffed, "If these boys are serious, they're making a very bad mistake. If they're not serious and are using the Olympic Games for publicity purposes, we don't like it."

The idea of a boycott started to gain some high-profile support. Jackie Robinson, who knew better than most the slights suffered by the black athlete, publicly backed the project, declaring, "I say, use whatever means necessary to get our rights here in this country. When, for three hundred years Negroes have been denied equal opportunity, some attention must be focused on it."

Reverend Andrew Young, Martin Luther King Jr.'s top lieutenant, weighed in with his leader's opinion only a few weeks before the assassination, writing, "Dr. King applauds this new sensitivity among Negro athletes and he feels that this should be encouraged. Dr. King told me that this represents a new spirit of concern on the part of successful Negroes for those who remain impoverished. Negro athletes may be treated with adulation during their Olympic careers, but many will face later the same slights experienced by other Negroes. Dr. King knows that this is a desperate situation for the Negro athlete, the possibility of giving up a chance at a gold medal, but he feels that the cause of the Negro may demand it."

But support among prominent black athletes wasn't unanimous. Jesse Owens had struck his own blow for black racial pride when he won four gold medals at the 1936 Berlin Olympics, which were organized by the Nazis as a showcase for Aryan superiority. After his unprecedented achievement, however, he was reduced to racing against horses and other humiliating ventures to earn a living. Nevertheless, Owens publicly opposed the boycott, stating, "I deplore the use of the Olympic Games for political aggrandizement."

In February, Brundage and the IOC, intent not to appear weak in the face of the protests, voted to readmit South Africa into the Olympics. Any black athletes who were still wavering made up their minds then and there not to go to Mexico City. But the U.S.S.R. and Mexico immediately pressured Brundage to hold a special meeting, warning they could not tolerate the appearance of the white supremacist state. South Africa was once again expelled. The most important of the OPHR demands had been met.

In September, at the Olympic trials, Edwards called a meeting of the twenty-six male black athletes favored to make the team. He had decided that if less than two-thirds favored a boycott, he would change his strategy. Only thirteen—exactly half—voted to boycott. To maintain unity, the OPHR agreed that blacks would participate in the Games, try their hardest to win and, then, make an appropriate gesture on the victory stand.

Brundage immediately warned that any protest in Mexico would result in a quick trip home.

The Games began with only three black athletes boycotting the event (among them basketball star Lew Alcindor, later known as Kareem Abdul-Jabbar), who decided to make their own stands in order to highlight the unmet demands of the OPHR.

The protest appeared to have fizzled, but just the opposite was true —it was about to explode onto the front pages of newspapers the world over. On October 16, two black Americans won medals in the 200-meter dash. Before the games began, Harry Edwards had explained that "The Star Spangled Banner," the U.S. national anthem, would be the focal point of the expected victory-stand protests. "For the black man in America," he explained, "the national anthem has not progressed far beyond what it was before Francis Scott Key put his words to it—an old English drinking song. For in America, a black man would have to be either drunk, insane, or both, not to recognize the hollowness in the anthem's phrases."

The three 200-meter medalists took to the podium. As the first strains of the national anthem wafted from the loudspeakers, American gold medalist Tommie Smith drove his right fist high in the air. It was enclosed in a black glove. U.S. bronze medalist John Carlos immediately followed suit, raising his glove-enclosed left fist over his head. Each wore black socks with no shoes and a black scarf around his neck. The 65,000 spectators knew they were witnessing something historic, even if they didn't know exactly what.

After the ceremony, Smith explained to Howard Cosell the significance of their actions:

> I wore a black right-hand glove and Carlos wore the left-hand glove of the same pair. My raised right hand stood for power in Black America. Carlos's left hand stood for the unity of Black America. Together, they formed an arc of unity and power. The black scarf around my neck stood for black pride. The black socks with no shoes stood for black poverty in racist America. The totality of our effort was the regaining of black dignity.

The photograph of their gestures was beamed around the world, becoming perhaps the most lasting symbol of Black Power. Largely unreported was the fact that the silver medalist, white Australian Peter Norman, had stood on the podium with his head bowed, wearing the OPHR badge on his track suit in solidarity. The Olympic establishment was furious. As fast as Muhammad Ali was stripped of his title eighteen months earlier after his own defiant action, Smith and Carlos were evicted from the Olympic Village and permanently banned from Olympic competition. The U.S. Olympic Committee president apologized to the IOC and warned other athletes not to follow their example.

Two days later, three black Americans swept the 400-meter race. On the victory podium, each wore a black beret and raised their closed fists as their names were called. The USOC displayed its hypocrisy when it failed to reprimand or expel these three athletes as it did Smith and Carlos. They made up three-quarters of the 4 × 400-meter relay team, which had yet to compete. In contrast, Smith and Carlos had no more events to run when they were evicted.

Muhammad Ali watched on television with satisfaction as Smith and Carlos followed his defiant example in Mexico City. A few days later, watching the boxing finals, Ali and millions of others witnessed a different kind of political display by a black American athlete. After winning the gold medal, the new Olympic boxing champion George

Foreman ran around the ring waving a little American flag and yelled "United States Power" in a deliberate dig at the Black Power demonstration of his teammates. It would take six years for Ali to let Foreman know what he thought of his action.

▶ ▶ ▶

As America careened through its own turbulence and turmoil, Ali's legal case moved slowly through the court system. On May 6, 1968, the U.S. Court of Appeals upheld his conviction. Judge J. P. Coleman appeared less than sympathetic to the case, ruling, "There has been no administrative process which Clay has not sought within the Selective Service System, its local and appeal boards, the Presidential appeal board and, finally, the federal courts, in an unsuccessful attempt to evade and escape from military service of his country."

The court agreed with the claim by Ali's lawyers that blacks were under-represented on draft boards throughout the country. In the next breath, however, the three-judge panel decided this was irrelevant to Ali's conviction, ruling that "even the systematic exclusion of Negroes from draft boards would not render their acts null and void." More important to the case, the court ruled against Ali's ministerial deferment claim, insisting he was a professional boxer, not a minister.

It was yet another legal setback, and it left the Supreme Court as Ali's sole hope for staying out of prison. Even then, the chances of convincing the nation's highest court to hear his case were remote. Increasingly, Ali was growing frustrated at having his fate in the hands of a legal system that every day seemed more and more out of step with the times and the transformations that were wracking American society.

After the decision, he defiantly announced, "You done rolled the dice on me. Now we're going to have to finish the game. We've gone too far to turn back now. You can't cop out on me. You've got to either free me or put me in jail. I'm going to go on just like I'm doing, taking my stand."

Ali would see the inside of a jail cell sooner than he thought. A year earlier, he had been driving his Cadillac when he was stopped in Miami for speeding. Upon verification, it was found that he was driving without a license. Once again, it seemed Ali was a modern-day incarnation of Jack Johnson, who had left a legacy of possibly apocryphal driving stories. On one occasion, it is said, Johnson was stopped on a highway and handed a fifty-dollar fine. He peeled off two fifty dollar bills and handed them to the traffic cop, who asked what the second bill was for. "I'm coming through again," the notorious boxer said. Ali was well on his way to gaining such notoriety on the nation's roads when Elijah Muhammad took away his license and assigned him a driver several months before the Miami incident. It didn't stop him, however, from occasionally slipping away and indulging his passion for speed.

When he didn't show up in court on the traffic violation, a warrant was quietly issued for his arrest in Dade County, Florida. Then, in December 1968, he was again stopped on a Miami street by a motorcycle cop, who found the outstanding warrant and escorted him to the local courthouse. There a judge sentenced him to a ten-day term in the Dade County jail. Considering his otherwise clean record, a large fine would have been the standard punishment for such an offense, prompting his lawyer to charge, "He got sentenced for being Cassius Clay. Everyone is caught up in the hate-Clay hysteria."

So just before Christmas, Ali got a small taste of what lay ahead of him, barring Supreme Court salvation. He was assigned the kitchen detail, where for forty cents an hour, he sliced vegetables, washed dishes, and brought trays of food to his fellow inmates, who were excited to have a celebrity in their midst.

"Jail is a bad place," he later recalled. "You're all locked up; you can't get out. The food is bad, and there's nothing good to do. You look out the window at the cars and people, and everyone else seems so free. Little things you take for granted like sleeping good or walking down the street, you can't do them no more. A man's got to be real serious about what he believes to say he'll do that for five years."

Still, the week in jail—he was let out three days early under a Christmas amnesty—didn't change his mind about his stand, even after the government let it be known that it wasn't too late to make a deal.

Indeed, if anything the stint behind bars revived Ali in some ways. His poetizing, which had been temporarily (and some would say mercifully) suspended during his exile, was stimulated again by his jail experience. To the oft-repeated question, "Are you still willing to go to prison?" he began to respond in rapping verse:

> *Hell no,*
> *I ain't going to go.*
> *Clean out my cell*
> *And take my tail*
> *To jail*
> *Without bail*
> *Because it's better there eating,*
> *Watching television fed,*
> *Than in Vietnam with your white folks dead*

Meanwhile, Herbert Muhammad, his manager and the Messenger's son, thought he had found a loophole in the legal obstacles that kept Ali from boxing in any of the fifty states. He had approached an Arizona Indian reservation—which wasn't governed by the same licensing laws as the states—and proposed a fight between Ali and Zora Folley. The closed-circuit rights alone would have been worth millions and would promise a financial cushion for the still-struggling boxer.

"The Indians have suffered at the hands of the white man just like we have," Ali said, anticipating the fight. "They're with me."

He spoke too soon. The Gila River Tribal Council, citing its military and historical heritage, voted to deny the use of the reservation for the fight.

"The reason I oppose having this fight here is that it would desecrate the land some of our brave boys have walked on," announced Mary Anna Johnson of the Tribal Council, noting that many Gila River Indians had fought bravely for the United States, including Ira Hayes, a Medal of Honor winner as a marine during World War II.

Ali's legal prospects weren't looking any better. The case had been submitted to the United States Supreme Court. There, before it would receive a full hearing, a majority of the nine justices would have to agree that an error in law or interpretation was likely to have been a factor in the lower court judgments. If no such majority existed, the decision of the lower court would stand and Ali would immediately go to prison. When the justices convened in closed session in March 1969, only Justice Brennan believed the appeal was compelling enough to grant a writ of certiorari (or approval to hear the case). By an overwhelming eight-to-one margin, Ali's argument had failed; the boxer appeared to have run out of legal options. When, a week later, the Court released the list of cases it would ponder that spring, *Cassius Marsellus Clay vs. United States of America* would be absent, forcing Ali to turn himself in to serve his five-year term.

The long battle appeared over; Ali, it seemed, had lost his biggest fight. Then, out of the blue, he caught a break. In June 1968, Congress had passed a law legalizing electronic eavesdropping by federal agents with court approval in cases of national security and certain criminal contexts. A byproduct of the bill was that any eavesdropping on other grounds that had taken place before that date was considered illegal. The Justice Department was forced to concede that, indeed, conversations involving Ali had been illegally listened to at least five times before that date. Among the other high-profile cases affected by the decision were convictions against Teamsters Union president Jimmy Hoffa, antiwar protester and pediatrician Dr. Benjamin Spock, and Black Panther H. Rap Brown—each of whom had also been illegally wiretapped.

The Supreme Court could have overturned Ali's conviction on this basis alone. Instead, it granted him a different form of reprieve. On March 11, 1969, the Court ruled that Ali's case would be sent back to a lower court to determine if the wiretaps had had any influence on his prosecution.

"It wasn't the best thing which could have happened," says his lawyer Charles Morgan, "but it kept him out of prison and gave us another chance to pull something out of our hat."

Ali's new hearing was scheduled for Federal District Court on June 4, 1969. Two days before the hearing was scheduled to begin, Morgan filed a motion demanding the government produce complete records of the wiretap information against Ali or drop the case. The U.S. Attorney agreed to allow Morgan to inspect four of the five transcripts, but the fifth was being withheld "for national security."

Two days later, the hearing got underway with an explosive revelation. Under examination by Charles Morgan, FBI agent Robert Nichols took the stand and testified that the Bureau had maintained a telephone surveillance of Martin Luther King Jr. for several years before the civil rights leader's assassination. For the many people who had long suspected that King was being monitored, this represented the first official confirmation.

Nichols then produced the transcript that affected Ali's case. It contained a condensation of a September 1964 telephone conversation between Ali and King that had been initiated by lawyer Chauncey Eskridge, who represented the two men. It read, in sum:

> Chauncey to MLK, said he is in Miami with Cassius, they exchanged greetings. MLK wished him well on his recent marriage. C. invited MLK to be his guest at his next championship fight. MLK said he would like to attend. C. said that he is keeping up with MLK, that MLK is his brother and is with him 100 percent but can't take any chances and that MLK should take care of himself, that MLK is known worldwide and should watch out for them Whities, said that people in Nigeria, Egypt, and Ghana asked about MLK.

But Ali's lawyer Chauncey Eskridge, who had also represented King, then testified that he had placed this particular call from Ali's Miami home to Dr. King's home in Atlanta, and that Ali had talked from an extension. He said the conversation had lasted forty-five minutes and included a discussion about Ali's religious activities. This prompted Morgan to demand a complete transcript of the entire conversation; however, the FBI agent claimed the original recording had been destroyed.

On the initial copy provided to the court, the FBI had altered the document to take out Nichols's handwritten name and remove the comma at the end of the transcript, to make it appear that the conversation was much shorter than it had, in fact, been.

"They were committing legal fraud," recalls Morgan. "Luckily we caught them at it and we forced them to produce the original log. But we still only got ten lines of a forty-five-minute conversation."

Among the other conversations the FBI released were several between Ali and Elijah Muhammad, whose phone had been bugged since 1960. In one, the Messenger told Ali that he would "not be a good Minister" until he gave up boxing.

The fifth conversation remained a mystery. The judge concurred with the U.S. Attorney that divulging its contents would compromise "national security," a decision that helped fuel rumors that the conversation involved a member of a foreign government. If this was indeed the case, its disclosure would confirm that the U.S. government was illegally bugging foreign embassies, which would have resulted in a highly embarrassing international incident.

The next day, FBI agent Warren L. Walsh testified that two of Ali's bugged conversations had been sent from the FBI's Phoenix office to the Bureau's office in Louisville, the location of Ali's draft board. But Oscar Smith, former head of the Justice Department's Conscientious Objector Section—the man who ruled against Ali's conscientious objector claim—denied that he had ever heard of the monitored conversations.

This was enough for Judge Joe Ingraham, who ruled the wiretap evidence was irrelevant to Ali's draft case and re-sentenced the boxer to five years in prison and a ten-thousand-dollar fine. Before handing down his sentence, the judge asked if Ali had anything to say.

"No, sir," came the polite reply. "Except I am sticking to my religious beliefs. I know this is a country which preaches religious freedom."

Soon after the hearing, Ali was invited to the opening of a new Broadway play called *The Great White Hope,* with James Earl Jones starring as Jack Johnson. As he approached the theater, Ali looked up at the blown-up photograph of a black man with a shaved skull in bed with a white woman.

"So that's Jack Johnson," he said to himself, pursing his lips in a silent whistle. "That was a b-a-a-a-d nigger!"

As the curtain rose, Jones appeared on stage in the persona of the notorious black boxer, mocking sportswriters at a press conference. He told the reporters that the reason he smiled so much in the ring was because "Ah like whoever ah'm hitting to see ah'm still his friend." When Jones told a white opponent that he looked as if he were "about ta walk da plank," Ali laughed and said to his seatmate, "Hey! This play is about me. Take out the interracial love stuff and Jack Johnson is the original *me.*" It appeared to be the first time Ali had ever made the connection.

Sparring with James Earl Jones during the Great White Hope about Ali's boxing hero, Jack Johnson.

At the end of the first act, Johnson decides to leave the country rather than be sent to prison and be stripped of the title he won in the ring.

As Ali stood in the lobby signing autographs during intermission, he said, "Hey, that Jack Johnson just gave me an idea."

"If you went to Canada," said a white middle-aged businessman, "I wouldn't blame you."

"Sssh," Ali said, looking around in mock terror and then smiling. "I couldn't do that. They'd raise hell with my people."

A while later, he repeated his joke about going to Canada to a young black woman.

"Oh don't do that," she pleaded. "We need you *here* in this country."

When a reporter asked him if he could ever really contemplate fleeing the country, he said, "You understand? They done picked up my passport and took my job. But I couldn't leave this country like Jack Johnson did even if I wanted to. But you know I've been visiting jails just to get used to it. Man, that is a bad place, jail. All cooped up, nothing to do, eating bad food. Oh, man."

After the play, Ali visited the cast backstage. He said to Jones, "You know, you just change the time, the date, and the details and it's about me."

"Well, that's the whole point," said the actor.

Ali's tone became somber. "Only one thing is bothering me."

"What?"

"Me," he said. "Just what are they gonna do fifty years from now when they gotta write a play about me." He paused and thought about it. "I just wish I knew how it was gonna turn out."

CHAPTER NINE:
Return from the Wilderness

B Y THE SPRING OF 1969, two years of exile from the ring had left a mark on the marginalized champion. His grueling lecture tours brought in barely enough money to pay his outstanding lawyers' bills and his recent week-long jail stint had forced him to confront the reality of what likely lay ahead. He had long since been dismissed as a boxing footnote by the time his old friend Howard Cosell invited him to appear for an interview on ABC's *Wide World of Sports* in early April.

Revisionist history notwithstanding, Cosell had yet to publicly call for the reinstatement of Ali's heavyweight title almost two years after he had refused induction. During the course of the interview, however, he asked his old verbal sparring partner if he had any desire to return to boxing. Ali's answer was offhand and curt. Still, it was enough to tear apart his world.

"Yeah, I'd go back if the money was right," he responded. "I have a lot of bills to pay." As Ali spoke, Elijah Muhammad watched the interview at his Chicago mansion with his lieutenant John Ali. That week's edition of *Muhammad Speaks* had already been sent to the printers. The Messenger made a phone call and stopped the presses. Two days later, the Nation's 500,000 members were stunned by the front-page headline, WE TELL THE WORLD WE'RE NOT WITH MUHAMMAD ALI. In a signed editorial, Elijah wrote:

> Muhammad Ali is out of the circle of the brotherhood of the followers of Islam under the leadership and teaching of Elijah Muhammad for one year. He cannot speak to, visit with, or be seen with any Muslim or take part in any Muslim religious activity. Mr. Muhammad Ali plainly acted the fool. Any man or woman who comes to Allah and then puts his hopes and trust in the enemy of Allah for survival is underestimating the power of Allah to help them. Mr. Muhammad Ali has sporting blood. Mr. Muhammad Ali desires to do that which the Holy Qur'an teaches him against. Mr. Muhammad Ali wants a place in this sports world. He loves it.

The next edition of the newspaper took the shocking punishment a step further, announcing that the Nation's most famous recruit would be referred to by his old slave name Cassius Clay rather than be recognized "under the Holy Name Muhammad Ali."

The paper carried a statement from the Messenger's son, Herbert Muhammad, that he was "no longer manager of Muhammad Ali (Cassius Clay)" and furthermore that he was no longer "at the service of anyone in the sports world."

Sensitive to the widespread assumption that the boxer's huge fortune had been plundered by the Nation of Islam, John Ali wrote that the champion's need to fight to pay off debts resulted from his own "ignorance and extravagance" by failing to follow the teachings of Elijah Muhammad, who advised all of his disciples to be prudent in handling their money.

"Neither Messenger Muhammad, the Nation of Islam, nor the Muslims have taken any money from Muhammad Ali," stated the movement's National Secretary. "In fact, we have helped Muhammad Ali. Even Muhammad Ali's sparring partners made better use of their monies than Muhammad Ali, who did not follow the wise counsel of Messenger Muhammad in saving himself from waste and extravagance."

It would be the last reference to Muhammad Ali in the newspaper for almost three years. It is difficult to accurately gauge the Nation's motives in disassociating itself from its most celebrated member, but Elijah Muhammad's biographer Claude Clegg doesn't buy the Messenger's official explanation. "That Ali's stated desire to be financially rewarded for his boxing talents was suddenly offensive to Muhammad is not credible," writes Clegg. "For the past five years, the fighter had made his living in the sport. By 1969, Muhammad's tolerance of the exceptionality of Ali among his followers was simply no longer necessary. In the era of Black Power, the boxer was no longer an essential factor in the appeal of the Nation to young African Americans, and his ouster would not have a significant impact on membership. On another level, the suspension of Ali was reminiscent of the isolation of Malcolm X during 1964. It seemed to raise many of the same issues of authority, generational tensions, and jealousies. Arguably, the punishment was meant to be a reassertion of Muhammad's dominion over the Nation—a reminder to followers who had become a bit too enamored of Ali."

According to Jeremiah Shabazz, one of Ali's earliest spiritual advisers, the comment angered Muhammad, "because to him it was like Ali saying he'd give up his religion for the white man's money."

Eugene Dibble recalls his friend's reaction to the suspension. "He was shattered. The Muslims were his life. First he got his title taken away and they threatened to send him to prison but that was nothing compared to his suspension from the Nation. He acted like a little boy who had been spanked for being bad."

For years the Nation of Islam had controlled every facet of Ali's life. Suddenly, he was on his own. Elijah Muhammad had been like a father to him—so much so that he had virtually shunned his own father for more than five years. Now Cassius Clay Sr. re-entered his son's life and was shocked to discover his son's financial state. This only confirmed his longstanding suspicion of the Muslims, who he believed had stolen his son's money.

For his part, Ali was shaken by the suspension but believed it was just one more test by Allah. On the lecture circuit he continued to invoke the name of Elijah Muhammad and constantly praised his spiritual leader. He seemed to show genuine remorse for his words, but

continued to call himself Muhammad Ali despite the Messenger's prohibition.

"I made a fool of myself when I said that I'd return to boxing to pay
my bills," he told one student who asked about the suspension. "I'm
glad he awakened me. I'll take my punishment like a man and when
my year's suspension is over, I hope he'll accept me back."

Suddenly shorn of his Muslim entourage, Ali enlisted his old fight
publicist Harold Conrad to drum up some paying gigs. The ever-strug-
gling Ali had virtually disappeared from the national radar screen.
Before long, though, appearances on national TV shows such as *What's
My Line?* and *Merv Griffin* reminded Americans that Ali was still
around and still defiant.

Typically, his TV appearances were lighthearted. On the *Tonight*
Show, he unveiled a poem he had written that has been acknowledged
by the *Guinness Book of World's Records* as the shortest in history—
"Whee! Me!" But the famous conservative intellectual William F.
Buckley Jr., well known for his debating skills, was anxious to challenge
Ali's views on race and booked him on his weekly TV show for a more
serious discussion. In a memorable exchange that proved Ali could
hold his own against any opponent, in or out of the ring, Buckley fired
the first salvo: "You have said that the white man is your enemy. Well,
I happen to know this is not true. I believe you have been poisoned by
your leader."

Ali jumped right in. "How can you say Elijah Muhammad is poison-
ing us to believe the white people are our enemy? It's *you* who taught
us that you're our enemy. It was white people who bumped off Martin
Luther King, it was white people who bumped off Medgar Evers, it was
white people who bumped off Adam Clayton Powell. We didn't imagine this."

Buckley has rarely, if ever, publicly admitted being wrong. More
inconceivable still would be an admission that he was bested by a mere
athlete. But after the debate he told an interviewer, "I started out thinking he was simply special-pleading on his own behalf, but I ended up
thinking he was absolutely correct."

Two years earlier, at the height of the nation's hostility toward Ali,
Bertrand Russell had assured him, "The air will change, I sense it."
Now it finally seemed the philosopher's prophecy was coming true.

A number of high-profile media figures were beginning to register their own doubts about the war, including "the most trusted man in America," CBS anchor Walter Cronkite, who in 1968 said on the air, "The bloody experience of Vietnam is to end in stalemate." This prompted President Johnson to tell his advisers, "If I have lost Walter Cronkite, I have lost Mr. Average American Citizen."

Soon after Tet, a draft resister named Raymond Mungo told his draft board that the United States was the "greatest force for evil, the worst hater of mankind, unscrupulous murderer, alive today," charging that the country was on the verge of a civil war. Mungo compared America's leaders to Nazis and defiantly told the board, "I don't intend to play Jew for any of you."

On November 15, 1969, more than 250,000 protesters gathered in Washington, D.C., for the largest-ever anti-war demonstration. A month later, polls showed for the first time a majority of Americans disapproved of America's participation in the war. Richard Nixon had been elected president a year earlier on a platform vowing to bring U.S. troops home, and by the end of the year, the United States had begun to de-escalate.

For the increasing numbers of Americans who were turning against the war, Ali's stand no longer seemed treasonous; instead it was principled, even prophetic. For many, however, the issue was still hugely divisive. As boxing writer and long-time Ali supporter Budd Schulberg observed, "By this time, the name of Ali was a recognized shibboleth. He divided sheep from goats, peaceniks from gung-hoers, leftists and liberals from conservatives and reactionaries. Did Ali have the right to practice his brawny and brutal trade while his celebrated case was still being judged by higher and higher courts? If your answer was negative, we would know how you stood on a dozen front page issues, on the ABM and the SST [missiles], on the CIA, the FBI, and Kent State, on the Nixon doctrine and the law-and-order bills. Never before had there been a heavyweight champion who provided this kind of touchstone. Never before in this ideological sense had there been a champion of the world. Never before a champion fighting for millions of people in the United States against the government of the United States."

Perhaps the best illustration of the new attitude toward Ali came from his long time detractor, sportswriter Jimmy Cannon. In early

1970, Cannon seemed to capture the spirit of both the boxer and the era when he wrote, "The athlete of the decade has to be Cassius Clay, who is now Muhammad Ali. He is all that the sixties were. It is as though he were created to represent them. In him is the trouble and the wildness and the hysterical gladness and the nonsense and the rebellion and the conflicts of race and the yearning for bizarre religions and the cult of the put-on and the changed values that altered the world and the feeling about Vietnam in the generation that ridicules what their parents cherish. . . . The sixties were a bad time, but some of the years were wonderful. And, because I make my living writing sports, Cassius Clay is the sixties for me."

For the first time, it was relatively safe to defend Ali. Howard Cosell began to support the former champion loudly and publicly. But Robert Lipsyte, Jerry Izenberg and a handful of others had never stopped—even at the height of the boxer's vilification—and they were gratified to see the tide turning.

"At some point, you could sense a change in attitude toward Ali," recalls Izenberg. "I never stopped getting hate mail, so he was still very controversial, but now there was a sense that he had some support for his stand. I don't know how much of it had to do with America's changing attitude about the Vietnam War or whether people started to respect his principles. It was good to see but what I didn't like is that it seemed to start the canonization of Ali. As much as I like and respect Muhammad, he was no saint, believe me."

The unspoken implication of Izenberg, and many others who knew Ali well, was that—like his two fathers, Cassius Clay Sr. and Elijah Muhammad—the remarkably handsome and charismatic boxer was a notorious womanizer. While his wife Belinda cared for his new baby daughter, Maryum, back in Chicago, Ali spent more than half the year on the road, where the temptations were constant.

"The women would throw themselves at him wherever he went," says his friend Lloyd Wells, who frequently arranged trysts for Ali. "His only rule was that he wouldn't ever sleep with a white woman."

The revelation of Ali's womanizing stands him in sharp contrast with his former mentor Malcolm X, who abided so strictly to the Muslims' strict moral code that he felt utterly betrayed by Elijah Muhammad's adultery. What some have called Ali's hypocrisy was highlighted by his frequent lambasting of blacks who were not willing to "live a righteous life." In a 1966 profile, Jack Olsen of *Sports Illustrated* attempted to capture the enigma of the man he once described as a "symphony of paradoxes":

> Figuring out who or what is the *real* Cassius Clay is a parlor game that has not proved rewarding even for experts. Clay's personality is like a jigsaw puzzle whose pieces were cut by a drunken carpenter, a jumbled collection of moods and attitudes that do not seem to interlock. Sometimes he sounds like a religious lunatic, his voice singsong and chanting, and all at once he will turn into a calm, reasoning, if sometimes confused, student of the Scriptures. He is a loudmouthed windbag and at the same time a remarkably sincere and dedicated athlete. He can be a kindly benefactor of the neighborhood children and a vicious bully in the ring, a prissy Puritan, totally intolerant of drinkers and smokers, and a foul-mouthed teller of dirty jokes.

In early 1970, *Esquire* magazine—one of Ali's few media supporters—ran a cover story featuring more than one hundred prominent Americans who supported the former champion's reinstatement. Under the headline, WE BELIEVE THAT MUHAMMAD ALI, HEAVYWEIGHT CHAMPION OF THE WORLD, SHOULD BE ALLOWED TO DEFEND HIS TITLE, a virtual who's who of writers, artists, entertainers, and activists signed their names. Among the high-profile signatories were Norman Mailer, George Plimpton, Elizabeth Taylor, Richard Burton, Sammy Davis Jr., Truman Capote, Isaac Asimov, Marshall McLuhan, Kurt Vonnegut, Henry Fonda, Harry Belafonte, and Jim Morrison. Two surprise names on the list were Jackie Robinson and Joe Louis, who both had been critical of Ali's efforts to stay out of the army. The most ironic and controversial name on the roll was the director Elia Kazan, who had long been shunned by the liberal establishment for naming names and perpetuating the notorious Hollywood blacklist twenty years earlier.

According to one well-known American who was asked to lend his name to the *Esquire* story but refused, "I had this sense that Ali was just the latest liberal cause for these people. They were supporting him because it was fashionable, sort of like having a Black Panther at your cocktail party. I didn't want to be part of that."

America wasn't the only place where the tide was turning against the war and in support of Ali. In late 1969, *Time* reporter Wallace Terry traveled to Vietnam to conduct a follow-up to his 1967 survey of black soldiers. This time he found a radically different attitude than he had encountered two years earlier.

In 1967, blacks in Vietnam overwhelmingly condemned the anti-war stand of Muhammad Ali and Martin Luther King Jr. Now he found Ali—along with Malcolm X and Eldridge Cleaver—was a hero to the increasingly militant black soldiers, with an approval rating of 69 percent.

Terry also discovered that half the black soldiers were so bitter about their treatment that they would consider taking up arms against white society when they returned home. "When you come back to the States and the Man's going to say, 'Sorry, son, but I'm going to give you these rights, but you ain't ready for the rest of them yet after I put my life on the line. Uh-uh. The man who says that, I'm going to kill him. If I can't kill him, he's going to wish he were dead," Marine Sergeant Randolph Doby told Terry.

Some 45 percent of the soldiers Terry surveyed said they would likely have joined in the race riots that had recently swept the nation. "There's going to be more violence back in the world because we're going back," another black Marine told Terry. "Hell yes, I'd riot. If they're kicking crackers' asses, I'm going to get in and kick a few myself. I'm just doing what my grandfather wanted to do and couldn't."

Today, Terry believes the black community didn't have the luxury of following Ali's stand. "He was a rich athlete with a lot of resources to back up his convictions," he says, "but the average black person would have found himself in jail with no supporters if they had done what he did."

Terry believes the black community still hasn't recovered from the experience of Vietnam. "Look what happened when they returned, a lot of them ended up homeless, addicted to drugs, committed suicide. They had no support. The left considered them baby killers, the right believed they lost the war. It caused a lot of social unrest. That all stemmed from their experiences in Nam," he says. "I think white America has recovered but blacks are still feeling the impact."

▶ ▶ ▶

Coincidentally or not, Ali's financial fortunes improved dramatically following the Nation of Islam's disassociation from the exiled boxer. With Cassius Sr., Gene Dibble, and lawyer Chauncey Eskridge supervising Ali's business affairs, the two-year period of austerity quickly came to an end.

Ali signed on for two high-profile ventures, each designed to bring in about $10,000. The first committed him to participate in a laudatory documentary project called *A/K/A Cassius Clay*, in which he appeared in several scenes.

The second project, one Ali would always regret, involved a computer fight against former heavyweight boxing champion Rocky Marciano, who had retired from the ring thirteen years earlier. The two boxers filmed seventy-five staged one-minute rounds, each one with a different scenario. A variety of different endings were filmed. In one, Ali knocked out Marciano. In another, the former champion knocked out Ali. Another had Ali being stopped on cuts. The idea was that data on each boxer would be fed into a computer and the computer would

Ali signs autographs for sailors during his exile from boxing.

determine the winner. The resulting ending would be shown in theaters. In the end, however, it was political considerations, not the computer data, that would determine the outcome. In the version shown in the United States, where Ali had been vilified, Marciano emerged the victor, knocking out his opponent in the thirteenth round. But the version shown in Europe, where Ali was still popular, had Ali beating Marciano on cuts.

When the fictional American version showed the undefeated Ali getting a come uppance that no American had seen in real life, the *Philadelphia Inquirer* celebrated the outcome, informing Ali:

> The Computer knows who's who in the equation. Take you, a loud-mouth black racist who brags 'I'm the Greatest! I'm the King!' You won't submit to White America's old image of black fighters, you won't even submit to white America's Army. . . . Every self-respecting made-in-American knows how to add that up. They killed you off but can't get rid of the ghost you left behind. And there's not a white fighter around to chase it away. . . . They want your ass whipped in public, knocked down, ripped, stomped, clubbed, pulverized and not just by anybody, but by a real great white hope, and none's around. That's where the computer comes in.

Soon after, Ali's new advisers dropped Richard Fulton Inc. as his Speaker's agent and signed on with the American Program Bureau, headed by Robert Walker.

"Ali was afraid to fly," recalls Walker. "We promised him that we could get him a private jet to go from speech to speech. He loved that idea. He signed on and he was immediately our most popular speaker. He was in huge demand on the campuses. We were getting him $15,000 to $25,000 a speech, which was unheard of back then. It would be like the equivalent of $225,000 today. The Student Unions had a lot of money and they all wanted him." Under Richard Fulton—a contract negotiated by the Nation of Islam—he had only been receiving $1,500 to $2,000 a lecture.

Ali tells assembled crowd he has no looming fear of his prison sentence as he visits the set of the TV show Land of the Giants *in 1970.*

At the end of 1969, Ali was approached by a Broadway producer named Ron Rich about appearing in a "Black Power" musical called *Buck White* on Broadway. The money was right and Ali would have a new outlet for his theatrical instincts.

To everyone's surprise, the boxer-turned-actor could actually sing. Sporting an Afro wig and a beard, he took to the stage every night with a musical message very similar to the one he had been espousing in real life. In one number, he sang:

> *We came in chains, we didn't volunteer*
> *And yet, today, the fact remains*
> *We're still held captive here*
> *Now we say, cut us loose*
> *Though that may go against your grain*
> *Still, there is no excuse*
> *We came in chains, and now your choice must be*
> *To either blow out all our brains*
> *Or else just set us free*

Better now than later on,
Now that fear of death is gone,
Never mind another dawn.

Notwithstanding the fact that the *New York Times* had always been hostile to Ali's stand against the war, its theater critic Clive Barnes was impressed by the neophyte actor's talents. "How is Mr. Clay?" he wrote in the review. "He emerges as a modest naturally appealing man. He sings with a pleasant slightly impersonal voice, acts without embarrassment, and moves with innate dignity. He does himself proud." The rest of New York's demanding theater critics were equally kind to Ali's performance, if not to the play itself, which closed after only three weeks.

Meanwhile, Chauncey Eskridge had negotiated a deal that seemed destined to make the recently impoverished ex-boxer a rich man again without setting foot back into the ring. Ali lent his name and image to a chain of hamburger restaurants called "Champburger" in return for six-percent ownership in the company and one-percent of gross sales. When Champburger stock was issued in 1969, Ali received a check for $900,000.

The first thing he did with his windfall was to buy himself a gray Cadillac limousine at a cost of $10,000. For a man who cared little for material possessions, the purchase was symbolic of his battle against adversity, a way to tell the establishment they couldn't beat him, no matter how hard they tried.

He made this explicit one day when he arrived in Manhattan for a meeting at Random House, which had recently offered to publish his autobiography. As he pulled up at the publisher's midtown office, a small group of people recognized the ex-champ and gathered around his shiny new car.

"See my new limousine?" he asked them. "They think they can bring me to my knees by takin' away my title and by not letting me fight in this country, and by taking my passport so I can't get to the $3 million worth of fight contracts that are waiting for me overseas. Shoot! I ain't worked for two years and I ain't been Tommin' to nobody and here I'm buying limousines—the President of the United States ain't got no better one. Just look at it! Ain't it purty? Y'all go and tell everybody that Muhammad Ali ain't licked yet. I don't care if I never get another fight.

I say, damn the fights and damn all the money. A man's got to stand up for what he believes, and I'm standin' up for my people, even if I have to go to jail."

A week later, Random House gave him a $200,000 advance for the book that would appear five years later as *The Greatest*. Ali was once again a millionaire. This time he was determined that his funds would not be frittered away as they had the last time. During his two-year stint as an impoverished celebrity, he had dreamed about what he would do if he ever came into the kind of money he had before. Once again, however, his trusting nature proved his undoing.

"As soon as he was back on his feet again," laments Gene Dibble, "the vultures came right out of the woodwork. And Ali never seems to learn. He had all this money from the hamburger chain and he was starting to make big bucks on the lecture circuit. He wanted to use his money to help the poor blacks in the ghetto. He had been talking to people like Jim Brown and reading a lot about economic justice, helping blacks start their own businesses, stuff like that. He was very excited about it, he thought he was going to eliminate poverty. All these lawyers got involved helping him put together a foundation or something but in the end it was the same story. They ripped him off."

Ali was so passionate about his dream that in early 1970 he decided that he had no desire to ever box again. Instead, he would devote his life to his plan for black economic justice. In May, *Esquire* magazine—a long-time supporter of his anti-war stand—offered Ali its pages to outline his economic plan and explain what he would do if he were President of the United States. In a five-page treatise headlined I'M SORRY, BUT I'M THROUGH FIGHTING NOW, he announced that the only way he would go back into the ring would be to fight a series of exhibitions with the current heavyweight champion Joe Frazier to help relieve poverty.

"We can go to Jim Brown, Lew Alcindor, Arthur Ashe, and all the top black athletes, and all of us can go down to Mississippi and do something to help the poverty people," he wrote. "We'll take all this fame the white man gave to us because we fought for his entertainment, and we can turn it around. Instead of beating up each other, and playing ball games, and running miracles for the entertainment of white folks, we will use our fame for freedom. I want Joe Frazier to join me. I'm getting together a dope-addict program, rehabilitating addicts. And there are some black welfare women in Los Angeles who want my help because they don't have clothes for their children. They're trying to buy a shop where they can make their own clothes, but they can't get the money. All they've got is the seven dollars the government gives them to live on. Me and Joe could put on one boxing exhibition and get them more sewing machines than they could use in a life-time."

In response to the question of what he would do if he were President, he envisioned his State of the Union address to the American people: "Now, fellow Americans, we owe these black people for four hundred years of back labor," President Ali would announce. "They've done a lot for us. They died in the Japanese war, the German war, the Korean War, the Vietnam War. We're repaying them. I'm going to take this $25 billion I was gonna spend on helicopters in Vietnam, and it's going to Alabama and Georgia and Mississippi, and pay for $25 billion worth of houses, nice brick houses. Each black man who needs it is going to be given a home. Now, black people, we're just repaying you. We ain't giving you nothing. We're guilty. We owe it to you."

At the time, much critical attention was being given to the American government's policy of destroying huge quantities of food and paying farmers not to grow crops as a means of keeping agricultural commodity prices artificially high. President Ali reserved his harshest words to address this situation: "Now, after all the boys get back to America [from Vietnam], I'm going to tell you people that's been getting paid for not growing food that you'll get the electric chair if I catch you destroying any more food. We need that food. I'm gonna hire a bunch of people with all those billions we've been spending on the war. I'm going to pay them $300 a week to help their brothers. And I'm gonna say, 'General Motors, listen here. I want you to make 50,000 diesel trucks. I'm gonna fill those trucks up with canned goods and all the food that you people have been throwing away. We're gonna take it all down to the people of Mississippi and charge them nothing.'"

For the rest of his career, Ali would continue to speak out on and fight for economic justice, later extending his efforts to help poor whites as well. He also repeatedly challenged other successful black celebrities to help revitalize the ghettoes. But this side of Ali's personality and character, perhaps the most serious and important, was consistently ignored by the media or denigrated as "naive."

Once, after witnessing one of Ali's anti-poverty speeches, which were traditionally relegated to a paragraph on the sports pages if they were written about at all, celebrated American author Roger Kahn complained, "Christ, I thought, here is someone who wants to give away a fortune. Here is a man who cannot read without the most painful pauses between words making a stirring and even profound speech. Here is a black millionaire, socialist, populist and revivalist and most of all idealist. Yes mostly that. Idealist. And in a society that forever confuses value and net worth, this aging, baby-faced champion, this dreamer finely tuned to reality, throws out a mighty blow with his checkbook. What do the papers report? Ali to concentrate on body blows [in his next bout]."

Jerry Izenberg was also intrigued by Ali's burgeoning economic philosophy. "He told me something very interesting around this time," recalls the sports columnist. "He told me that his boxing career was only a tool. He said, 'Fighting hunger, fighting illiteracy, these are the things I really want to do. That's what my boxing fame made possible.'"

▶ ▶ ▶

Ali may have been publicly announcing his intention never to box again professionally, but his friends had other ideas. They sensed that the political and social climate had changed sufficiently since 1967 and that America was ready to accept the exiled fighter back in the ring.

Fight publicist Harold Conrad especially believed he could arrange a comeback. As far back as 1968, he had put out feelers, approaching twenty-eight different states about granting Ali a license, only to be turned down each time. He came closest to success in California, where the chairperson of the state athletic commission polled its members and discovered they had enough votes to let Ali fight. Before the decision was announced, however, California Governor Ronald Reagan got wind of the impending fight and declared, "That draft dodger will never fight in my state, period."

Chicago Tribune sports editor Arch Ward's description of Ali as the "unpopular, undefeated, heavyweight monster-in-exile" seemed to capture the mood as Conrad persisted in his quest. One of the most ironic rejections he suffered during this period came from Nevada. The governor believed an Ali fight would be good for tourism and was ready to sanction the Las Vegas bout. At the time, however, the Chief Executive didn't pull that much weight. Instead, the desert state was controlled by two forces: the mob and right-wing billionaire Howard Hughes. The former had no problem with the fight. Not so Hughes. He had strong political connections with Richard Nixon and let it be known that he strongly disapproved of Ali's politics and would not tolerate the boxer's presence in Las Vegas—the American capital of gambling, prostitution, and vice. Once again, Conrad was rebuffed. When Ali was informed of the decision, he seemed genuinely puzzled. "Me corrupt Las Vegas?" he asked with a bemused grin.

Meanwhile, on the legal front, the United States Court of Appeals had rejected Ali's appeal of the wiretap ruling, leaving him only one chance to stay out of prison, the U.S. Supreme Court, which had once before refused to hear his case. A decision was not expected until early 1971, giving the boxer at least one more year of freedom.

Conrad's next stop was an unlikely setting—Mississippi, America's most racist state, where there was no love lost for Ali, at least among the governing elite. Still, after two weeks of negotiations, the intrepid promoter had an agreement with the state's governor and the mayor of Jackson along with a bona fide boxing license. In return, Ali had to pledge to donate the entire gate receipts of the fight to the Salvation Army.

The long exile appeared to be finally over. But when the citizens of the state and, in particular, the American Legion got wind of the deal, the political firestorm was too much for the politicians to bear. Despite the fact that his signature appeared on the license already in Conrad's possession, the governor promptly denied its existence.

A similar deal came close to being struck in Michigan before the governor there also pulled a hasty about-face after public opposition once again made the fight politically unpalatable. The *Detroit Free Press* described the atmosphere that continued to thwart Conrad's efforts. "Approving a fight for Clay would appear to the public to be approving of his way of life," the paper editorialized, "and this includes draft evasion. This is a difficult thing for anyone to do, especially a public figure . . . the public sentiment against him seems to be so strong that no one wants to take the responsibility for sanctioning a fight against him."

But Ali was never convinced public opposition was really behind the repeated attempts to deprive him of his livelihood. When Conrad informed him of his latest setback, blaming public opinion for his troubles, Ali cut him off.

"It's not the public," he protested. "It's never been the public, not the mainstream of the people. I travel all the time. Wherever I go, whether the Deep South like Alabama or Louisiana, or from Maine to California, since the day I left the draft board, people white, black, Protestant, Catholic, Jewish, welcome me, crowd around me, tell me they're with me. They tell me how ashamed they are about what's happening to me. . . . It's not the public, it's political, from somewhere big."

Ali was only partially right in this assessment. Despite growing support for the exiled fighter throughout the country, millions of Americans still reviled him. But, as he sensed, there also seemed to be powerful political forces behind the continuing rejections.

In May 1970, Conrad appeared to have finally found a city to host his fight. Charleston, South Carolina, had approved a charity boxing exhibition involving Ali and a fighter to be named later. The contracts had been signed and it looked inevitable that Ali would finally get his chance to step into a ring. Suddenly, however, the Charleston city council announced the fight was off. It seemed that the mayor had received a phone call from longtime Ali detractor and South Carolina Congressman L. Mendel Rivers, who headed the powerful House Arms Appropriation Committee. "You're making me the laughing stock of Washington by letting that draft-dodging black sonofabitch fight in my hometown," Rivers complained. The fight was off.

If America didn't want the fight, however, plenty of other places were all too happy to host Ali's comeback. Tijuana, Mexico, only minutes away from the American border, offered its bullring for a match. Ali would have only been required to leave the United States for two hours. The State Department refused to grant permission.

Toronto, Canada, made a similar offer. This time, Chauncey Eskridge petitioned the Supreme Court for approval. He offered to put up a $100,000 cash bond. Ali would travel by car, which the Justice Department could staff with as many U.S. marshals as it deemed necessary to assure the boxer's return. Seventy percent of the total one-million-dollar purse would be put in escrow. In his petition, Eskridge pointed out that Ali had never failed to make an appearance in federal court since he was indicted three years earlier. Justice Hugo Black was unimpressed and turned down the petition. These rejections were particularly suspicious because there was ample precedent of Americans being given permission to leave the country while their sentences were being appealed. Only the year before, radical activist Abbie Hoffman was allowed to travel to communist Cuba for twenty-six days while his own five-year sentence for inciting a riot at the 1968 Democratic National Convention was being appealed. Once again, it appeared that Muhammad Ali, whose only previous offense was a traffic violation, was being singled out for special treatment.

Just when it appeared that any further attempts to secure a license were futile, Ali received a call from Georgia State Senator Leroy Johnson, the first black to be elected to the state senate in the South since Reconstruction. Johnson let it be known that he was in a position to arrange an Ali-Frazier title bout in Atlanta if the right strings were pulled. Georgia was one of the few American states without a state licensing commission. A year before, when Conrad had secured an agreement with the city of Macon, Georgia, to stage an Ali bout, it had been vetoed by the state's conservative firebrand governor Lester Maddox On that occasion, Maddox vowed, "I'll give Clay a license after he serves his term in the Army, or his term in jail. Then maybe I'll think of allowing him in Georgia."

But Johnson was insistent that he had the clout to arrange the Atlanta match. The senator was indeed influential. He had recently delivered the votes that enabled a liberal Jew named Sam Massell to win the Atlanta mayoral race. Massell's support would be crucial to securing the fight and Johnson could assure it. For years, Leroy Johnson trumpeted his role in arranging the fight as altruistic. But Harold Conrad would later reveal that Johnson insisted on being cut in for a piece of the action.

When the idea of an Atlanta match was first floated, memories of the Macon rejection still lingered. *Chicago Sun-Times* columnist John Carmichael poured water on the prospect, writing, "I advise Muhammad Ali to call it quits. He is an outcast, a fistic pariah. Maddox, will never let him fight in Georgia."

But Carmichael and the other doubters underestimated Johnson's clout. His ability to control the state's black vote intimidated even Maddox, and the governor surprised everyone when he took to the airwaves and announced his approval for the fight. "There has been a lot of controversy about this fellow Clay. When he rejected the draft, I'm sure it hurt him. He's paying for it. We're all entitled to our mistakes. This is the way I see it. I see nothing wrong with him fighting here."

The governor's approval took everybody off guard, from the state's large racist population to Ali's detractors in Washington, who believed Maddox had betrayed patriotic Americans. Within days, the governor was inundated with hate mail from his constituents and phone calls from members of Congress demanding he reverse his decision. Reports out of the Georgia Statehouse had Maddox fielding a call from the U.S. Justice Department exerting pressure on the governor to stop the fight by any means at his disposal.

Meanwhile, Joe Frazier—the reigning heavyweight champion and pretender to Ali's old throne—announced he would not fight Ali in Atlanta. Instead, promoters enlisted a leading white contender, Jerry Quarry—a genuine "Great White Hope." It was to be the first time Ali would fight a white opponent since 1962. The prospect of a white boxer silencing the uppity Negro added significantly to the anticipated fight revenues.

The pressure being exerted on Maddox finally became too much for him to resist. Two weeks before the scheduled bout, the Governor's office issued a statement announcing that Maddox "urges all Atlantans to boycott the fight of Clay and Quarry. He further urges all patriotic groups in the city to let promoters know how they feel about it. We shouldn't let him fight for money if he didn't fight for his country."

Jerry Izenberg was in Atlanta to cover the fight.

"Maddox was feeling a lot of heat," he recalls. "One moment he was supporting the fight, the next he was trying to stop it. The pressure was coming from pretty high up. We didn't know if the fight was going to actually take place. I remember I was in his office when he declared the day of the fight to be an official 'Day of Mourning.' It was a bit much."

With the license issued, it seemed to be too late to stop the fight. What Maddox didn't know was that Atlanta still had an old ordinance on its books that would have made the Ali-Quarry fight illegal. Section

28 of the *Rules and Regulations Governing all Boxing Contests in the City of Atlanta* stated, "No mixed bouts shall be permitted between white and black contestants in the city of Atlanta and said rules shall be binding and made a part of the agreement of all matchmakers and promoters."

When Leroy Johnson learned of the obscure regulation, which dated back to the post-Civil War period, he quickly moved to get the city council to delete it before Maddox got wind of the loophole and declared the license null and void.

The fight was on, scheduled for October 26, 1970. But in Georgia, and across the nation, news of Ali's return to the ring sparked intense and divisive emotions. The night before he was scheduled to leave for Atlanta, Ali received a gift-wrapped package, which was opened by his sparring partner. Inside the box was a black chihuahua with a severed head. A message accompanying the package read, "We know how to handle black draft-dodging dogs in Georgia. Stay out of Atlanta." It was signed with a small Confederate flag.

While he was staying at the cabin of Leroy Johnson a few days later, Ali was woken by gunshots ringing out of the Georgia night. Moments later, the phone rang. "Nigger, if you don't leave Atlanta tomorrow, you gonna die. You Viet Cong bastard! You draft-dodging bastard! We won't miss you the next time!"

On the day of the fight, the anticipation was boiling over. The implications of the upcoming match were not lost on the array of black celebrities—including Bill Cosby, Sidney Poitier, Harry Belafonte, and Julian Bond—who flooded Atlanta, the birthplace of Martin Luther King Jr., to see the black knight begin the long march back to reclaim his throne.

"If he loses tonight," declared Jesse Jackson, who had been one of King's top lieutenants, "it will mean, symbolically, that the forces of blind patriotism are right, that dissent is wrong; that protest means you don't love the country, this fight is Love-it-or-leave-it vs. Love-it-and-change-it. They tried to railroad him. They refused to accept his testimony about his religious convictions. They took away his right to practice his profession. They tried to break him in body and in mind. Martin Luther King used to say, 'Truth crushed to the earth will rise again.' That's the black ethos. And it's happening here in Georgia of all places, against a white man!"

Ali understood more than anybody the burden he carried. "I'm not just fighting one man," he said before the fight. "I'm fighting a lot of men, showing them here is one man they couldn't conquer. Lose this one, and it won't be just a loss to me. So many millions of faces throughout the world will be sad. They'll feel like they've been defeated. If I lose, for the rest of my life I won't be free. I'll have to listen to all this about how I was a bum, how I joined the wrong movement and they mislead me. I'm fighting for my freedom."

On the morning of the bout, Ali ran into Joe Louis, who was hired to participate in the pre-fight promotion.

"Who are you picking, Joe?" he asked his boyhood idol.

"Why?" responded the legendary boxer, aware he was being taunted.

"Because if you're picking me, I'm scared to death. Everybody you pick is a loser. When I fought Liston the first time, you picked Liston' When I fought Liston the second time, you picked Liston; When I fought Patterson, you picked Patterson. When I fought Chuval Terrell, Cleveland Williams, Bonavena, you picked them."

"Well," said Louis, "if we go by that, Quarry's the next champion because I'm picking you."

That afternoon Coretta Scott King, widow of the slain civil rights leader, presented Ali with the first Martin Luther King Memorial Award for his contribution to the "cause of human dignity," proclaiming that the boxer was carrying on her husband's legacy as "a champion of justice and peace."

As Ali entered the ring for the fight, cheered on by the 90 percent black crowd, his corner man Bundini Brown yelled out, "Ghost in the house, ghost in the house." The ghost he was referring to was Jack Johnson, who had emerged from his own exile to fight a white boxer sixty years earlier. For the last few days, Ali had been watching old Jack Johnson fight films to inspire him for the Quarry fight. Later he would say, "I grew to love the Jack Johnson image. I wanted to be rough, tough, arrogant, the nigger the white folks didn't like."

It had been forty-three months since Ali last set foot in a ring, what his trainer Angelo Dundee refers to as the "lost years," when the exiled champion would have been at his peak as a fighter and which he could never win back. Still, it took him only three rounds to dispose of Quarry and lay to rest any lingering doubts as to whether he was still a force to be reckoned with after such a prolonged absence. He was a little slower, his timing wasn't what it once was, but he still had it.

▶ ▶ ▶

Beyond its symbolic importance, the Quarry victory was actually quite meaningless. The only fight that counted was against Joe Frazier, to determine who had the right to call himself the true heavyweight champion. Before that could happen, however, Ali would have to win another battle—against the New York State Athletic Commission to get back the license they had stripped from him three years earlier.

Before going the legal route, Ali had tried another tactic to gain back his New York license. In 1969, he appealed for help to Jackie Robinson, who had supported Republican New York Governor Nelson Rockefeller in his election bid. Rockefeller had only to say the word and Ali would be given his license back by the politically appointed athletic commission. But Robinson told the boxer it was no use asking Rockefeller. He was too close to Richard Nixon and, according to the aging baseball great, Cassius Clay was "Nixon's pet peeve."

In 1967, shortly after the commission's arbitrary decision to revoke his license, Ali's legal team had been approached by Michael Meltsner, a lawyer from the NAACP Legal Defense Fund. The Fund—which was actually a separate entity from the NAACP—specialized in civil rights litigation dating back to the historic *Brown vs. Board of Education* decision in 1954. Meltsner believed he could employ a strategy to win back Ali's license under a provision of the law called Civil Disabilities, which seeks to remedy the indirect consequences of a criminal conviction— in this case the withdrawal of a boxing license. At the time, Meltsner was rebuffed by Ali's original lawyer, Hayden Covington Jr., who wasn't interested.

Two years later, the legal team—now minus Covington—reconsidered. Chauncey Eskridge contacted Meltsner and gave him the go-ahead to pursue his strategy. In 1969, the Fund brought a case against the New York State Athletic Commission, claiming that Ali's Constitutional rights had been violated by the denial of his ring license. Among the many arguments in the initial motion was what appeared at the time to be a minor point—that other criminals had received licenses in the past. In late 1969, a District Court judge ruled against Ali but didn't dismiss the case out of hand, suggesting he was willing to hear further evidence on the history of licenses being granted to criminals.

"I grew up in New York City listening to the Friday night fights," explains Meltsner almost thirty years later. "My father was an intense sports fan and if you followed boxing, you knew that just about every famous boxer had spent time in jail. It almost seemed that being a felon was a requirement for being a champion. So when the Athletic Commission tried to argue that they took away Ali's license to keep boxing safe from felons, it was absurd. The case was obviously political."

Meltsner assigned a young Defense Fund lawyer named Ann Wagner to comb the records of the New York State Athletic Commission to confirm his suspicions.

"Ann was an extremely dedicated young attorney who had worked as a clerk and was quite familiar with legal files and documentation," says Meltsner. "She spent months searching through the records and it paid off. She struck pay dirt."

What Wagner found shocked Ali's legal team. In the course of her research, she discovered 225 convicted felons who had been granted boxing licenses by the commission in the past. Of these, ninety had committed murder, armed robbery, sodomy, or rape. And, since Ali had been charged with a military offense, Wagner produced fifteen cases of men convicted of military crimes, such as desertion or assaulting an officer, who had also been granted licenses.

When Meltsner presented a list of these offenders, Judge Walter Mansfield could barely contain his anger and immediately ruled in Ali's favor, saying he was "astounded" by what he had heard.

"The action of the Commission in denying Ali a license because of his refusal to serve in the armed forces, while granting licenses to hundreds of other applicants convicted of other crimes and military offenses involving moral turpitude appears on its face to be an intentional, arbitrary, and unreasonable discrimination against plaintiff, not the even-handed administration of the law which the Fourteenth Amendment requires," the judge said.

The commission's lawyers attempted to differentiate Ali's case from the hundreds of examples cited by Meltsner, arguing that, unlike the list of convicted felons, Ali had not yet served his time. Mansfield was in no mood to hear this nonsense, declaring, "Defendants have offered no evidence tending to refute or rebut the overwhelming and undisputed proof of arbitrary, capricious, and unfounded discrimination furnished by plaintiff."

His license restored, Ali only had one comment. "Bring on Frazier."

▶ ▶ ▶

The hype leading up to the Ali-Frazier fight took on a life of its own. The drama of the occasion spoke for itself. Two legitimate champions would decide once and for all who had a genuine right to wear the crown.

The fight was being billed as the "Patriot vs. the Draft Dodger," which infuriated Ali, who seemed to take his anger out on the soft-spoken Frazier, by all accounts a decent guy.

In the weeks leading up to the fight, Ali engaged in his usual psychological baiting—but this time with a slightly sadistic edge, repeatedly calling Frazier an "Uncle Tom" and equating him with the white establishment that desperately wanted to see Ali beaten. "Frazier's no real champion," he taunted. "Nobody wants to talk to him. Oh, maybe Nixon will call him if he wins. I don't think he'll call me. But ninety-eight percent of my people are for me. They identify with my struggle. Same one they're fighting every day in the streets. If I win, they win. If I lose, they lose."

In a boorish moment which angered even his black supporters, Ali called his opponent "gorilla"—a taunt which Frazier has never forgiven.

In what was becoming a tradition, Joe Louis turned up in Frazier's camp, as he did with all Ali's opponents, hoping his nemesis would finally get what he deserved.

Ali wanted to donate closed-circuit proceeds of the fight to help ghetto children, but Frazier's camp rejected the idea, fuelling Ali's accusations even further.

Television personality Bryant Gumbel would later describe the emotions he felt as a young black teenager anticipating the first Ali-Frazier fight: "If Ali lost, it was as though everything I believed in was wrong . . . . He was a heroic figure, plain and simple. In every sense of the word, he was heroic. So what you had that night were two undefeated heavyweight champions. One was the very symbol of black pride, parading black feelings about black heritage, speaking out against racial injustice. And the other guy was more like your parents were. He just kind of went along. He did his job. He wasn't a proponent of the old order, but he didn't fight it either. One guy was dead set against the war, the other didn't seem to have much feeling about it, but was supported by those who backed the war. We'd all seen those pictures of the people with flags and hard hats beating up kids with long hair who were protesting, and this was our chance to get even in the ring. Our side was right, and their side thought it was right, and whoever won the fight, damn it, that's how it was. There was no middle ground."

The fight itself was one of the most epic battles ever fought in the squared circle. Ali had anticipated the scene with one of his typical poems:

> Joe's gonna come out smokin'
> But I ain't gonna be jokin'
> I'll be pickin' and pokin'
> Pouring water on his smokin'
> This might shock and amaze ya
> But I'm gonna destroy Joe Frazier

The crowd made it clear from the start who they were supporting. "It was like good vs. evil," recalls Jerry Izenberg. "I think they wanted Frazier to kill him."

For the first time in his professional career, Ali seemed to have met his match. Each boxer absorbed devastating punishment throughout the fight. Ali had rarely if ever been really hit by an opponent before. As voices from the crowd—reminiscent of the Liston fight—cried, "Pound that nigger, Joe!" Frazier proved his fighting abilities, taking whatever Ali delivered and returning a brutal volley of blows. In the eleventh round the momentum clearly went to Frazier, who stunned Ali with the hardest punch he had ever received, a left hook that sent him reeling. Still, Ali survived and proved why he had been undefeated for more than seven years. He recovered from the setback and summoned a few crushing blows of his own, taking the fight to Frazier until the final round, when the younger boxer once again sent a left hook against Ali's jaw, knocking him on his back for the first time in his professional career. To the amazement of the onlookers, however, Ali sprung right back up to his feet and held his own until the final bell.

The fight was so close that nobody in Madison Square Garden that night knew who won until the decision of the judges was announced. When the referee held Frazier's arm up, signaling his victory, tears ran down the cheeks of many blacks in the crowd and millions more throughout the country. Cornell University's black student leader Donald Reeves later summed up his feelings in the *New York Times*, writing, "When Ali tasted defeat for the first time, I was crushed. Few things have so destroyed my spirits as to see Ali lose. I had so much of myself in Ali that I think he took his defeat better than I did."

In the White House, Richard Nixon was ecstatic, jumping up and down and celebrating the defeat of "that draft dodger asshole," according to his chief of staff. His joy echoed the feelings of a large segment of the population who had finally seen the uppity Ali put in his place.

Ali was gracious in defeat, congratulating Frazier and calling him a "fine champion." To his friends, he couldn't help but voice his opinion that he thought he had won. This may have been more than sour grapes. In the *New York Times*, veteran sportswriter Robert Lipsyte voiced the first suspicion that the ring officials were at least subconsciously biased by the conviction that a Frazier victory would be good for boxing and for America. Judging a boxing match involves a great deal of subjectivity, so there may be something to Lipsyte's charge.

Certainly, anybody who saw the two boxers after the fight couldn't have guessed the victor. Ali's face was unblemished. He went to the hospital for an Xray, which turned up nothing serious, and left an hour later. In contrast, Frazier's face was grotesquely swollen, and he ended up spending three weeks in the hospital recovering.

Longtime boxing writer Larry Merchant covered the fight and, like Lipsyte, believes the judges may have been biased. "In any boxing match, there is what is known as the house fighter, the favorite," he explains. "Sometimes being the house fighter can help you win one or two close rounds. There is no question Frazier was the house fighter that night. I was scoring the fight myself and I'm one of the few writers who actually had Ali ahead. I had no problem with the decision of the judges, it was certainly close, but I thought Ali had won."

When Ali fought a rematch against Frazier three years later, Merchant—who now covers boxing for HBO—was still uneasy about the result of the first fight: "Just before the rematch, I decided to screen the film of the first fight with a friend of mine, another boxing writer. Originally, at Madison Square Garden, I had Ali beating Frazier but my friend thought Frazier had won. So we decided it would be interesting to sit there and score the fight again round by round, punch by punch. Well, the results were telling. After we screened the fight, I came away convinced more than ever that Ali was robbed and my friend changed his mind completely and also thought Ali had won. I know, people will say you can't score a fight that way, and I'd normally be the first to agree. But this was quite blatant. In one round, I think Ali landed nineteen punches, many of them solid, to Frazier's three, and one of the judges scored it a draw. Come on. How unfair can you get? In the original scoring, the referee only had Frazier winning eight-six with one draw. That means Ali would have only had to win one more round for the fight to be a draw. Some of those rounds were damn close, nobody can tell me with any credibility that Frazier won the fight hands down. The eleventh round, maybe, but let's get serious."

While his supporters and detractors continued to debate who won the Frazier bout, Muhammad Ali knew that his most important fight still lay ahead—and it would not be decided in a ring.

CHAPTER TEN:
Vindication

WHEN THE CASE OF *Cassius Marsellus Clay vs. the United States of America* came before the Supreme Court in January 1971, little had happened to change the minds of the justices since they first voted not to hear it almost two years earlier. At that time, only the last-minute revelation of illegal government eavesdropping had prevented the Court from announcing its decision, allowing Ali's conviction to stand and sending him to prison.

But even if each justice had already made up his mind in March 1969 and not changed it since, Justice William Brennan was conscious of the country's changing social climate, especially on racial issues. He believed it was important to at least give the high-profile appellant a hearing so that justice would be seen to be done.

There was also a new precedent to consider. During the interim, the Court had decided another conscientious objector case that might have a bearing on the Ali appeal. In the 1970 decision *Welsh vs. United States,* the Court had ruled in favor of a young man named Elliot Welsh who refused to serve in Vietnam because of his deeply held *moral* opposition to war. Previously, a conscientious objector was required to object on religious grounds and hold a belief in a Supreme Being. In the *Welsh* decision, Justice Hugo Black wrote:

> What is necessary for . . . conscientious objection to
> all war is that this opposition to war stem from . . . his
> moral, ethical or religious beliefs about what is right
> or wrong and that these beliefs be held with the
> strength of traditional religious convictions . . . .

To most of the justices, the *Welsh* decision seemed irrelevant to Ali's case, because it required a moral objection to *all* wars and each justice believed that Ali's objection was limited to selective wars. Nevertheless, Brennan convinced his reluctant colleagues to grant cert (approval to hear the case) on the basis of *Welsh*. None of them, including Brennan, expected Ali to prevail.

"Cert would never have been granted if the petitioner was not Muhammad Ali," reveals Thomas Krattenmaker, who at the time was a clerk for Justice John Harlan. "It was a very high profile case so they agreed to hear it. Nobody believed he'd win."

Jonathan Shapiro had recently joined the NAACP Legal Defense Fund in New York after two years trying civil rights cases in Mississippi. The Fund, which was already involved in the case to restore Ali's boxing license, had been asked by Chauncey Eskridge to join the appeal of the boxer's conviction. Shapiro had unsuccessfully argued the wiretap ruling in the Federal Court of Appeals a year earlier and was convinced that it was this issue that might reverse Ali's conviction before the Supreme Court.

"I thought our wiretap argument was the strongest chance of a reversal," recalls Shapiro, who today practices law in Boston. "In the original hearing, the judge refused on the grounds of national security to let Ali hear one of the conversations, which supposedly took place with an official of a foreign government. I thought that clearly violated his Constitutional right to be confronted with the evidence against him. In my petition to the Supreme Court, this is what I argued. I thought they would grant us cert on that issue. Just in case, though, I threw in some other arguments including the denial of his conscientious objector claim. I was very surprised when that was the issue they decided to hear."

The nine men who would decide Ali's fate on the Supreme Court— arguably the most powerful body in the country—were also the most unpredictable. When Richard Nixon was elected three years earlier, his first order of business was to tilt the previously liberal Court to the right. Using a series of his infamous dirty tricks and targeted appointments, he did just that. But as many presidents had already learned to their dismay, justices become notoriously independent as soon as they donned their robes, and it was often impossible to peg how one would vote on many issues.

Nevertheless, Nixon's choice for Chief Justice, Warren Burger, had so far proven himself very loyal to Republican ideology, siding with the Administration on many key issues. Although the justices were supposed to decide cases according to the Constitution, interpreting the intentions of the founding fathers, their own political views could often be counted upon to sway their judgment.

Burger had a clear ideological agenda, believing he had a mission to undo many of the groundbreaking decisions ushered in by his predecessor, the liberal Earl Warren. Burger's own power lay in his ability to choose who would author the legal opinions of the majority. These opinions contained the Court's legal and Constitutional justification for particular Court decisions and were often more important than the decisions themself, influencing the entire federal judiciary in future legal decisions.

According to Bob Woodward and Scott Armstrong's groundbreaking 1979 exposé of the Supreme Court, *The Brethren*, Burger sized up his ideological enemies on the Court and made sure to keep important decisions away from them, particularly cases involving criminal law, racial discrimination, and free speech. The Ali case would involve all three of these areas. Tops on the Chief Justice's list of enemies were William Douglas and Thurgood Marshall.

Douglas had been appointed by Franklin Roosevelt in 1939 and was among the most liberal members of the Court, vowing to act as a vanguard against Burger's conservative agenda. On the surface, Douglas should have been among the most prominent defenders of Ali's right to conscientious objection. But, ideology aside, these issues were never cut and dried.

For more than five years, Douglas had been lobbying for the Court to hear a case on the constitutionality of the Vietnam War. He believed that, unlike America's previous wars, Vietnam was a war of aggression.

But he had considerable difficulty in getting his colleagues to intervene. They had their chance in 1967 in a case involving the constitutionality of the Tonkin Resolution, but Douglas could never find enough votes to grant cert (four votes are needed on the Court to decide whether to hear a case). His only ally was Potter Stewart, who had been appointed by the Republican President Dwight Eisenhower in 1958.

The most surprising holdout on these war-related cases was Justice Hugo Black, another Roosevelt appointee. Black had opposed American intervention in World War II right until the bombing of Pearl Harbor. He was always against the Korean War and had opposed Vietnam from the beginning, lamenting to his colleagues "A waste, a mistake. We're going to pay a high price for that. Big heroics today; wait until the death lists come in."

But Black firmly believed that these decisions were not the domain of the Court: they should be decided by Congress. The Court, he believed—along with many others—should not be involved in matters of war powers, national security, or foreign policy.

Among the other traditional liberals on the Court, Thurgood Marshall and Byron White could not be counted on to oppose the war. White was appointed by John F. Kennedy, the man who plunged the country into Vietnam in the first place. The Justice was fiercely loyal to his mentor's policies.

Marshall might not have been expected to share the same loyalties towards the president who appointed him, Lyndon B. Johnson. Marshall, the first black justice in the history of the Court, was a pioneer civil rights activist in the battle against segregation. In 1965, when Johnson appointed a reluctant Marshall as the United States Solicitor General, the president appealed to the legendary lawyer by arguing, "I want folks to walk down the hall at the Justice Department and look in the door and see a nigger standing there." Despite L.B.J's racial insensitivity, however, he proved himself to be a committed champion of civil rights legislation. When Johnson eventually appointed Marshall to the Supreme Court in 1967, the new justice demonstrated a fierce loyalty to the president's agenda and made no secret of the fact that he supported the war. However, Marshall had been Solicitor General when Ali was originally convicted, so he was forced to recuse himself from the case.

The final moderate was William Brennan, another Eisenhower

appointee who turned out to be a committed liberal on many issues. Brennan was morally opposed to the Vietnam War but didn't believe the Court could take up a "political" question like the war unless Congress opposed it and the president continued to conduct it. He needed such a conditional excuse to justify the Court's involvement.

Among the conservative majority, Burger's chief allies on most issues were his fellow Nixon appointee Harry Blackmun, Eisenhower appointees Potter Stewart and John Harlan; and, surprisingly, the Kennedy appointee Byron "Whizzer" White, a former NFL football star whose views were becoming increasingly conservative over the years.

The justices were a disparate lot. Their ideology or political connections were often less important than a wide range of other factors. Nowhere was this more evident than in the bizarre weekly ritual called "movie day." Every Friday afternoon the justices would convene in a basement storeroom and watch dirty movies. This practice went back to an old court ruling that material couldn't be considered obscene if it has "redeeming social importance." Since this term was so vague and subjective, it was left up to the Supreme Court to decide on a case-by-case basis. As Justice Stewart once said when asked what constitutes obscenity, "I know it when I see it."

On Friday afternoons, the clerks and justices would screen exhibits in obscenity cases involving banned films, creating a comical spectacle. Many of the clerks, and an occasional justice, would complain bitterly if the films didn't contain enough hardcore material for their tastes. Justices Black and Douglas refused to attend these screenings, arguing that nothing should ever be banned. But the rest of the justices often relied on their own prudish instincts and morality to decide what was obscene rather than any legal basis. Dirty movies aside, the powerful judicial body was a force to be reckoned with and had a major influence on American political and social landscape.

On April 19, 1971, the Court turned to weightier matters as the Ali case finally reached its chambers.

Chauncey Eskridge, representing Ali, began arguing the case of *Cassius Clay vs. the United States of America* before the eight justices. Representing the government was the U.S. Solicitor General Erwin Griswold. Earlier that week, Lieutenant William Calley had been convicted at his military court martial of ordering the brutal massacre of more than three hundred Vietnamese civilians three years earlier. Calley was given a life sentence.

In Congress, Representative James Mann of South Carolina argued that he could not understand the justice in Calley's conviction while "Muhammad Ali still walks the streets of America, a couple of million dollars richer by virtue of his failure to serve."

A poll conducted for Richard Nixon the same week revealed that, despite the rapidly changing social climate, America still had a long way to go in its attitude about the war. Only 7 percent of Americans agreed that Calley should have been convicted while a full 78 percent registered their disagreement with the verdict.

Similar attitudes seemed to be reflected on the bench of the highest court of the land. While Eskridge pleaded his case before the justices, his arguments were met with considerable skepticism, even hostility.

Solicitor General Erwin Griswold, arguing the case for the government, noted that Ali had left little doubt that "if the Vietcong were attacking his people, the Muslims would become involved in that war." Griswold cast doubt on the boxer's selective objection to war, saying, "The petitioner just doesn't want to fight the white man's war, and I can understand that. But that's not the same as being a pacifist."

Ali, he said, had been quoted in newspaper accounts saying, "I am a member of the Muslims and we don't go to war unless they are declared by Allah himself. I don't have no personal quarrel with those Vietcongs." Since Ali would participate in a Holy War, Griswold argued, he was not a true conscientious objector. The justices appeared responsive to this argument to the extent that under questioning by the court, the Solicitor General felt confident enough to concede that Ali had been sincere in his beliefs, which were religiously based. This concession would be crucial later on.

Arguing for Ali, Eskridge noted a 1955 Supreme Court ruling that Jehovah's Witnesses could be classified as conscientious objectors even though they expected to participate in warfare at the time of Armageddon. He compared this to references about warfare in Black Muslim literature. In both cases, he argued, the references are quite "hypothetical." Eskridge also made sure to differentiate the Nation of Islam from traditional Islam, assuring the Court that Black Muslims would not take part in a war involving Moslem countries.

"Chauncey didn't have a lot of trial experience," recalls Shapiro, "but we thought that it was better the case was argued by a black man than by myself, a liberal New York Jew. After he was finished, it was obvious that it hadn't gone well. I was very pessimistic. I was pretty sure we were going to lose."

His fears were well-founded. When the justices convened on Friday, April 23, to discuss the case, only the three most liberal members, Justices Brennan, Stewart, and Douglas, urged the reversal of Ali's conviction. Justices White, Blackmun, Harlan, Black, and the Chief Justice Warren Burger believed the conviction should stand. Thurgood Marshall recused himself because he was Solicitor General of the United States at the time of the original conviction. By a vote of five to three, therefore, the Court upheld the conviction. Ali was headed to prison.

If the chief justice is on the side of the majority on a given Court vote, tradition dictates that he assigns another member of the majority to write the Court's opinion—the legal and Constitutional justification for their decision. Usually the Chief will assign the member of the Court whose views on the issue most closely parallels his own. In this case, Burger assigned the majority opinion to John Harlan, confident that he would make a convincing argument for Ali's conviction. But when justice Harlan huddled with his clerks that evening to discuss the preparation of the opinion, he discovered that they had their own strong views on the matter.

In those days, at the height of the Vietnam War, most of the clerks were considerably more radical than the justices they served and most of them strongly opposed the war. In *The Brethren*, Woodward and Armstrong noted that in a vote on whom to invite to a question-and-answer lunch, one of the clerks' top choices was radical anti-war actress Jane Fonda, one of the few prominent Americans more widely reviled at the time than Muhammad Ali. Because they write most Court opinions, the clerks have considerable influence on the justices. In this case, Harlan's clerks persuaded him to take home a copy of Elijah Muhammad's book *Message to the Blackman in America* to gauge for himself the Muslim teachings.

Harlan had been appointed to the Court by President Eisenhower fifteen years earlier and had a reputation as a fair-minded jurist, despite his Republican views.

"He had been a high ranking officer in World War II so he definitely supported the military," says one of his clerks at the time, Thomas Krattenmaker. "But he was very torn by the Vietnam War, he thought it was an ill-defined adventure. He was not the kind of guy to say 'my country right or wrong.'"

A short while previously, Harlan, who was dying of cancer, had demonstrated a strong commitment to free speech in the case of *Radich vs. New York*, in which the proprietor of a Manhattan art gallery had been convicted of displaying American flags in a "lewd, vulgar and disrespectful way." The flags were actually thirteen different impressionistic sculptures, each portraying the Stars and Stripes in the shape of a penis. Harlan presumed the display was a protest against the war and lobbied hard—unsuccessfully—to convince his colleagues to overturn the conviction.

It was with this sort of open mind that Harlan took home *Message to the Blackman in America*. By the next morning, he had done a complete about-face. Without informing his colleagues or the Chief Justice, he immediately set about drafting a memo arguing that the government had mistakenly painted Ali as a racist and misinterpreted the doctrine of the Nation of Islam pertaining to Holy Wars, even though the Justice Department's own hearing examiner, Judge Lawrence Grauman, found that Ali was sincerely opposed to all wars at the original hearing in 1966. In that decision, Grauman ruled, "I believe that the registrant is of good character, morals and integrity, and sincere in his objection on religious grounds to participation in war in any form. I recommend that the registrant's claim for conscientious objector status be sustained."

If the government had followed Judge Grauman's advice at the time, Harlan believed, this whole case could have been avoided. In conversations with his colleagues, Harlan had hinted that he was having second thoughts about the case, but none were aware of how serious he was.

"The most important thing that caused him to change his mind was that he now understood the Muslim concept of Holy War," explains Krattenmaker. "Basically, a Holy War was more of a purely philosophical religious speculation. Ali was saying that if Allah came down and commanded it, he would fight a war. You knew that wasn't really going to happen. It was almost exactly the reason the Jehovah's Witnesses won their conscientious objector cases during World War II."

On June 9, Harlan shocked the Chief Justice by sending him a copy of his memo along with the following cover letter:

> Dear Chief:
>
> My original Conference vote was to affirm, and it was of course on that basis you assigned the opinion to me. As I tentatively indicated to the Conference a week or so ago and in later conversation with you, subsequent work on such an opinion brought me serious misgivings, and I am now convinced the conviction should be reversed.

In his memo, Harlan cites the religious doctrine of the Nation of Islam, quoting Elijah Muhammad's *Message to the Blackman in America*, which states:

> The very dominant idea in Islam is the making of peace and not war; our refusing to go armed is our proof that we want peace. We felt that we had no right to take part in a war with nonbelievers of Islam who have always denied us justice and equal rights; and if we were going to be examples of peace and righteousness (as Allah has chosen us to be) we felt we had no right to join hands with the murderers of people or to help murder those who have done us no wrong. . . . We believe that we who declared ourselves to be righteous Muslims should not participate in any wars which take the lives of humans.

The justice believed this passage proved that Black Muslims were legitimately opposed to all wars on religious grounds. But in recommending against Ali's conscientious objector claim, the government had maintained his objection rested "on grounds which primarily are political and racial. These constitute only objections to certain types of war in certain circumstances, rather than a general scruple against participation in war in any form." In his memo, Harlan called these arguments "misreadings and overdrawings."

Harlan's switch meant the justices were now deadlocked four to four. A tie vote meant that Ali would still go to prison. But Burger was furious, telling one of his clerks that Harlan had become "an apologist for the Black Muslims." If Harlan had his way and stressed the government's twisting of the facts, Burger believed, it might mean that all Black Muslims would be eligible for conscientious objector status.

Burger was among the most conservative of the justices and strongly supported President Nixon's obsession with stifling anti-war dissent. The day after the Court heard arguments in Ali's case, the chief justice accepted an emergency petition from the Justice Department to evict from their makeshift campsite on the Washington Mall hundreds of peaceful army veterans who were protesting the war. Burger upheld the government's claim that the veterans represented a threat to national security.

Neither Burger nor the other members of the original majority had any intention of changing their vote. If the deadlock stood, Ali would go to prison. A tie vote is not accompanied by a decision, so he would never know why he lost.

Justice Potter Stewart believed a clear injustice was about to be perpetrated. First, Ali had been convicted for political reasons; now the Court was about to send him to prison because they were afraid of the political consequences of setting him free.

Meanwhile, Ali awaited the Court's decision with the same aplomb he had displayed for the last four years. "If the judges look at me in what I believe, they'll vindicate me," he told an interviewer. "But if they send me to jail, I'm not going to leave the country. You don't run away from something like that. When you go to jail for a cause, it's an honor. If I have to go, I'll be a famous prisoner."

Stewart and his clerks studied the case carefully until they discovered a compromise alternative.

In order to satisfy a claim for conscientious objection, an applicant must satisfy three basic requirements. He must show that he is conscientiously opposed to war in any form. He must show that this opposition is based on religious training and belief, as interpreted in two key Supreme Court rulings. And he must show that his objection is sincere.

In 1966, after a hearing officer ruled that Ali's claim was sincere, the Justice Department sent a letter to the Selective Service Board—which eventually ignored the hearing officer—disputing his finding. In the letter, the Department implied that it had found Ali had failed to satisfy each of the three tests of conscientious objection.

To the requirement that the registrant must be opposed to war in any form, the letter said Ali's beliefs "do not appear to preclude military service in any form, but rather are limited to military service in the Armed Forces of the United States."

To the requirement that the registrant's opposition must be based on religious training and belief, the letter said that Ali's "claimed objections to participation in war insofar as they are based upon the teachings of the Nation of Islam, rest on grounds which primarily are political and racial."

To the requirement that a registrant's opposition to war must be sincere, the letter contained several disparaging paragraphs reciting the timing and circumstances of Ali's conscientious objector claim and concluded that "the registrant has not shown overt manifestations sufficient to establish his subjective belief where his conscientious-objector claim was not asserted until military service became imminent."

Stewart pointed out that, in oral arguments before the Court, Solicitor General Griswold himself had conceded that Ali's beliefs were based upon "religious training and belief." Presenting the government's case against Ali, Griswold had been asked by Justice Douglas whether he personally believed Ali had been sincere in his beliefs. He admitted that he believed so, which proved to be a critical legal lapse.

This kind of mistake by an accomplished legal scholar like Griswold—the government's highest-ranking prosecutor—is unusual. It is possible that, because of the changing political winds since the original conviction and growing public sympathy for Ali, Griswold deliberately decided to give the Court an "out"—an excuse to reverse the conviction and avoid the inevitable outcry that would have resulted from Ali's imprisonment.

Stewart had found his compromise. "Since the Appeal Board gave no reasons for its denial of the petitioner's claim," he wrote to his colleagues, "there is absolutely no way of knowing upon which of the three grounds offered in the Department's letter it relied. Yet the Government now acknowledges that two of those grounds were not valid and. . . the Department was simply wrong as a matter of law in stating that the petitioner's beliefs were not religiously based and were not sincerely held."

Stewart's clerks spent all night researching court precedents until they found the 1955 case of *Sicurella vs. the United States,* which involved a similar error in an advice letter by the Justice Department. In that case, the Court ruled the error was sufficient to overrule a conviction.

This technicality—the Justice Department's wrong advice to the Appeal Board—was sufficient excuse for every justice except Burger to reverse Ali's conviction. Even the previously reluctant justices were willing to set Ali free as long as it didn't give carte blanche for every Black Muslim to evade the draft.

"It's what Justice Harlan always called a 'peewee,'" explains his former clerk Krattenmaker. "It was a way of correcting an injustice without setting a precedent and changing the law."

The only holdout was the Chief Justice. According to Woodward and Armstrong in *The Brethren,* the compromise left Burger with a problem. If he dissented, his might be interpreted as a racist vote. He decided to join the others and make it unanimous. An eight-to-nothing decision would be a good lift for black people, he concluded somewhat patronizingly.

The Court's decision was released on June 28, 1971. Gene Dibble was with Ali in Chicago when his newly vindicated friend heard the news. "We were driving in his car and we stopped at a store," he recalls. "When he stepped out of the car, a guy came running out of the store and said he just heard on the radio that the Court had freed him. For once, Ali didn't know what to say. I could tell he was happy. I know he thought he was going to prison."

A swarm of reporters was waiting for the exonerated boxer at his motel, anxious to get his reaction to the news.

"It's like a man's been in chains all his life and suddenly the chains are taken off," he told them. "He don't realize he's free until he gets the circulation back in his arms and legs and starts to use his fingers. I don't really think I'm going to know how that feels until I start to travel, go to foreign countries, see those strange people in the street. Then I'm gonna know I'm free."

A reporter asked whether he would take legal action to recover damages from those who hounded him into internal exile. His answer displayed the same dignity he had maintained through his seven years as a national pariah.

"No. They only did what they thought was right at the time. I did what I thought was right. That was all. I can't condemn them for doing what they think was right."

Ali's greatest fight was over. Now that American society had begun to catch up to him, now that he had stripped it of some its prejudices and ignorance, he could turn back, rehabilitated, to what had brought him fame in the first place. While his most glorious days as a boxer still lay ahead—his recapturing of the heavyweight crown still to come—as a fighter in the world outside the ring, as a catalyst for change, and as a hero to his people, Muhammad Ali would never have the same impact again.

Zaire, 1974. Ali uses the rope-a-dope to win back his title from George Foreman.

AFTERWORD

The Legacy

THROUGH THE AFRICAN NIGHT CAME the repeated cries, "Ali Bomaye! Ali Bomaye! (Ali, kill him!)." In the ring below, George Foreman's supposedly indomitable punching power was being thwarted by Ali's improvised rope-a-dope strategy, designed to exhaust the powerful champion.

In the weeks leading up to the fight, he had signalled a return of the old Ali, promising the skeptics he was in top form. "I rassled an alligator, I done tassled with a whale/I handcuffed lightening/threw thunder in jail. That's bad! Only last week, I murdered a rock, injured a stone/I'm so mean, I make medicine sick!"

Behind the tallyhoo, however, was an accute understanding of the significance of the fight and what it meant for so many.

"I'm going to win the fight for the prestige," he vowed, "not for me but to uplift my brothers who are sleeping on concrete floors today in America, black people on welfare, black people who can't eat, black people who have no future. I want to win my title so I can walk down the alleys and talk to wineheads, the prostitutes, the dope addicts. I want to help my brothers in Louisville, Kentucky, in Cincinnati, Ohio, and here in Africa regain their dignity. That's why I have to be a winner, that's why I'll beat George Foreman."

Hardly a pundit in Zaire that night in 1974 believed an aging Ali could overcome the overwhelming odds. But cunning triumphed over clout and in the eighth round Foreman went crashing to the canvas. Muhammad Ali had reclaimed the heavyweight championship, seven years and four months after it was stripped from him. It was a feat that his forbears Jack Johnson and Joe Louis were never able to accomplish.

But it was more than a boxing title he won that night. Suddenly, a nation that reviled him only a few years earlier signaled that all was forgiven. The first sign of the changing attitude came when *Ring* magazine bestowed on Ali the "Fighter of the Year" designation it had refused him in 1967 because he set a bad example for American youth.

Then, a little more than seven years after he received a letter from President Johnson ordering him to report for induction, Ali received a different kind of White House invitation. Gerald Ford beckoned the redeemed champion to the Oval Office in what was billed as a great gesture of reconciliation after the trauma of Vietnam and Watergate.

It was more likely a cynical Republican ploy to court black voters. Years later, Ford explained to Thomas Hauser why he issued the invitation. "When I took office, we as a nation were pretty much torn apart. There were conflicts between families, in colleges, and on the streets. We'd gone through some serious race problems; the Vietnam War had heightened differences; and of course there was the heritage of Watergate. And one of the major challenges my administration faced was how we could heal the country. Not that everybody had to agree, but at least we should lower our voices and listen to one another and having Muhammad Ali come to the Oval Office was part of our overall effort. . . and he was a man of principle. I know there were some who thought he evaded his military responsibility, but I've never questioned anybody's dedication to whatever religion they believe in. I give people the maximum benefit of the doubt when they take a stand predicated on conscience. That's always been my philosophy, so I never joined the critics who complained about what he did and didn't do during the Vietnam War. I accepted his decision."

Ford, who served in Congress during Ali's exile period, may not have publicly joined the critics who denounced the champion's induction refusal, but the record shows he never used his influential moral platform to support the boxer's stand or praise him as "a man of principle."

INDEX

The Revolt of the Black Athlete, Harry Edwards (Free Press, 1969).

One Man, One Voice, Morgan.

"Great Black Hope," Pete Hammill, Esquire, March, 1969.

Gorn, "Ali as Sixties Protest Symbol", Thomas Hietala

Out of Bounds, Jim Brown (Kensington, 1979).

CHAPTER NINE

Hauser interview with Jeremiah Shabazz, Bryant Gumbel.

"I'm Sorry but I'm Through Fighting Now," Muhammad Ali (*Esquire*, Feb. 1970).

CHAPTER TEN

The Brethren: Inside the Supreme Court, Bob Woodward and Scott Armstrong (Simon & Schuster, 1979).

"Champ in the Jug?," Robert Lipsyte (*Sports Illustrated*, April 10, 1967).

Gorn, "Ali and the Age of Bare-Knuckle Politics," Thomas Hietala

Gorn, "Victory for Allah," David Wiggins

Gorn, "Ali as Sixties Protest Symbol," Jeffrey Sammons

"I'm Free to Be Who I Want," Robert Lipsyte, *New York Times Magazine*, May 28, 1967).

"Cosell," Howard Cosell (Playboy Press, 1973).

Gorn, "The Politics and Economics of Televised Boxing", Randy Roberts

"I Am Not Worried About Ali," Bill Russell, (*Sports Illustrated*, May 10, 1967).

The Greatest, Ali.

One Man, One Voice, Charles Morgan Jr. (Holt, Rinehart & Winston, 1979).

Johnson Presidential Files, L.B.J. Presidential Library.

CHAPTER SEVEN

Hauser interviews with Howard Cosell.

CHAPTER EIGHT

Hauser interviews with John Condon, and Aminah Boyd.

Holy Warrior, Atyeo and Dennis.

Congressional Record.

Sportsworld, Lipsyte.

CHAPTER FOUR

Hauser interviews with Jim Brown, Harry Markson, and Robert Lipsyte.

King of the World, Remnick.

The Holy Warrior, Atyeo and Dennis.

Muhammad Ali Reader, edited by Gerald Early, "The Redemption of the Champion," Gordon Parks; "Miami Notebook: Cassius Clay and Malcolm X," George Plimpton (Rob Weisbach Books, 1998).

Declassified Presidential Files, Lyndon B. Johnson Library.

CHAPTER FIVE

Hauser interviews with Jerry Izenberg, and Carl Walker.

Soul On Ice, Eldridge Cleaver (McGraw-Hill, 1968).

SNCC: The New Abolitionists, Howard Zinn (Beacon Press, 1965).

Fighting on Two Fronts: African Americans and the Vietnam War, James E. Westheider (New York University Press, 1997).

Vietnam and Black America: An Anthology of Protest and Resistance, Clide Taylor (Anchor Press, 1973).

Chicago Tribune Archives.

Clay v. United States, Suzanne Freedman, Landmark Supreme Court Cases (Enslow, 1997).

CHAPTER SIX

Voices of Freedom, Hampton, Fayer, and Flynn.

Sportsworld, Robert Lipsyte (Quadrangle, 1975).

In the years to come, many people would attempt to jump on the bandwagon of Ali's growing popularity by retroactively supporting his stand. But despite their historical revisionism, at the time Ali desperately needed these people's support, only a handful were there.

For Ali, a decade of pariah status had taken its toll and in his typically generous way he welcomed the new acceptance. But some of his supporters were not so forgiving.

"When Ali came back from exile," recalled Jim Brown, "he became the darling of America, which was good for America because it brought black and white together. But the Ali that America ended up loving was not the Ali I loved most. I didn't feel the same about him anymore, because the warrior I loved was gone. In a way, he became part of the establishment. And I suppose, in a sense, there's nothing wrong with that, because if you can come to a point where you make all people feel good, maybe that's greater than being a fighter for black people, but I didn't like it."

But Ali's longtime defender, columnist Jerry Izenberg, has a different view of the boxer's new social acceptability. "It wasn't that Ali changed," he explains. "He was the same as he always was. It was the rest of America that changed. The country went through Watergate and Vietnam and the turbulence of the '60s and it had a profound impact. Ali kept preaching the same message but now America could listen to it without going through convulsions."

Indeed, as the resurrected boxer continued to rack up victories in the ring—including two magnificent triumphs over Joe Frazier to avenge his first defeat—the money rolled in and Ali vowed to use his earnings to fund his dream of black economic justice. But one thing hadn't changed.

"After the Foreman fight," recalls Gene Dibble, "there were millions of dollars pouring in, huge sums of money, more from one fight than Ali had made in his entire career. He was very excited about using the money in the ghettoes for community economic development to eliminate poverty. These lawyers took the money to invest and start a foundation in Chicago. Next thing you knew, the money was gone. It was the same old story."

When he wasn't being robbed blind by those around him, says Dibble, he was giving his money away. "I remember one night I got a call from Ali, who was in New York. He had been watching the local news and he saw a report about this Jewish senior citizens' community center in the Bronx which served Holocaust survivors. They were about to shut down because they owed $100,000. Ali had called them and said he was sending a check over to bail them out. Trouble is that, as usual, he didn't have two nickels to rub together. He wanted me to figure out where he was going to get the money he had promised them. I called a friend at the Chase Manhattan Bank and arranged a loan against Ali's next fight purse. The center was saved."

On February 25, 1975, the association that had brought Ali spiritual meaning and sense at the same time as it caused him terrestrial grief and ostracism came to an end with the death of Elijah Muhammad. The Nation of Islam didn't disappear with its guiding light and leader, but it did fracture—and Ali chose to follow its most moderate faction. This decision made the boxer that much more palatable to mainstream society.

The Messenger's son Wallace Muhammad immediately took the movement in a new direction. Wallace, who was at one time a close friend of Malcolm X, had been suspended from the Nation by his father several times for questioning Nation doctrine and had a very different philosophy. His first action was to change the name from the Nation of Islam to the World Community of Al-Islam in the West. He resurrected the memory of Malcolm and stressed his positive contributions. But most significantly, he de-emphasized racial issues and aligned the movement to traditional orthodox Islam, announcing the new organization would accept people of all races for membership.

Many militant members of the Nation were infuriated by the shift in direction. But Ali immediately embraced the changes, declaring on the CBS news show *Face the Nation* that it was necessary for Elijah Muhammad to speak of white devils because during much of the first half of the twentieth century, black Americans were "castrated; lynched; deprived of freedom, justice, equality; raped." But as the result of the improved racial conditions in society, "Wallace Muhammad is on time. He's teaching us it's not the color of the physical body that makes a man a devil. God looks at our minds and our actions and our deeds."

In fact, the new philosophy closely reflected what Ali had believed and preached from the beginning, and what Malcolm X espoused during the last year of his life.

But despite Ali's endorsement, not everybody accepted the new ways. Louis X changed his name to Louis Farrakhan and led a breakaway movement of followers who refused to reject the old teachings.

To this day, Farrakhan's movement continues to thrive in America's inner cities, combining Elijah Muhammad's philosophy of economic self-help and racial pride with a fanatical anti-semitism much stronger than anything heard under the Messenger's regime. "Hitler was a great man," Farrakhan said on one occasion, before claiming to have been quoted out of context. On another, he declared: "The Jews are responsible for the majority of wickedness in the world."

At first, Ali was silent about Farrakhan's leadership. But after a particularly anti-semitic outburst was reported in the media, Ali declared, "What he teaches is not at all what we believe in. We say he represents the time of our struggle in the dark and a time of confusion in us and we don't want to be associated with that at all."

As his boxing skills waned, many of Ali's friends and supporters urged him to retire while he was on top. But for the vultures and hangers-on, this would have meant the elimination of their cash cow. Each time the aging boxer publicly contemplated retirement, he was convinced to put on the gloves "one more time."

After losing to a journeyman boxer named Leon Spinks, in 1978 he became the first three-time heavyweight champion by winning the rematch seven months later, insisting Spinks had merely "borrowed" his title. The Spinks defeat wasn't humiliation enough and, like a parody of the fighter who doesn't know when to quit, Ali left retirement and returned to the ring twice more to put on ever-sadder spectacles and enrich the parasites in his entourage.

Almost as disturbing to his old friends was his brief political flirtation with Ronald Reagan, the man who did more to set back the cause of civil rights than any other politician. To the chagrin of the black community, Ali endorsed Reagan for President in 1980, citing the right-wing candidate's promise to restore prayer to public schools. He later blamed this decision on "bad advice."

In September 1984, Ali checked into the Columbia-Presbyterian Medical Center in New York for a series of routine diagnostic tests, complaining of slurred speech and trembling hands. A week later, the results were released. Ali was suffering mild symptoms of Parkinson's Syndrome, an ailment which is *not* the same as the degenerative, and more serious, Parkinson's Disease.

Even more significant than what the test diagnosed is what it ruled out. The supervising physician, Dr. Stanley Fahn, declared, "Ali does not suffer from dementia pugilistica, commonly referred to as 'punch-drunkenness.' Ali's mind is impressively alert and well-oriented."

This diagnosis is especially significant because, in the ensuing years, the myth that Ali's condition is related to the punishment he suffered in the ring during his later career has been widely accepted. In public appearances, his trembling hands and slurred speech—which has become more pronounced over the years—has caused the once spell-bindingly articulate and expressive man to be portrayed as a tragic figure, suffering from brain damage—a prisoner inside his own body.

In fact, anybody spending more than a few minutes with him today soon discovers Ali's mind is completely intact. His quick wit and practical jokes are still there and apparent to anybody who takes the time to listen to his slowed speech, muted to a near whisper. Parkinson's Syndrome, in fact, can be controlled by medication but Ali is often reluctant to take chemical substances and it is often a losing battle to get him to take his medicine.

Despite the self-righteous tones of those who use Ali's condition to call for a ban on boxing, significant scientific evidence has emerged in recent years that his Parkinson's Syndrome was caused not by too many blows in the ring, but by too much exposure to pesticides. During the last decade of his career, Ali trained in a complex at Deer Lake, Pennsylvania. Each of the buildings was made of wood, which neccessitated liberal coatings of a chemical pesticide to keep away termites. A number of medical studies have linked this and other pesticides to Parkinson's, although there is still an ongoing debate in the scientific community, and boxing certainly hasn't been ruled out as the cause of his condition.

In 1975, sportswriter Gary Wills contemptuously downplayed Ali's social and political significance, arguing that his only contribution to society came from his boxing skills. "For some reason, people don't want fighters just to be fighters," he wrote. "They have to stand for an era, for the color of hope, for a metaphysics of spirit. . . . Ali will be a celebrity as long as he lives—like the Duke of Windsor. But he only *rules* from the ring. He has nothing, really, to say, except with his fists."

After he retired once and for all in 1981, however, Ali proved just how wrong Wills was. Rather than rest or reflect on past glories, the former champion turned his energies full-time to a crusade that had been a life-long passion—social justice.

Perhaps the best evidence of Ali's continued energy, in spite of his disability, is the fact that he still spends more than two hundred days a year on the road as a roving ambassador for human rights.

For a man who is afraid to fly, his travel itinerary is impressive. During the past decade, he has visited more than fifty countries, crusading against world poverty and oppression. His latest passion is the Jubilee 2000 campaign—an international movement to cancel Third World debt. His access to world leaders makes him an especially effective advocate, a fact proven in 1998 when he convinced British Prime Minister Tony Blair to support the movement. Both Nelson Mandela and Fidel Castro have called Ali their "hero."

Polls continue to show Ali is the most recognized and admired man in the world and huge crowds assemble wherever he travels, giving him a continued platform for his message of tolerance and economic development.

In the introduction to his 1998 book, *The Muhammad Ali Reader,* Gerald Early attempts to deflate the significance of Ali's induction refusal, arguing "Ali cannot be taken seriously as a Martyr." He points out that other athletes such as Jackie Robinson, Joe Louis, Ted Williams and others lost several years of their athletic prime serving in the Armed Forces during their careers. "No one seems to think this was tragic," he complains, noting Ali didn't end up paying a price for his dissent.

Early, who condescendingly writes that Ali hadn't a single idea in his head, clearly misses the point and fails to acknowledge that Ali was fully prepared to pay a harsh price by going to prison for his beliefs.

Activist Dick Gregory's assessment seems closer to the mark.

"I don't know of anyone who's had as great an impact on people as Ali. Not just black people; not just Muslims. . . . He got our attention; he made us listen. And then he grew within people who weren't even aware he was there. Whatever the Universal God Force meant for him to do, it's out of the bottle, and it isn't ever going back. Ali is inside all us now, and because of him, no future generation will ever be the same."

When he entered his exile period in 1967, Ali regularly reflected on how history would view his stand, on what his legacy would be.

Unquestionably, his actions helped spark the Revolt of the Black Athlete, characterized by the 1968 Olympic protests and other principled actions which followed. But thirty years later, such stands are increasingly rare in the world of sports. Many are especially troubled by the association of superstars such as Tiger Woods and Michael Jordan with the Nike Corporation, a company that has been accused of brutally exploiting Third World labor to manufacture its elite running shoes, especially in Asia. Jordan has made millions of dollars as the symbol of the world's most successful marketing campaign, refusing repeated calls by human rights groups to demand the company improve its labor conditions. Meanwhile, his endorsement has allowed Nike to gain a stranglehold on the black community's buying habits.

When Jordan retired in 1998, award-winning sports columnist Jack Todd compared the basketball icon's attitude to the example of Muhammad Ali. In an article headlined NOBODY EVER CALLED HIM CARE JORDAN, Todd writes, "Jordan's legacy will forever be tainted by the marketing connection that marks the chasm between him and a truly great athlete like Muhammad Ali. How can a man who most certainly does not need the money go on pushing Nike after he learns about their sweatshops in Southeast Asia? Ali understood the political dimension: he refused to go to Vietnam because he understood the irony of exploited young black, Hispanic, and poor white males being sent halfway around the world to fight poor Asian boys involved in a war of national liberation that had nothing to do with the U.S. or its national interests. A decade after the end of the Vietnam War, Jordan willingly became a worldwide spokesman for a U.S. corporation that exploited the children of the Asian boys Ali refused to fight. In the global context, that is far more significant than anything he achieved on the basketball court. . . . Remember, a generation grew up wanting to 'Be Like Mike.' Maybe that's why their aspirations today don't extend beyond the next video game, or the next new pair of Nikes. Once you get past the highlight film, it's not much of a legacy."

Todd, an American who moved to Canada to dodge the Vietnam War, is one of the rare sportswriters who understands the unparalleled influence sports has on society. By extension then, an athlete—especially one who so utterly dominates his sport like Ali or Jordan—must be judged on more than his athletic accomplishments.

Although Ali's principles don't seem to have trickled down to the current generation of athletes, Martin Luther King Jr.'s former lieutenant Andrew Young believes his legacy is undeniable. "Ali's lasting impact is that he was the first athlete to make us aware of the world in which we lived," says Young, who served as U.S. Ambassador to the United Nations under President Carter. "He forced us to think internationally. Ali saw that the globe is dominated by those who are oppressed because of their color. His influence is and was enormous."

Ali's political and religious views weren't the only aspects of his life to become more socially acceptable as the years passed. His personal life did too—but not because of an evolution in collective values. Rather, after years of womanizing, Ali settled down in 1986, when he married Lonnie Williams, an old Louisville friend he had known since she was five years old. By all accounts, the marriage is the best thing that ever happened to Ali. Besides providing domestic stability, Lonnie, who has an M.B.A., finally banished the vultures and parasites who had mismanaged and stolen Ali's assets for more than two decades.

She has brought a happiness and structure to his life, which has gratified many of his old friends, long troubled by the exploitation of the trusting champion. At their home on Ali's Michigan farm, their days are spent quietly with Ali studying the Koran and personally answering each and every letter and request for an autograph, or donating hundreds of pieces of memorabilia to charity auctions. "Each good deed is counted," he explains. That is his life when not traveling the world—an enterprise that takes up the lion's share of his time.

His human rights work has taken Ali to every state and every continent. No trip, however, was as significant as the journey he made to Vietnam in 1994, a trip that brought closure to the most tumultuous chapter in his life while also bringing together the families of American and Vietnamese servicemen missing since the war.

Wherever he went in the country, thousands of Vietnamese turned out to greet the man who, almost three decades earlier, had stood up to his country and sacrificed so much for his principled refusal to declare war on a people he had no quarrel with. With tears in their eyes, the cheering throngs shouted out the English words they had carefully memorized: "Thank you!"

ACKNOWLEDGMENTS

THIS BOOK WOULD NOT HAVE BEEN possible without the support of numerous individuals who contributed their assistance, advice, and inspiration. Thanks first, of course, to Muhammad and Lonnie Ali; Thomas Hauser for his guidance and navigation; Phyllis Bailey; Damon and Dustin Bingham; my attorney, Ron DiNicola; Bernie Yumans; Mel Wallace; Daniel Sanger for his superb editing skills; Marc Baller and George de Kay of M. Evans & Co. for making the publication process a painless task; our agent Noah Lukeman, one of the best in the business, for persistence and patience; and the following people and institutions: Elizabeth Barthelet, Evan Beloff, Julian Bond, Jacquie Charlton, Esmond Choueke, Ramsey Clark, Ian Halperin, Coretta Scott King, Coretta Bather, Paul Bather, Stokely Carmichael (Kwame Toure), Ali Cohen, Gene Dibble, Harry Edwards, Julien Feldman, Jack Greenberg, Betty Hawkins, Jerry Izenberg, Jesse Jackson, Betty Johnston, Thomas Krattenmaker, Lyndon B. Johnson Presidential Library, Bob Lipsyte, Michael Meltsner, Larry Merchant, Charles Morgan Jr., NAACP Legal Defense Fund, James Nabrit III, David Nanasi, Brenda Plant, George Plimpton, Pat Putnam, Darcie Rowan, Betty Shabazz, Jonathan Shapiro, Tom Syvertsen, Wayne Smith, Mort Susman, Wallace Terry, Jack Todd Jamel Touati,, Margaret van Nooten, Robert Walker, Jeremiah Wall, Hope Wallace, Lloyd Wells, Bobby White, Sandy Wolofsky, Morag York, and Andrew Young.

SOURCES

WE CONSULTED HUNDREDS OF BOOKS, newspaper, and magazine articles to research this book and interviewed hundreds more people associated with Muhammad Ali's life and the events documented in this book. Instead of a detailed bibliography, we list here the major sources consulted for each chapter.

The book is most of all indebted to Thomas Hauser's definitive biography/oral history *Muhammad Ali: His Life and Times* (Simon & Schuster, 1991), which provides a number of the quotes used throughout the book, many of which were facilitated by Howard Bingham, to whom Hauser dedicated the book.

CHAPTER ONE

A History of Blacks in Kentucky, George Wright (Kentucky Historical Society, 1992).

The Greatest, Muhammad Ali with Richard Durham (Random House, 1975).

The Holy Warrior: Muhammad Ali, Don Atyeo and Felix Dennis (Simon & Schuster, 1975).

King of the World, David Remnick (Random House, 1998).

Hauser interviews with Skeeter McClure, Joe Martin, Chuck Bodak.

CHAPTER TWO

"White America Views Jack Johnson, Joe Louis, and Muhammad Ali," Frederic Cople Jaher, in *Sport in America: New Historical Perspectives,* edited by Donald Spivey (Greenwood Press, 1985).

Loser and Still Champion, Budd Schulberg (Doubleday, 1972).

Beyond the Ring, Jeffrey Sammons (University of Illinois Press, 1988).

Bad Nigger!: The National Impact of Jack Johnson, Al Gilmore, (Kennikat Press, 1975).

"Ali as Sixties Protest Symbol," Thomas Hietala, in *Muhammad Ali: The People's Champion,* edited by Elliott Gorn (University of Illinois Press, 1995).

Gorn, "Muhammad Ali and the Revolt of the Black Athlete," Othello Harris

Voices of Freedom: An Oral history of the Civil Rights Movement from the 1950s through the 1980s compiled by Henry Hampton and Steve Fayer with Sarah Flynn (Bantam Books, 1990).

CHAPTER THREE

Hauser interviews with Neil Leifer, Abdul Rahman, and Harold Conrad.

The Assassination of Malcolm X, George Breitman, Herman Porter, and Baxter Smith. (Pathfinder, 1991).

An Original Man: The Life and Times of Elijah Muhammad, Claude Andrew Clegg III (St. Martin's Press, 1997).

The FBI and Martin Luther King, Jr., David J. Garrow (W.W. Norton, 1981).

Malcolm X: FBI Surveillance File (Scholarly Resources, 1978).

The Autobiography of Malcolm X, Malcolm X, with the assistance of Alex Haley (Ballantine Books, 1973).

Beyond the Ring, Sammons.